Freefall
of the AMERICAN
UNIVERSITY

Freefall

of the AMERICAN UNIVERSITY

How Our Colleges Are CORRUPTING THE MINDS AND MORALS *of the Next Generation*

JIM NELSON BLACK

WND BOOKS
A Division of Thomas Nelson Publishers
Since 1798

www.thomasnelson.com

Published in Nashville, Tennessee, by WND Books.

Library of Congress Cataloging-in-Publication Data

Black, Jim Nelson.
    Freefall of the American university : how our colleges are corrupting the minds and morals of the next generation / Jim Nelson Black.
        p. cm.
    Includes bibliographical references and index.
    ISBN 0-7852-6066-8
    1. Education, Higher—Moral and ethical aspects—United States. 2. Universities and colleges—Moral and ethical aspects—United States. I. Title.
    LA227.4.B53 2004
    378.73--dc22

                                                                                    2004015147

Printed in the United States of America

04 05 06 07 08 QW 5 4 3 2 1

To my father,
Joseph Nelson Black Sr.,
a World War II veteran and
a man who is upright in all his ways.

Contents

Part III:
FINDINGS

Foreword

A Moment of Truth

Despite the work of many fine writers who have addressed the problems of the academy over the past two decades, often to great fanfare, evidence of declining academic standards abounds. Grade inflation, the proliferation of junk courses, and the loss of a core curriculum still pose serious problems for learning today. At the same time, historical revisionism, moral relativism, and an emphasis on the flawed ideologies of race and gender continue virtually unchallenged. Like the weather, it seems, everybody talks about it, but nobody does anything about it. It's time for that to change.

In this volume my purpose is to add new evidence and a renewed sense of urgency to the campaign to transform and reform the American university. I come to this task not as an academic but as a citizen, a parent, a professional researcher, and a writer whose principal focus the past twenty years has been the collapse of cultural and moral standards in this country. My role in most respects has been that of a reporter and a concerned witness who has examined the documentary evidence and spent many hours interviewing the men and women most affected by these issues—in this case, students and their professors on some of the premier campuses across this land.

Beyond merely reporting these discoveries, however, my aim is also to awaken debate and to stir those who have been footing the bill for the indoctrination and reeducation of the next generation to take action to stop the madness, and to begin the process of discovery that may lead to dramatic changes in the structures, governance, and methods of the universities. To that end, I have offered several concrete suggestions with approaches and action steps, a number of which were recommended by individuals who find themselves in the middle of the controversy.

In the first four chapters of this book, which make up Part I, I offer a broad perspective of the critical issues confronting students and their parents today, along with an assessment of the risks to the universities and the nation. In particular, I examine the connection between the collapse of primary and secondary education and the aimlessness of modern higher education. My interview with Dr. Harvey Mansfield in Chapter Four focuses specifically on these issues. In Part II, dealing with corruptions of the curriculum and the social environment on campus, the discussion is enlivened by my conversations with Professors Robert George of Princeton and Donald Kagan of Yale, as well as some exceptionally perceptive young men and women.

The final chapters are in many ways the heart of this work. Not only have I included substantially more interviews with students and faculty, but I offer an interpretation of the important conclusions and findings of this research project. In addition to my interviews with Professors Dallas Willard, J. Budziszewski, and Gerard Bradley, and a brief exchange with Dr. Donald Kagan, I've focused on patterns that emerged from this analysis, looking at the long-range implications and the burden of responsibility that each of us must shoulder if there are to be changes in the way the nation prepares the "best and brightest" for leadership. I'm convinced that genuine change can come, but only when enough of us care enough to act.

During my own graduate studies, and especially during my doctoral research at the Sorbonne in the late seventies, I investigated the nature of chaos in contemporary culture. My thesis and my interview with the novelist Anthony Burgess addressed the writer's moral vision and his characterization of the tenuous equilibrium between good and evil, right and wrong, and the poles of political opinion. Subsequently, I discussed the changing social order after the Second World War and the fragmentation of the moral imagi-nation in greater detail in my dissertation in the University of Texas system. As a publisher, educator, and executive director of a Washington, DC, research institute, I have continued to pursue these issues, and my apprehensions have only increased over time.

All these things play a part in my analysis of intellectual and academic trends in these pages, but they do so principally in terms of establishing points of reference and evaluating the implications. But my analysis is practical and not merely academic. Rather than offering realistic solutions to the problems that plague American culture, academic answers often tend to complicate matters or make them worse. The intellectual approach is theoretical and equivocal, whereas the issues here are concrete and very real. Consequently, my plan in this volume has been to offer review and analysis combined with common-sense solutions, which I believe is the only way of dealing with our predicament and of changing the conditions on campus in which the men and women in academia find themselves today.

If we really care about the world our children will inherit, something must be done. The crisis in higher education is not only the risk of indoctrination through the vagaries of pluralism, tolerance, and diversity but also the fact that "value-neutral" socialization and radical sexual indoctrination are robbing many young Americans of their future, their competitiveness, and their cultural inheritance. Leftist ideology is stripping the nation of future leaders and subjecting millions of the most vulnerable young women and men to physical and mental harm. Statistics concerning disease and related health risks on campus are staggering. Obviously, those who are poorly educated in the essential facts of this country and its heritage will be ill-prepared to lead the nation. But the risks students face today go far beyond mere academic attainment. Some of their challenges are also life-threatening and fearfully real.

DEALING WITH DENIAL

Sociologist Christopher Lasch, in the final work of his distinguished career, laid the charges against the academy as well as it has ever been done. In *The Revolt of the Elites*, Lasch writes:

Talk of pluralism and diversity provides no comfort when young people can't seem to learn how to read or write, when they graduate with no more than a smattering of culture, when their stock of general knowledge grows more meager every day, when they can't recognize allusions to Shakespeare or the classics or the Bible or their own country's history, when SAT scores keep falling, when American workmanship and productivity are no longer the envy of the world, and when superior education is widely cited as the reason for the economic success of countries like Japan and the former West Germany. These are the developments that trouble ordinary people, and any serious talk about education has to speak to those developments.[1]

Most remarkable is the fact that these things were troubling enough for Lasch—who was himself a lifelong liberal—to provoke him to betray the confidence of his colleagues and admit the devastation that leftist ideologies had wrought upon the nation. In order to realize some higher ideal of social justice, academics have stripped away the tried and true from the university curriculum and inculcated millions of students in untested, unproven, and unproductive schemes that put them at odds with their own interest as citizens.

Aristotle famously observed that "Educated men are as much superior to uneducated men as the living are to the dead." He also said that "Education is the best provision for old age." A good education, founded upon the search for truth, prepares one both for life and for death. But in the rush to create a world that is free of "hurt feelings" and honest *debate*, modern educators have sentenced millions of bright young people to lives of mediocrity and disappointment. And as Lasch pointedly observes, many recent graduates are morally unfit—handicapped and unprepared for living meaningful lives. As he goes on to say:

Many young people are morally at sea. They resent the ethical demands of 'society' as an infringement of their personal freedom. They 'create their own values,' but they cannot explain what that means, aside from the right to do as they please. They cannot seem to grasp the idea that 'values' imply some principle of moral obligation. They insist that they owe nothing to 'society'—an abstraction that dominates their attempts to think about social and moral issues. If they conform to social expectations, it is only because conformity offers the line of least resistance.[2]

How many parents, preparing to send their children off to some prestigious institution, have considered the possibility that the four-year indoctrination program for which they will spend a hundred thousand dollars or more will yield a product they no longer recognize as their own offspring? How many parents will appreciate the de-education and de-moralization that will be forced upon their children?

The cogency of Lasch's remarks is that he focuses, not on institutions, tactics, or ideologies, but on the real concerns of parents: the young people who are being shortchanged by this system. Surely this is something Mom and Dad do understand, and this is precisely why I have decided to include a large number of personal interviews with students, alumni, and faculty in this work. It is also important to provide facts and figures, to recite the evidence of knowledgeable observers, so along with these interviews I have also included statistical information, survey results, expert analysis, and other types of documentation to help elucidate the nature of the problem.

It's essential for those who foot the bills, and who have a vested interest in what they're receiving for this investment, to hear from students and faculty who must confront the one-sided programming on campus and somehow carry on. In these pages I will examine the impact of "the shadow university," as Alan Charles Kors and Harvey Silverglate have termed it, on American culture, and the degree to which the elements of a university education have changed over the past forty years. But to put the long-term decline of the university into better perspective, consider these words from the catalog of Columbia College in the year 1785:

No candidate shall be admitted into the College . . . unless he shall be able to render into English Caesar's Commentaries of the Gallic War . . . the four Orations of Cicero against Catiline . . . and the Gospels from the

Greek . . . and to turn English into grammatical Latin, and shall understand the first rules of Arithmetic, with the rule of three.

How things have changed! Today, after two centuries of "progress,"
American high school graduates about to enter the university have almost no
knowledge of their nation's history and only a functional command of the
English language—let alone any knowledge of Greek or Latin. In comparative testing of American high school seniors with students of other nations
over the past twenty years, as it has often been reported, American students
rank consistently near the bottom in head-to-head comparisons. Ironically,
they have the highest "self-esteem" and lowest academic performance. This
should be a matter of concern for every American.

As we embark on another century of progress, our prospects for developing future leaders with real knowledge, understanding, competitive job
skills, and respect for citizenship and community have never been worse.
More than forty million American adults are illiterate in this country, and
fifty million have only survival-level academic skills. Two-thirds of school
children are unable to read at grade level, while educators and their unions
are in denial.

The university campus is no longer a center of higher learning but a
socialist conspiracy that feeds on itself, fueled by fear-mongering on the Left
and apathy on the Right. Responsible academics and concerned parents are
riddled with uncertainty, unsure of what is actually happening on campus
and ignorant of what they can do about it. Many are stymied by the myth
that professors and administrators are beyond the reach of the common man,
while others are merely passive in the naïve belief that if they ignore the
problems long enough things will get better by themselves.

BREAKING THE SILENCE

The university today is an academic system that rewards novelty, extreme
positions, and radical theories, and it favors any intellectual trope that pan-
ders to the prevailing anti-American bias of the academy. Administrators

who have been compromised and corrupted by this system have been drawn into the conspiracy and are, for the most part, incapable of changing the downward drift of the academy. It would not be stretching the truth to say that within every faculty in every college and university in this country there is a cadre of militant activists who have an aggressive agenda of social change and a revolutionary zeal to undermine the traditional foundations of Western culture. And they're doing it without resistance.

Thanks to the decades-long descent of primary and secondary education, students coming into the university today are, for the most part, poorly educated and poorly prepared for the challenges they will face. Most are already infected by the leftist, anti-American, and anti-intellectual bias of the academy. This attitude of distrust and antipathy has been disseminated by organizations such as the National Education Association (NEA) and the public school mafia, not to mention a host of well-funded left-wing organizations that prey on the idealism and ignorance of the young.

A reporter for the *Washington Post* once accused evangelical Christians in this country of being "poor, uneducated, and easy to command." The fact is, thanks to twelve years of social indoctrination in the nation's primary and secondary schools, the vast majority of young people entering college today are under-educated, disinterested in learning, morally and intellectually undisciplined, and sitting ducks for the mind-control agenda of the Left.

Within the universities there is a second tier of social programmers who manipulate students for personal, professional, sociological, and/or political reasons. Their favored means of control include (a) freshman orientation, (b) diversity indoctrinations (or brainwashing), (c) sexualization that is patently exploitative and abusive, enforced through campus housing and dormitory arrangements, and (d) forced compliance with the hyper-sexualized environment that includes the requirement to accept deviant behaviors and the loss of personal privacy.

To achieve all these objectives, student affairs directors employ tactics that are straight out of Chairman Mao's "Little Red Book," designed to force acceptance of practices that any normal American would find shocking and unacceptable. All in all, the universities are behind a disturbing frontal assault on freedom of speech, conscience, and religion. But within the gambit of this dismantling of the traditional culture, parents, scholarship providers, and other funding agencies also play a role either through ignorance, apathy, or their uneasy compliance with educators in the seduction of their children.

What we are witnessing is a deliberate and systematic suppression of dissent, especially of students who are often defenseless. Parents don't believe what they're told; fellow students are cowed into submission by the intense pressure to fit in; and, for many reasons, faculty and administrators will not come to their aid. The tactics being employed on many campuses are not just Orwellian but have a distinct totalitarian component. The radical notions of the sixties have not disappeared; they're very much in play, and they're Maoist by design. Behind all of this is a network of collaborators within the academy, the professional associations, the professoriate, the government, and especially the media, whose silence and complicity have made the entire conspiracy possible.

In these pages I present evidence for what's happening on America's college and university campuses as a direct result of the widespread policies of political correctness and social indoctrination. In addition to survey results, analysis of the issues, the history of the problems, and professional commentary from a number of highly regarded sources, this volume also presents the observations of individuals on the frontlines in their own words.

Over the past several months I have traveled across the country, from coast to coast, to meet and interview students and faculty members at some of the nations most distinguished universities. My conversations with students from Dartmouth, Stanford, Harvard, Yale, Princeton, MIT, Tufts, Amherst, Vanderbilt, Indiana, UCLA, USC, Cal Berkeley, Boston University, Columbia, Texas, Chicago, Akron, Michigan, Ohio State, Bowdoin, Colby, Georgetown, Notre Dame, and other campuses, have added depth and urgency to this story.

My discussions with both students and faculty have focused on what each of them has discovered about the political bias, sexuality, socialism, anti-capitalism, and overriding anti-American animus on campus today. All of this, I trust, will help to illustrate in categorical terms what is actually happening, and where all the hard-earned tuition money is actually going. In short, this book is offered as a chronicle of an intellectual and moral freefall that is taking place in the academy, right before our eyes.

The purpose of this book is not to attack higher education or to keep students from attending these schools. Rather, my task has been to pose questions that may cause parents, educators, and other concerned citizens to stop and reconsider the implications of what's happened to the academy since the sixties, and then to become involved in taking action to address these issues with a renewed sense of commitment. If there's any integrity, any sense of alarm, or any capacity for moral outrage left in this country, then men and women of conviction must rise up now and challenge the hegemony of the Left so that genuine learning can once again take place, and so that freedom of expression may at last be restored to the university campus. This is our moment of truth; we can't afford to blink.

JIM NELSON BLACK
Washington, DC

Part I
INDICTMENT

1

A Crisis on Campus

Fall registration, the first day of class, the beginning of another year at the university of your choice. Each year nearly fifteen million students enter colleges in this country where their hopes and dreams will be realized, their minds opened to new ideas, and their prospects for success in life either affirmed or denied. At least, that's the idea. But from Harvard to Stanford and on hundreds of campuses in between, the best and brightest of America's youth are being introduced to ideas that will shake the foundations of their beliefs, challenge their confidence and objectivity, and, one way or another, shape the future of this nation.

Most Americans today have some vague notion that all is not well on the university campus. Parents know that colleges are run by liberals, that silly ideas are being bandied about by tenured radicals left over from the sixties. They understand that the climate on campus these days is more sexualized than ever before, but they're not really sure what it's all about. They don't know what to worry about and what to ignore, and they're just not sure what to believe anymore. So they wait and hope for the best.

What they may not know is that of the 14.9 million students who will enroll in college this year, half of them will not graduate. Forty years ago only about half of America's high school graduates went to college. Today, more than two-thirds will go. During recent years the drill from Washington has been that "every American is entitled to a college education," and record numbers of students have enrolled in post-secondary programs of some kind; but only about half will actually earn a diploma. And more distressing,

3

thanks to the politicization of the academy, merely receiving a diploma no longer guarantees that the student has actually received a good education, or that he or she will be able to compete in the marketplace of ideas.

The cost of a college education has never been higher, and admissions standards have never been lower, but the entire calculus has changed. The university campus is no longer that idyllic place of the imagination where callow youths are educated and prepared for life in the real world. The campus is, indeed, a place of radical transformation, but not the kind that most parents expect.

To put it plainly, the university is not a safe place to send your child. The reason is that the university is only marginally about education today. For one thing, many senior faculty members have renounced classroom duties in favor of research, writing, and other non-pedagogical duties. Those with consulting practices, funded research projects, or access to a general audience can usually earn more through their off-campus activities than from teaching. Which leaves graduate teaching assistants and part-time faculty in charge, most of whom do not have the depth or the inclination to deal with the range of issues they're expected to teach.

But a far greater problem is that higher education today is now a pretext for concentrating large numbers of unsuspecting and often poorly-prepared students on campuses, away from their families and other mediating influences, where they may be socialized and manipulated by leftist faculty members and administrators for purely ideological reasons. Since the social revolution of the sixties, the agenda of the Left has been to transform the United States into a socialist utopia; consequently, the issue of greatest concern on America's most distinguished university campuses is no longer traditional learning but a new form of social and sexual indoctrination.

THE SHADOW UNIVERSITY

In one of the most comprehensive and disturbing studies published to date on the crisis of authority in the academy, *The Shadow University: The Betrayal of Liberty on America's Campuses*, professors Alan Charles Kors and Harvey

Silverglate report that something awful is happening in our great universities. "To know the betrayal of liberty on our campuses," they say, "one must understand what has become of their divisions of university life and student life, residential advisors, judicial systems, deans of students and their officers, and of their new and profoundly disturbing student rules and regulations."

It's in this arena, where administrators exercise absolute control over students, that one finds the enforcers of political correctness, the mandatory sensitivity classes, the seminars on race and gender, and the encounter sessions through which students are indoctrinated, often by invasive and manipulative means, including various kinds of role-playing, in the dogmas of "diversity" and "tolerance" that are a mask for the anti-American and hyper-sexualized agenda of the universities. The doctrines being forced on students is distinctly countercultural and contrary to any interpretation of traditional morality, and it is easily the most sinister element of what's happening today. "The ultimate force of the shadow university," say Kors and Silverglate, "is its ability to punish students and, increasingly, faculty behind closed doors, far from public and even campus scrutiny."

Parents who send their sons and daughters to universities trusting these academics and administrators to guard their children, through the university's *in loco parentis* (in the place of the parent) responsibilities, are in for a shock. There is a moral agenda on campus, but a very different sort than most people expect. "The shadow university hands students a moral agenda upon arrival, subjects them to mandatory political reeducation, sends them to sensitivity training, submerges their individuality in official group identity, intrudes upon private conscience, treats them with scandalous inequality, and, when it chooses, suspends or expels them." The impact of what's being done to today's undergraduates, largely behind closed doors, is "something truly chilling," Kors and Silverglate say. It is "a hidden, systematic assault on liberty, individualism, dignity, due process, and equality before the law." The universities, as these distinguished authors conclude, "have become the enemies of a free society."[1]

In truth, many excellent books have been written about the state of higher education in this country over the past two decades. Scholars and researchers have reported in great detail about the dangerous political agenda that has wreaked havoc on traditional learning. Allan Bloom's classic, *Closing of the American Mind*, alerted millions to the pernicious risks of political correctness and the change of attitude taking place in our institutions of higher learning. That book is still one of the most quoted sources on the subject. Equally important were books such as Roger Kimball's *Tenured Radicals*, Martin Anderson's *Impostors in the Temple*, and Kirk Kilpatrick's *Why Johnny Can't Tell Right from Wrong*, which examined the impact of the sixties' "free love, free everything" generation now ensconced within the faculties and administrations of our colleges and universities.

Dinesh D'Souza's *Illiberal Education*, John Silber's *Straight Shooting*, and Charles Sykes' *A Nation of Victims* each pointed out the racial component of the struggle; and more recent books—including *Experiments against Reality* by Kimball, *Incorrect Thoughts* by John Leo, and Alvin Schmidt's excellent overview, *The Menace of Multiculturalism*—have provided unimpeachable documentation and compelling evidence of the long-term damage being wrought by leftist tactics on campus and the even greater risks ahead for America if the historic foundations of higher education are not restored.

While every one of these works has added to our understanding of the problems, what they have lacked is the capacity to change the attitudes and habits of those who keep this corrupt system alive. That is, the mothers and fathers who send their sons and daughters to college each year, along with the many organizations that help to pay the tuition that supports it. They have either not listened, not believed the reports, or have not felt strongly enough the need to respond with anger and with force. The best books on the decline of higher education have been consumed by those with a professional interest in the subject, but middle America has yet to respond, and that must change.

As source after source has revealed over these many years, the American university is engaged in a conspiracy against the historic moral and social values of the American people. Sociologist Paul Hollander has said, "The university is the reservoir of the adversary culture."[2] On hundreds of campuses all across the country, legions of faculty members are at war with the rest of America, and the aim of these leftist professors is to create a phalanx of liberal culture warriors who are disaffected and angry, and who share the strongly anti-American sentiments of their intellectual masters. Who will stop them? Who will rise up and change the dreadful dynamic on the university campus?

A New Absolutism

Perhaps a certain lethargy is to be expected. After all, who would have thought it would come to this? The ivory tower, the academic cloisters, the ivy-covered halls lampooned for generations as a place where nothing of significance ever happens have become, in fact, the frontlines in a struggle for the soul of America. Professors, department heads, administrators, and well-meaning trustees and alumni preside over the wholesale deconstruction of American values, and they are responsible for the collapse of educational standards and a debasement of morality that is unprecedented in American history. Because of the importance we've given to universities in our culture, those who administer the system have helped created a situation that is potentially devastating to our future as free and independent people.

Columnist John Leo, who has consistently been one of the most outspoken critics of the dismantling of the traditional curriculum, points out that during most of our history it wouldn't have been necessary to look closely at what students were learning on campus. The elements of a college education were well known and widely agreed upon. Sadly, that's no longer the case. "Colleges are unsure of their mission," Leo writes, "buffeted by consumer pressures and ideological forces, and unwilling to say what a sound education might consist of."

As a result of bias, indecision, and poor leadership, students are increasingly at the mercy of politicized faculty members immersed in the latest academic fashions. Ivy League catalogs are as likely now to offer courses on pop music, pornography, standup comedy, and television sitcoms as any more orthodox subject matter. The University of Wisconsin offers a course in soap operas. Columbia offers "Issues in Rock Music and Rock Culture." Duke's catalog offers "The Physics, History, and Technique of Juggling," while the University of Pennsylvania offers a course called, "Vampires: The Undead." And it comes as no great surprise that courses in drug culture, sado-masochism, bondage, and civil disobedience appear in a growing number of catalogs these days.

Here's just a sample of some typical course offerings: University of California at Berkeley, "Male Sexuality"; Columbia, "Sorcery and Magic"; Dartmouth, "Queer Theory, Queer Texts"; Yale, "AIDS and Society"; Cornell, "Gay Fiction"; Princeton, "Sexuality, Bodies, Desires, and Modern Times"; University of Pennsylvania, "Feminist Critique of Christianity"; Brown, "Unnatural Acts: Introduction to Lesbian and Gay Literature"; Bucknell, "Witchcraft and Politics"; University of Iowa, "Elvis as Anthology"; Swarthmore, "Lesbian Novels since World War II"; Stanford, "Homosexuals, Heretics, Witches, and Werewolves"; Oberlin, "Feminist Criticism of Shakespeare"; Rutgers, "Women on the Fringe: Perceptions of Women as Social and Sex-Role Deviants in American Civilization"; Vassar, "Global Feminism"; Wesleyan, "Pornography Writing of Prostitutes"; University of Massachusetts, "Rock and Roll"; University of Indiana, "Star Trek and Religion"; University of Michigan, "Crossing Erotic Boundaries"; University of North Carolina, "Magic, Ritual, and Belief"; University of Wisconsin, "Goddesses and Feminine Powers."[3]

Even more disturbing are courses such as "How To Be Gay: Male Homosexuality and Initiation" at the University of Michigan; "Introduction to Lesbian and Gay Studies" at Yale; "Feminist Biblical Interpretation" at Harvard and the University of Florida; "Witchcraft in the Modern World" at Bowdoin; and "Black Marxism" at the University of California at Santa Barbara. At the University of Chicago, literature students can enroll in "Third Wave Feminism and Girl Culture" or "Contemporary American Monstrosity," while the history department offers "Fetishism, Gender, Sexuality, Capitalism" and "Love and Eros in Japanese History."

Does anyone see a pattern here? John Leo's assessment of the problem is precise and right to the point. "The junk courses creep in," he says, "because much of the professorate now believes that nothing can truly be known, so nothing truly matters. From this it follows," he adds, "that juggling, horror movies, and serious courses all have equal claims on students' attention. Alas, the academy today is obsessed with the trivial and trashy, relentlessly focused on sexual politics, and gripped by a deep antagonism to tradition that has degenerated into a new absolutism."[4]

Even as traditional learning is dismissed in many classrooms as reactionary, tainted by sexism, racism, and a legacy of authoritarian hegemony, the students' ability to reason, question, or challenge ideas is subverted, and efforts to think independently are everywhere undermined. The last thing leftist professors want is a roomful of students who are able to argue persuasively and challenge the bias of the typical lecture hall. Some students are able to rise above the dogma and preserve their self-respect and independence, but never without consequences. Many, on the other hand, are profoundly changed—intellectually scarred, morally neutered, socially and intellectually programmed—and sometimes physically or emotionally crippled for life.

A CRISIS OF VALUES

In their surprisingly frank assessment of the state of public education in the early eighties, the National Commission on Excellence in Education wrote, "If an unfriendly foreign power had attempted to impose on America the mediocre educational performance that exists today, we might well have viewed it as an act of war. As it stands, we have allowed this to happen to ourselves . . . we have, in effect, been committing an act of unthinking, unilateral, educational disarmament."[5]

Seven years after that report was published, the U.S. Department of Education conceded that, "Large proportions, perhaps more than half, of our elementary, middle, and high-school students are unable to demonstrate competency in challenging subject matter in English, mathematics, science, history, and geography. Further, even fewer appear to be able to use their minds well."[6] Albert Shanker, head of the nation's second largest teacher's union, the American Federation of Teachers, was compelled to admit that, "Ninety-five percent of the kids who go to college in the United States would not be admitted to college anywhere else in the world."[7]

When you combine the candor of such admissions with the fact that many universities are primarily concerned with the political and social indoctrination of students, the scope of the problem becomes apparent. There is a revolution taking place in our midst, and the insurgents are making the rules. The consequences of this situation are many and profound. Not least is the ignorance that pervades American society. More than forty million American adults are illiterate today, and fifty million have only survival level academic skills. Teachers in our elementary and secondary schools are often poorly educated themselves, the result being that two-thirds of school children are unable to read at grade level.

As we enter the twenty-first century, at least three generations of young Americans believe what they have been taught: that their own native land is populated by men and women who are homophobic, bigoted, misogynist, exploitative, environmentally insensitive, and morally corrupt. Politicians and public officials have failed to challenge the perpetrators of this ongoing educational fraud. Government, in fact, is still the largest supplier of funding for these universities, pouring billions each year into research, administration, and building projects; and of course the media, with their own liberal ax to grind, remain deceitfully silent. Is it any wonder that so many Americans are so poorly informed, and that so few college graduates are willing (or interested enough) to participate in a free, elective political system?

In his 1999 book, *The Conspiracy of Ignorance: The Failure of American Public Schools*, Martin Gross pointed out that none of this has happened by accident. The hippie generation that marched for peace and love in the sixties has become the generation of ivory-tower liberals holding forth today in the ivy halls. And the souls of America's youth are the prize they covet most. Writing in *FrontPage* magazine, David Horowitz offers an assessment of the impact of this radical takeover by quoting one of the icons of the Left, Richard Rorty, who says openly that:

The power base of the Left in America is now in the universities, since the
trade unions have largely been killed off. The universities have done a lot
of good work by setting up, for example, African-American studies programs, Women's Studies programs, and Gay and Lesbian Studies programs.
They have created power bases for these movements.

Rorty, identified by Horowitz as "a professor of philosophy at the University
of Virginia and one of the nation's most honored intellectual figures," is an
editor of the socialist magazine *Dissent* and a "moderate" in the ranks of the
Left. Yet, says Horowitz, "That such an intellectual should celebrate the con-
version of academic institutions into political 'power bases,' speaks volumes
about the tragedy that has befallen the university."[8]

To further illustrate how one-sided the political agenda on campus has
become, a recent study from the Center for the Study of Popular Culture,
of which Horowitz is founder and president, polled social science and liberal arts professors at Ivy League colleges to determine their political affiliations and civic affinities. Horowitz writes, "Only three percent of the
faculty in all the Ivy League identify themselves as Republicans. Forty-four
percent named an organization that represents their views as the ACLU.
Zero percent identify with the Christian Coalition, one percent with the
NRA." The Left bias of these men and women becomes patently clear,
which raises the question: Whose values are your children being exposed
to today?

WARNING SIGNS

Nothing is so dangerous to America's future as the assault on Western civilization taking place on our university campuses. The people we have
entrusted to educate and prepare the next generation for leadership in an
increasingly complex world have a visceral hatred for America and a profound disrespect for the achievements of Western culture. Thanks to
decades of socialist programming, the academic elites have created a mythology in their own minds based on faulty reasoning and bad information,

and they are now foisting these views on our sons and daughters—a view of history, science, and human nature that is not only counter to the hopes and dreams of their charges but also a betrayal of the trust we've placed in them. This villainy cannot help but have grave consequences.

In my study of nine great civilizations that have perished over time, I discovered a large number of symptoms that were early indicators of decline. Within each of the ten warning signs that I ultimately enumerated in my book, *When Nations Die*, drawing upon the works of scholars from Gibbon, Toynbee, and Spengler, to Solzhenitsyn and Russell Kirk (along with an extensive review of ancient sources), I found that there were subsets of disarray that could be seen as evidence of imminent decline.

Loss of respect for authority, for example, was evidence of changes both in the quality of leadership and in popular esteem for the responsibilities of citizens. An increase in promiscuous behavior among the common people was generally a reflection of dissipation among the ruling elites. And a loss of curiosity among the sons and daughters of the aristocracy led to a general collapse of education and the knowledge of history that was essential for national survival. In each case, the loss of a moral vision altered the framework of order that had made the culture sustainable.

By the end of my analysis, one lesson became perfectly clear: Any nation that turns away from its founding principles and repudiates the values upon which it was founded is destined for the ash heap of history. Whether in ancient Egypt where the governing authority was shattered by endless factional disputes or in Rome where the rule of law (the *Pax Romana*) lost its ability to restrain the excesses of either the masses or their masters, changes in the basic structures and value systems of the culture proved to be fatal. As the distinguished French scholar René Grousset expressed it, any nation that loses its reason for existence cannot long survive. Grousset writes:

> In general, no civilization is destroyed from without unless it has first brought about its own ruin; no empire is conquered by a foreign foe unless it has first committed suicide. And a society or civilization perishes by its

own hand only when it has ceased to understand its own *raison d'être*, when it has, as it were, become a stranger to the dominant idea around which it formerly grew up.[9]

At one time historians held that it was barbarian invaders who destroyed the great Roman empire, but this was not the case. By the time the Visigoths sacked Rome in the fifth century, the empire was already dying of self-inflicted wounds. Classics scholar Victor Davis Hanson has said much the same, observing that the final collapse of Rome "was a result not of imperial overstretch on the outside but of something happening within that was not unlike what we ourselves are now witnessing. Earlier Romans," he says, "knew what it was to be Roman, why it was at least better than the alternative, and why their culture had to be defended. Later in ignorance they forgot what they knew, in pride mocked who they were, and in consequence disappeared."[10] The comparison to our own situation is unavoidable.

"A nation does not have to be overrun by a foreign enemy to be utterly destroyed." Rather, as I observed in my book, "Sometimes the most dreadful aliens are those who dine at your own table. And a nation does not collapse only when it has been vanquished by barbarian hordes. Rome wasted away long before the barbarians ever arrived."[11] Another commentator, Jean-François Revel, offers this perceptive analysis:

There have been natural cataclysms in history, epidemics, droughts, earthquakes, and cyclones, and they have killed millions, destroyed cities and crops, annihilated artistic and intellectual treasures, devastated the infrastructures of nations. Yet these plagues are nothing compared to those that have been caused by human action. The most destructive catastrophes are man-made, and above all statesman-made. They come from his appetite for conquest and domination, from the dead-end political systems he thinks up, his uncountable religious or ideological fanaticisms, and, especially, his obsessive needs to reform societies instead of letting them change at their own pace.[12]

Such words offer a stern warning, but the most troubling implication is that this is precisely what the leftists in the Ivory Tower are attempting to carry off: to transform the fundamental value systems of America and Western society in general by discarding nearly four hundred years of democratic tradition and erecting in its place a socialist utopia built on a foundation of lies, ignorance, apathy, naïve misinterpretation, and unrealistic expectations. What we risk losing, as the most formidable repository of freedom in human history, is so much greater than what we could ever gain from their hands. Yet those who dominate the lecture halls and laboratories of our great universities have ignored the lessons of our collective past and are teaching our children a revisionist history and a view of human nature with no basis in fact.

PC INSANITY

John Leo of *U.S. News & World Report* has compiled lists of PC insanity. A student was charged with "Discriminatory Harassing" when he laughed at an anti-gay expletive. His sentence was physical labor, watching a video on "homophobia" and writing a paper about what he had learned. At George Mason University, flinching when a homosexual touches your arm is a punishable harassment offense; staring at gays, staying away from them, or even thinking that a homosexual might "come on" to you are all punishable offenses.

In his classic work, *Democracy in America*, Alexis de Tocqueville offered this warning:

> Because Roman civilization perished through barbarian invasions, we are perhaps too much inclined to think that that is the only way a civilization can die.
>
> If the lights that guide us ever go out, they will fade little by little,

as if of their own accord. . . . We therefore should not console ourselves by thinking that the barbarians are still a long way off. Some peoples may let the torch be snatched from their hands, but others stamp it out themselves.[13]

I believe this is the risk we face today as a nation. We can no longer assume that the chaos on the university campuses is merely innocent or naïve; the stakes are simply too high for that. We can no longer trust that our children will be able to see through the nonsense and move beyond it once their studies are complete; too many have already succumbed to ideologies that have put them and their futures at risk. For one thing, the risks are not merely ideological, they are also physical and emotional. The plummeting of moral standards has allowed sexually transmitted diseases to multiply among the best and brightest, and the suicide rate among these young men and women is out of control.

THE HIGH PRICE OF FAILURE

I don't doubt that people of all persuasions are concerned with the decline in educational standards, as well as the moral and emotional fallout that comes with it, but if there is to be any hope of ending the hegemony of leftist intellectuals and restoring the foundations of liberty and the values of a classical education on the university campus, then individuals and organizations with influence will have to rise up in protest, and soon. And to do that, we all need information, motivation, and the courage to respond. In light of the dangerous situation we find ourselves in at this late hour, only a massive uprising of concerned citizens—students, parents, and allies—will have any chance of making a difference in the prognosis of despair and decline.

By any measure, the price of a college education has skyrocketed over the last twenty years. A congressional panel on higher education chaired by Sen. Joe Lieberman reported that tuition at American universities has more than doubled since the eighties, for both public and private colleges. According to the American Council on Education, 71 percent of Americans believe "a four-year college education is no longer affordable." Sixty-five percent of those cited in the study listed the high cost of a college education as their top concern, ahead of violent crimes against children, children's healthcare, and quality of public schools.[14]

Clearly, a good education ought to be affordable. But it also ought to come with some basic guarantees, ensuring that what students actually receive for their tuition is what they came for: namely, an education that prepares them as contributing members of society. Unfortunately, that is not happening. In his new book, *Experiments against Reality*, Roger Kimball details the impact of postmodern ideologies on education over the past forty years. For decades, he says, America's colleges and universities have presided over nothing less than the overturning of Western culture. If a Michelangelo or a Shakespeare emerged today, says Kimball, he would evoke nothing but sneers from the cultural arbiters. Now it seems "art" has to be obscene and ugly to be taken seriously. So-called "serious" thinkers have long since abandoned any commitment to clarity of expression or the search for truth.

In his most recent book, *Incorrect Thoughts*, John Leo decries the scourge of "political correctness" on college campuses as a sinister social movement spreading a cancer through our colleges and schools. And in the bestselling book, *Slouching towards Gomorrah*, Judge Robert Bork addresses the rise of radical feminism on college campuses, calling it "the most destructive and fanatical movement to come down to us from the sixties. Totalitarian in spirit, it certainly deserves its own place in the halls of intellectual barbarism."[15]

And where has this led? Today the very fabric of American society is being unraveled by dangerous social engineering in our centers of higher learning. Under the guise of "sensitivity" and "consciousness raising," millions of young Americans are being systematically stripped of their beliefs, traditions, and values, and are being indoctrinated in social and political bias, hyper race-consciousness, and a type of Orwellian Newspeak that amounts to (as sources cited in this text will confirm) overt brainwashing.

Obviously, the educational systems in this country are in serious trouble. Almost every day we see new revelations that educational foundations are crumbling. Surveys published over the past five years indicate that America's school children have little or no grasp of their own history. Scores on standardized exams continue to plummet. High school and college students are incapable of precise written communications, and nearly half of all freshmen entering college in this decade will require remedial English or math.

For years educators and administrators have claimed that the problem is lack of funds, but three major studies from the Alexis de Tocqueville Institution show that these claims are false. As analyst John Berthoud observes, "No country or civilization in the history of the planet has spent more money educating its children." Yet for all this expense, young Americans are being cheated, systematically stripped of the most basic knowledge, mainly because the real concern of the unions and educrats is to secure benefits for themselves. "The net result," says John Berthoud, "is devastation for America's children."[16]

AN INSIDE REPORT

Early in my research for this book, I phoned Professor Steven Wallace* who teaches at a Boston-area university and arranged to compare notes on what's happening there. We met at the T station, the subway stop closest to my hotel, and walked to a nearby restaurant where we found a table in the corner. A new semester had just begun, and, as a prolific writer and speaker, Dr. Wallace is always busy. But his concern for the decline of the academy was apparent, and he was willing to talk about it.

"Steven," I said, "These problems aren't new, and a lot's been said and written about it. But I'd like to get your insights on how we got to this point."

"Part of it," he said, "has to do with the rise of the Baby Boom generation, when this tremendous surge of young people began attending college in record numbers, and I think there was a lot of deference and capitulation

---

* Not his real name. Many professors critical of the current university system are loath to be named, fearing reprisals from administrators and colleagues.

to young people in those days. There was a kind of worship of youth at that time, back in the mid-sixties, and a lot of people, including college administrators, wanted to appear friendly to youth. So they were unreasonably tolerant, and I think they overlooked a lot of bad behavior that wouldn't have been allowed by previous generations.

"Also at that same time," he said, "there was a sort of questioning of society and the establishment, partly because of the Kennedy assassination. Then Robert Kennedy and Martin Luther King were killed, and the acknowledgment of institutional racism and so forth played into it. Our involvement in the Vietnam War upset a lot of people, so there was a general defiance of authority at all levels. And what made the ultimate breakdown possible was that the authorities didn't feel sure of themselves anymore, particularly on the college campuses. Basic assumptions about social order were being overturned practically everyday, and everything else was just a logical working out of that."

I said, "Young people who were angry about what they saw as social injustice began to take things into their own hands, didn't they? That's when we began seeing radicals like the Students for a Democratic Society (SDS) taking over administration buildings on campus, and militant leaders like Jerry Rubin and Mark Rudd making headlines with their outlandish demands and violent protests."

"That's right," Steven said, "and that's what David Horowitz was talking about in his book about the sixties, *Destructive Generation*. That's when the world was really turned upside down. For the last forty years we've been seeing the results of that revolution, and that's really what it was, a revolution. Not just a sexual revolution, although we're still seeing the working out of that, but a revolution against all the accepted values and norms of society."

"The revolution on campus," I said, "not only subsumed the values of the revolutions that preceded it—the Bolshevik Revolution, the Cultural Revolution in China, and the Marxist revolutions in Cuba and South America—but all those forces fed right back into it. It taught the angry mobs on American campuses how revolutions are executed and won. Horowitz was very much a part of that, of course, just feeding them the party line. They didn't actually come out and say that they wanted a Marxist revolution, but that's basically what was happening."

EVERYONE JUST GOT SMARTER

In 1995 SAT scores were raised, apparently to give the impression of equality and to increase "self-esteem." The Verbal norm was raised from 428 to 500; Math from 479 to 504. Before the change, the "perfect" score of 1600 was only achieved by thirty-five students; now students don't have to answer every question correctly to make a perfect score. As a result, hundreds more students have suddenly gotten smarter.

"There's no question that a lot of the most prominent theorists paving the way for the sixties revolution were Marxists," Steven said. "Herbert Marcuse, Theodor Adorno, Antonio Gramsci, and others made up the intellectual vanguard that laid the foundations. If you read what they wrote, it's still shocking. They hated middle-class values. Adorno, for example, considered average American parents to be little better than Nazis. Just read any of the pamphlets from that era, and you'll see what they were really after, which was the total dismantling of the American republic and the creation of a Marxist state."

"Looking at the sad state of the university today," I said, "you have to wonder if it ever stopped. The young people who were screaming obscenities at the barricades and setting fire to offices and dormitories in the sixties, now mostly middle-aged and balding, are the same people who are in charge of the colleges and universities today. They didn't go away; they took over. This was, of course, Roger Kimball's point in his book, *Tenured Radicals*."

"Actually, one of the biggest problems today," Steven said, "is that most people think they did go away. They assume that law and order prevailed and the radicals all went home. When things calmed down in the mid-seventies, and when the campus returned to 'normal,' the average American decided it was safe to go back in the water. Now, parents sending their kids to Brown or Berkeley or Columbia have no idea that they're actually handing them over to the same radicals who were burning draft cards and holding college presidents hostage in 1968."

MISCHIEVOUS MYTHOLOGY

"If you look at what's happening today," Steven continued, "it looks like it's going to just keep on going. But I think we need to remember what happened in Russia and Eastern Europe in the late eighties. The Soviet Union looked like it was strong and would continue forever, but in a short period of time it all came tumbling down, and that's what may well happen to the universities . . . with any luck! There's no sign of the demise of political correctness on the campus at this moment, but when changes come, they come quickly."

"I like the sound of that," I said, "but I'm not sure we can count on it. What bothers me is that, especially with grad students who will go on to get their Ph.D.s and end up as tenured professors in a few years, they're still being taught the same old propaganda of the barricades. Certainly in the most liberal disciplines, they're being taught that America is a corrupt capitalist regime that deserves to be brought down. Isn't that a problem?"

"There's a certain amount of libertarian influence creeping in," Steven said, "the Straussian influence and that sort of thing, and that may help. Also, I think a lot of smart kids are becoming suspicious of the leftist jargon they're hearing on campus, and I think we're beginning to see changes among some of the younger academics. They don't necessarily subscribe to traditional values or religion, but they hold strongly libertarian values on a number of issues."

"Are you saying the Marxist influence is no longer a factor?" I said.

"Not at all," he said. "It's still very strong in the humanities and social sciences, and it's certainly visible in the antiwar movement and that sort of thing. But what I see now is primarily a watered-down version that's even filtering down to the high-school and elementary-school levels via multiculturalism. The faculties in the schools of business tend to be fairly conservative, because they're dealing with market factors; but humanities, sociology, psychology, and education departments are much more liberal than that. They tend to adhere to fairly liberal assumptions about human nature.

"This is particularly true in schools of education. They swallow the whole Rousseauvian philosophy, hook, line, and sinker," he said, "the noble savage and all that, which is the idea that children are naturally good, learning is a natural process, and therefore learning doesn't have to be pushed. It will come easily and naturally, they say, and if your children aren't starting to read, then just wait until they're ready to read. And this shades over into moral values, as well; if children are given enough freedom they'll find good values on their own, which is absurd, as any parent should know!"

"Like the kids at Columbine," I said. "They were left to find their own values, and they decided that killing everybody at school was a good idea."

"As if the problems on college campuses weren't enough," Steven said, "there's a direct channel from the colleges to the high schools and elementary schools, and what we're seeing is a much less intellectual but much more sinister kind of mind and behavior control filtering down to kids in the earliest grades. Much of this is carried out in the name of multiculturalism—a movement that basically substitutes ethnic warfare for class warfare."

"What about the chances of a counterrevolution?" I asked. "I mean, what percentage of the country are these people, after all? The number of actual radicals is very small, yet they seem to control all the major centers of influence—the universities, the media, the courts. They've been very successful in changing the culture, working very slowly over the last forty or fifty years. They've successfully de-educated the children in the public schools, but do you think this can continue indefinitely? Do you see any signs of change?"

"Yes, I think there are signs of hope here and there," he said, "but certainly not enough for a counterrevolution, as you suggest."

"Maybe it will take something like 9/11 to get people's attention," I said. "The only bright spot in that tragedy was that it made patriots out of people who never thought of being patriots before. I've spoken to a number of students who told me that, more than anything else, 9/11 changed their minds and helped them to see what was really at stake. Maybe something like that—some mega-event—will have to happen on the college campus to get people angry enough to take action."

"When 9/11 happened," Steven said, "I wondered whether multiculturalism would be able to survive. My feeling is that in its present form it shouldn't be able to survive. The mindset created by multiculturalism has rendered American society almost defenseless against infiltration by people who mean to do us harm. One of the essential tenets of multiculturalism is that all cultures are good, except Western culture. All cultures are innocent and well-meaning, they say, and we have a lot to learn from them."

"Back to Rousseau and the 'noble savage' again," I said.

"That's right," he said. "Multiculturalism perpetuates a mythology that's been there all along. And it's based on the doctrine of cultural relativism we've seen in the work of Margaret Mead, Ruth Benedict, and people like that who believe that all cultures are created equal and no culture can stand in judgment of the practices or beliefs of another. It's equivalent to saying, 'We can't really say what's right and wrong in the world,' which is a mischievous and very dangerous proposition."

A Reality Check

"When liberals in the faculty and the media came out and said we deserved what we got on 9/11, because we'd been forcing our values on others for so long, a lot of students didn't like the sound of that," I said. "A lot of them— people who had never thought about being patriotic—found out that they loved their country, and they really didn't like what the Left was saying."

"Multiculturalism is inconsistent," Steven said, "and that's going to be a thorn in their side. Let me give you an example. I was flying to California not long ago to give a speech, and there was a storm. The flights were all delayed, so I had to wait at Logan Airport for two or three hours. I got to talking to a young woman, a student from Taiwan, who was on her way for an interview at a small college on the West Coast. She was already a student at the University of Massachusetts, so I asked her why she was changing schools after just one year.

"She said, 'Well, it was the dorms. I was in a dorm that's supposed to be for girls, but there were all these boys coming in, day and night. There were boys in the bathrooms, boys in the showers, boys in other girls' beds, and I couldn't believe it. One night there was a fire alarm and about fifty boys came out of this all-girls dormitory, a lot of them in just their underwear.' What really bothered her, she told me, was that her roommate would have boys in to stay overnight, and that was very upsetting to this young woman.

"She had only come to this country a few years before," Steven added. "She'd been brought up in a traditional conservative culture where this sort of thing didn't happen. But when she went to the campus housing office and asked to change roommates, or to move to another dorm, they refused. They gave her a hard time and said she was being intolerant and sexist, so she just left the dorm and moved off campus on her own, at which point she was fined five hundred dollars for violating the rules. So much for tolerance and diversity."

"She was from another culture," I said, "but because she had moral scruples she was accused of being intolerant."

"Exactly," Steven said. "She belonged to an approved ethnic group, but she had the wrong values. So whenever I hear people talking about sensitivity, tolerance, and diversity, I think of that girl and how sensitive they were to her. What the universities are actually looking for is people of different colors who all think the same thoughts. Diversity means having liberal Jews, liberal blacks, liberal Asians, liberal Latinos, and liberal whites. It has nothing to do with freedom of thought."

"A young man I've been talking to during these interviews," I said, "is a graduate student in international relations at the University of Akron, which is apparently a hotbed of Left radicalism. He's a black conservative, and he said, 'They hate me here.' He was an editor of the campus newspaper as an undergrad, so he went to the editors and said, 'You have two or three people writing editorials from a liberal point of view; how about letting me be the token conservative? I'll write a weekly column from the right.' And they said, 'Absolutely not!' They wouldn't even consider it because, while he was a minority and politically correct on the outside, he had the wrong political opinions. He wasn't allowed to be a black conservative."

PARTY HEARTY?

According to the Education Law Reporter, 63 percent of college students rank drinking, including bar-hopping and partying, as their favorite activity. Risky sexual behavior tends to increase as the level of alcohol consumption increases. The Center for Science in the Public Interest says, "More of the nation's undergraduates will ultimately die from alcohol-related causes than will go on to get masters and doctorate degrees combined." Fully 95 percent of violent crime and 80 percent of all vandalism on campus is alcohol-related, and is implicated in 90 percent of all reported rapes.

—JOEL EPSTEIN, *A Parents Guide to Sex, Drugs and Flunking Out*

"It's a scandal," Steven said. "Look at the way the Left has treated Clarence Thomas and Ward Connerly. Justice Thomas is one of the brightest, most qualified, most articulate men in America, and a man every child in the black community should want to emulate. He's a role model and an example of someone who has achieved his potential. Ward Connerly is on the Board of Regents of the University of California system, a distinguished intellectual, an author and lecturer who understands that racial preferences have been a disaster for African Americans, but he's constantly vilified by the Left and the liberal media. It's a double-standard all the way."

"When you and I have spoken in the past," I said, "you've often said that it's the parents who have to be awakened to what's going on in the universities. What can I say to parents that will help them see what's happening to their kids? How can I make them care?"

"If they care about the kind of person their sons and daughters will become," Steven said, "they'd better be worried, because you can't separate your intellect from your total personality. And you can't pass through four years in an institution like this without undergoing some important changes. This is what colleges do. Like the army, the university has always been recognized as a transformative institution that changes people in powerful ways. The problem is that most universities today are in the business of changing students in ways that many parents would find very, very disturbing."

"So what's your advice for parents?" I said. "What can they do?"

"I'd say they have to do a lot of due diligence," he said, "and I'd say they ought to check all the options before sending their children off to one of these places. Eventually there will be more and more choices, like online universities for example, because the cost of a traditional college education is going through the roof. But also because all the political correctness is having a terrible effect on young people today. Parents are in the best position to make a difference, but they've got to wake up and do something about it.

"Those who contribute to colleges," he said, "ought to be very careful about the conditions under which they contribute. And those who are sending their kids to college need to do some research. Don't waste time on the *U.S. News & World Report* college guide; it's a sham. *National Review* puts out a much better one, and the Intercollegiate Studies Institute publishes a guide that's endorsed by Thomas Sowell and many top scholars. Sowell, who is one of the most distinguished conservative scholars in the country, wrote the introduction. If you're looking at Catholic or Christian schools, even there you can't assume they're going to be okay. There's only a handful that have a strong moral tradition."

"Places like Grove City College in Pennsylvania and Hillsdale College in Michigan come to mind," I said. "Can you name any others?"

"I know the Catholic ones best," he said, "and of those I'd recommend Christendom College in Front Royal, Virginia; Thomas Aquinas College in Santa Paula, California; Franciscan University in Steubenville, Ohio; Thomas More Institute in New Hampshire; and Ave Maria University in Naples, Florida. Notre Dame is better than most of the major colleges, but even there you'll need to be careful. And I always suggest that new students make it a point to get in with a group of kids who share their views on the important issues."

"Dorms are a big part of the college experience," I said, "as you were saying about the girl at the University of Massachusetts. How do parents deal with that situation?"

"First of all," he said, "they should read Wendy Shalit's excellent book, *A Return to Modesty*. That would be very helpful, because it's all about dorm life at a women's college. After that, they need to stay in contact with their children and meet with administrators if need be to make sure that their kids are treated with dignity and with respect for their privacy. In some cases, it's probably best to just stay out of the dorms altogether."

"I've heard that a lot of young people aren't even going to college these days," I said. "They've found out that they don't need a university degree because major corporations are telling them they can learn what they need from the companies they work for. I read one article about corporations that are telling young people, 'Forget college; we'll just have to reeducate you anyway. Come work for us and we'll teach you what you need to know.'"

"Yes, that's true," Steven said. "I do think, however, that a university should be more than just a vocational school; it's not just about learning how to do a job. On the other hand, what's happening to young people in the colleges is a travesty, and if something doesn't happen soon, I think there's a good chance we're going to see a major revolution in the academic world, and it's not going to be a return to the sixties. It's going to be much bigger than that, and it will basically change the way we do higher education in this country."

A NEW SENSE OF URGENCY

My conversation with Steven was stimulating and frightening. Thinking about his compelling insights, I had to ask myself: *When will it stop and who will stop it?* The motivation for this book is the belief that America cannot continue as a world leader so long as our young people are being short-changed in this way. Substandard education and PC speech codes are putting everything we value at risk. Democracy, liberty, truth, justice, honor, compassion, integrity, and the willingness to sacrifice for a great cause: these are among the finest attributes of the American character. But for at least two generations, young Americans—from kindergarten through graduate school—have been denied access to this greatest repository of virtue. And it has been done to them by the very teachers and academicians to whom they've been entrusted by their parents.

Maybe the solution is contained in the problem. For years parents have sacrificed their own well-being and virtually indentured themselves for the sake of their children's education and future success. In so doing, however, they've unwittingly placed their offspring into the hands of socialist reprogrammers whose radical agenda is to subvert the family values, beliefs, and aspirations of their charges, and to render the next generation of Americans as unquestioning pawns of the state. This has to stop.

If there's to be any hope of turning things around, parents, alumni, fraternal and private organizations, public servants, and legislators at all levels of government, along with scholarship providers and the funding agencies who have been bankrolling this dangerous resocialization of the next generation, will have to summon a new sense of urgency about the severity of the crisis. They need to recognize what's being done to our finest young men and women, and then demand immediate and widespread changes throughout the system. We must insist on academic freedom and an end to the intellectual tyranny that passes for knowledge on our campuses.[17]

Yes, it's that serious. As the other students and faculty members interviewed in these pages will attest, the university is in crisis today, in the midst of an unprecedented intellectual and moral freefall. There are signs of revolt among the students on many campuses, and there are emerging trends in the general population that could help to undo the work of the academic Left. But unless and until changes of this magnitude begin to happen on college campuses all over America, we stand to lose the most important struggle we shall ever face as a nation: the battle for the hearts and minds of our children.

If we are to restore the foundations of responsible civic education, half measures will not do. Make no mistake, we are facing a challenge of monumental proportions, and it will take everything we can do to slow, and then, by some miracle, to stop the tyranny that's running rampant in the American university at this hour. To help precipitate that awakening and to provoke such a rebellion is the overriding mission of this book.

2

A Trajectory of Decline

A solid education in the facts of our shared experience has always been considered an important qualification for citizenship. As Stephen Balch, president of the National Association of Scholars (NAS) has said, a comprehensive education should give students the "cultural furniture that allows them to be better citizens." Unfortunately, students are not being educated in actual facts and figures but in attitudes and "feelings" about their society, and the lessons they're being taught are generally critical of America's role in the world. Consequently, at least two generations of American students are poorly equipped to participate in a democractic society.

Evidence of this decline can be seen in a 2002 Zogby poll of randomly selected college seniors, comparing their level of knowledge with that of high school graduates in the fifties. The result? College seniors of today have no better grasp of general knowledge than high-schoolers a half century ago. According to the NAS, which commissioned the poll in concert with the Los Angeles-based Center for the Study of Popular Culture, "The average amount of knowledge that college seniors had was just about the same as the average amount of knowledge that high school graduates had back in the 1950s." Balch also notes that high school grads of the fifties actually performed better than today's college seniors on questions involving American history.

More than anything, the poor performance of today's university students reflects the deemphasis on general knowledge at all levels of education. Today's students are every bit as intelligent as those of earlier generations, but they've been miseducated and poorly prepared for the task of learning. If this knowledge gap is to be filled, our schools and universities will have to change the way they teach. Subjects such as history, literature, civics, foreign language, and basic math and science were standard fare until the sixties. "This is fundamental knowledge that everyone should have," says Balch. Unfortunately, there is almost no emphasis on these traditional subjects in either high school or college today, and the students themselves have no idea what they're missing.

Most universities do not require students to take American history or to be tested in specific history and government knowledge; consequently, those who enter college with vast areas of ignorance are likely to remain so unless they determine on their own to explore this territory. The NAS study raises many questions about the caliber of general education offered in high schools, but colleges and universities must bear the burden of responsibility for this deterioration of learning. As Balch says, "I think it probably has a lot to do with the dumbing down of curriculum, both at the college and high school level. It looks good, certainly, to say 'more people are graduating from college,' but is there any real intellectual yield from it?"[1] Apparently the answer is no.

THE LONG MARCH

In 1962, the year I graduated from high school, America was a very different place. There was peace on earth and, for the most part, goodwill toward men. It was the year memorialized in the 1973 film, *American Graffiti*, a year of bobby-soxers, satin prom gowns, drive-in movies, and long goodbyes. John Kennedy was in the White House, in the second year of a popular presidency, and many months away from the tragedy that would bring an end to what, in hindsight at least, would be remembered as "Camelot."

The U.S. crash-landed an unmanned spacecraft on the moon that year, and John Glenn, aboard Friendship 7, circled the earth three times in just under five hours, making splashdown in the Atlantic Ocean. Walter Cronkite became the anchor of *CBS Evening News*, and Chris Schenkel launched a radio feature called *ABC's Wide World of Sports*. Jack Parr finished his run as host of NBC's *The Tonight Show*, replaced by an upstart named Johnny Carson; and a rock band making waves in Liverpool made their radio debut and signed their first recording contract that year—although it would be yet another year before the Beatles became better known on this side of the Atlantic.

Late that year, satellite photos revealed that Russia was, in fact, building missile silos just ninety miles from our coast, in Cuba. The Kennedy administration challenged Soviet Premier Nikita Khrushchev to remove the missiles, and U.N. Ambassador Adlai Stevenson demanded an answer, declaring that he was prepared to wait "until hell freezes over" to get it. The Cuban Missile Crisis ended soon after, and America was spared a nuclear confrontation.

Former first lady Eleanor Roosevelt died in 1962, as did screen star Marilyn Monroe and novelist William Faulkner. And, not to go unnoticed, on June 25, by a vote of six to one, the United States Supreme Court—in the case of *Engel v. Vitale*, majority opinion rendered by Justice Hugo L. Black—banned prayer in America's public schools. No one suspected in those days the enormity of the changes that were ahead.

For all the apparent calm of that time, the seeds of change were already germinating in the subsoil of the American culture. In his landmark work on the history of conservative thought in the West, Russell Kirk reports that as early as 1950 intellectually subversive forces had invaded the academy and were searching for adherents to take a message of social transformation to the public. The takeover of higher education was not immediate, however. There were pockets of resistance. "If the university generally submitted to the liberal intellectuals' ascendancy," Kirk writes, "still the sympathetic public for conservative thinkers was larger than the liberals'."[2]

In the years after World War II, both Americans and Europeans were wary of the *armed* doctrine of the Communist League. Freedom-loving Americans were justifiably suspicious of socialism's egalitarian premise, and fully three-fourths of the American public described themselves as conservatives or "moderates." But as peace wore on and prosperity surged throughout

Western society, resistance to leftist ideologies and the nostrums of change grew perceptibly weaker. Enlightenment ideals that had infiltrated the academy would become the soil in which the radicalism of the Sixties Revolution would take root.

Ultimately, it was middle-class complacency that led to the lowering of intellectual standards and to the compromise of the traditional foundations of higher education. Those who entered university in the fifties and sixties were largely unaware of the tensions that had been mounting among faculty members and administrators, where intense ideological battles were being waged. By the end of the sixties, however, involved as we were in the all-encompassing maelstrom of protest and revolt engendered by the Vietnam War and related issues, it soon became apparent that the system was broken and the invasion of "tenured radicals" had begun.

When I began my college career, the undergraduate curriculum was long established and clearly prescribed. It was inconceivable, in fact, that anyone might someday change it. History, mathematics, English, foreign language, government, physical sciences, physical education, and academically relevant electives—including philosophy, music, and art—were all required. Survey courses in history, literature, and government assured that all students had at least a foundation of general knowledge and a basic understanding of our common heritage. Grading was rigid, and the competition was intense.

In its detailed comparisons of graduation requirements for English majors in 1964, the NAS found that more than half of the twenty-five elite schools in the study required survey courses in English and American literature for their students. By 1997, however, only a handful still had such requirements. In his summary statement, NAS President Balch observed that "the great majority no longer even try to provide their students with a serious overview of the Anglo-American literary tradition, or a systematic exposure to its greatest writers and works; that is to say, to the literary 'big picture.' Instead, they leave their students to wander among a hodgepodge of courses on narrow subjects and esoteric theory, often containing stiff doses of ideology, and frequently preoccupied with sex and cultural controversy."[3]

Traditional curricula have been scrapped in favor of cultural critique and politically-loaded social issues, such as "Queer Studies," rhetoric, linguistic deconstruction, and a new politically correct trivium: the politics of race, class, and gender. The consequence of such changes in the curriculum was not merely that second-rate authors were being studied, but that the "great tradition" had been demeaned and discarded. Chaucer, Dante, Milton, Shakespeare, Tolstoy, Melville, and Twain were out, and any writer with a racial, sexual, or political ax to grind was suddenly in.

By the mid-seventies, a staggering array of French intellectual fads had invaded university classrooms. Deconstructionists such as Roland Barthes, Jacques Deridda, Michel Foucault, and Gilles Deleuze, whose ideas borrowed heavily from the sociology of Freud and Marx, were suddenly the darlings of the literary elite. Marching beside them were the acolytes of the New Left—anarchists captivated by the revolutionary zeal of Frantz Fanon, Malcolm X, Che Guevara, and Chairman Mao—and all of them in the thrall of the neo-Marxist radicals of the Frankfurt School, which included Antonio Gramsci, Herbert Marcuse, Jurgen Habermas, Theodor Adorno, Max Horkheimer, and others less celebrated but no less dedicated to insurrection and the violent overthow of capitalist society.

FORGETTING WHO WE ARE

In just a little over a decade, "reading, writing, and arithmetic" had succumbed to the fashions of radical revisionism. No longer did the curriculum focus on American achievements in democracy, language, culture, science, and industry, but on our national failures: slavery, chauvinism, allegations of misogyny and cultural imperialism, as well as sexual prudery and repression. The object of literature and language for the new intellectual was no longer to uplift the human spirit but to tear down and deconstruct the literary text—to debunk, unmask, and demystify the act of communication and, thus, to rip away any sense of the transcendent.

Commenting on the general loss of memory in the schools and universities, columnist Mona Charen asks, "If the words Yorktown, bleeding Kansas, reconstruction, Ellis Island, *Marbury vs. Madison*, 'Remember the

Maine,' the Spirit of St. Louis, Midway, 'I shall return,' the Battle of the Bulge, the Hiss/Chambers case, and *Ich bin ein Berliner* mean no more to most Americans than to the average Malaysian, what is it that makes us Americans?" A big part of what makes this country unique, she says, is our common history and shared beliefs.

It's not possible to become a Frenchman, a Swiss, or a Russian by moving to those countries and adopting their beliefs. Nationality there is too bound up in blood, ethnicity, and land. "But every immigrant who arrives in the United States can become an American by adopting our beliefs," says Charen. The goal of the revisionists, on the other hand, was specifically to discredit the idea of American social and cultural dominance in order to elevate the status of, in Fanon's words, "the wretched of the earth," and to create a crisis of cultural dissonance.

There was a time when we had so much confidence in the superiority of the American way of life, as Charen points out, that we taught these values to new immigrants and insisted that they master the basics of American history, language, and government before becoming eligible for citizenship. Today, however, we're not even teaching those things to our own children. As a result, we're plagued by "a truly frightening collective ignorance." Those who don't know their own history, as Bruce Cole has said, are more inclined to believe any bizarre version of history served up by liberal loudmouths like Oliver Stone, Michael Moore, or Al Franken. That's why the organization Bruce Cole was appointed by President George W. Bush to lead, the National Endowment for the Humanities, has begun promoting a new series of initiatives to improve the teaching of history in America's classrooms.[4]

In a poll commissioned by the American Council of Trustees and Alumni (ACTA), researchers examined knowledge of American history among seniors at the top fifty-five liberal arts colleges in the country. The questions were all straightforward, what teachers in the sixties would have considered high-school-level knowledge. Fully 81 percent of college seniors received a grade of D or F on the exam. Only one student made a perfect score. As a brief sampling, 35 percent guessed that the phrase, "To each according to his needs, from each according to his ability, " comes from the

U.S. Constitution. In fact, the phrase is a principle of Marxist socialism. More than half of the students tested thought that Germany, Italy, or Japan was an ally of the United States during World War II. Less than 30 percent knew that the Reconstruction period had to do with the Civil War. And 30 percent thought the president has the authority to suspend the Bill of Rights in wartime.

WHAT ARE YOU PAYING FOR?

"The College Board reports that the average cost of the current school year (including tuition and fees, books and transportation, room and board) is $13,833 at a state university and almost $30,000 at a private college. If the past is any guide, those costs will rise next year and the next and the next. The $50,000 baccalaureate at a public school soon will cost more than that, while the $120,000 bachelor's degree at a private school is here today — but only if you prepay the whole amount. College no longer is like buying an expensive car but, rather, like a house...."

—Terry Eastland, *National Review*, 12 May 2004

At least 40 percent of the students could not place the Civil War in the correct half-century, and just 42 percent knew that the words "first in war, first in peace, first in the hearts of his countrymen" refers to our first president, George Washington. Only about 25 percent could identify James Madison as the "father of the Constitution," while only 22 percent recognized the words, "Government of the people, by the people and for the people" as coming from President Abraham Lincoln's Gettysburg Address.

If you wonder how there can be such a general lack of general knowledge in the nation's universities, you need to know that, of the fifty-five schools surveyed by ACTA, not one of them requires a single survey course in American history.[5] The implications of such studies should be obvious, but by and large American universities and the professional education establishment in Washington have chosen to ignore the problems, or to define them away. But historian Diane Ravitch, who served as an assistant secretary of education in two presidential administrations, sees the issue differently. She says, "Our ability to defend, intelligently and thoughtfully, what we as a nation hold dear depends on our knowledge and understanding of what we hold dear."⁶ But make no mistake: those who created this situation know precisely what they're doing.

Columnist Don Feder has written that the fact young Americans are oblivious to their heritage has not happened by accident. "Ignorance of our past has been carefully cultivated by the educational establishment," he says. "The result is a cut-flower generation, severed from its roots." The evidence of what has happened can be seen in many places. As just one example, the National Assessment of Educational Progress (NAEP), described as "the nation's report card," reveals that 60 percent of American high-school seniors lack even the most basic knowledge of U.S. history. But how could they know it when it's not even being taught in the schools?

On July the 4th, 1999, a reporter for the *San Francisco Examiner* asked teens at local malls what they thought the July 4th holiday was supposed to commemorate. One student said it had something to do with Pearl Harbor. Another said, "They put some flag up. It's like the freedom. Some war was fought and we won, so we got our freedom." Even when their answers came close, the reporter said, it was obvious that these typical middle-class students had no idea what had actually happened, how the Republic had been founded, or the price that was paid for our liberty. Feder says:

> This epidemic of ignorance is due in part to a crowding-out effect. Schools are so busy telling everyone else's story, there's no time for our own. At its 2001 convention, the National Education Association passed resolutions supporting multicultural education and global education. Absent was any suggestion that students should receive an American education. When they absolutely must teach something about the United States, educrats prefer niche history—the experiences of African Americans, Asian

Americans, Hispanic Americans. The idea of *E Pluribus Unum* (out of many, one) is anathema to them. Teaching American history—our common story—as opposed to group-identity history, is rejected as ethnocentric and jingoistic.[7]

This mindset was dramatically revealed at a forum of the National Council for Social Studies. The council represents twenty-six thousand teachers of history, social studies, and related subjects. To a teacher who said that in the wake of September 11 her students wanted to know more about their nation's past, one panelist responded, "We need to de-exceptionalize the United States. We're just another country and another group of people."[8]

Commenting on the deconstruction of American history in the schools and universities, President Reagan once warned, "If we forget what we did, we won't know who we are." He said, further, that "the eradication of American memory" will eventually lead to "an erosion of the American spirit." How right he was. If we contrast the level of general knowledge of students in the fifties and sixties with that of the typical high school or college student today, we will have a snapshot of two very different Americas. The first was an optimistic, naïve, even euphoric nation, standing on the cusp of the space age; the other is an agonizing, politically and spiritually divided, emotionally insecure, and ethically challenged nation attempting to deny its magnificent historical legacy and skulking silently in the shadows of self-doubt and self-denial.

TAKING STOCK

When Stephen Balch and researchers at the National Association of Scholars began to assess what they'd learned from their survey of curriculum changes since the sixties, they decided to prepare an outline of their findings. The list is sobering.

The majority of departments surveyed had abandoned any requirement for survey courses in English or American literature. Of the twenty-five departments that had such courses in the sixties, only four did by 1997.

Courses dealing with major authors, periods, and genres had dropped to just over a third.

Only two colleges still required English majors to study Shakespeare. The number of elective courses increased by 74 percent.

In 1964, twenty of the twenty-five programs examined demanded that students pass a comprehensive exam before graduation. In 1997, only two still had such requirements.

Also evident, the importance and influence of British literature had been lost, overshadowed by contemporary American works. Shakespeare, Chaucer, Milton, Pope, Wordsworth, Keats, Byron, and Swift had disappeared from most catalogs, while lesser-known women and ethnic writers soared to the top of the list.

Most literature programs today focus on subjects that might better be considered in a sociology department. The catalog description for a course called "Reading Television," at Wesleyan University, informs students that, "Despite the fact that the course focuses on what has been called 'mind-candy,' prospective students should know that this will be a rigorous course, requiring a serious commitment of time to reading about, watching, and analyzing television texts." Another course, called "Rebel Without a Cause/Sweet Little Sixteen: The Social Construction of the Teenager in American Culture, 1948-64," explored "the social construction of the teenager . . . in an attempt to understand why postwar America constructs this category and defines it as a consumer culture." With such fare, it's not hard to see why the level of academic achievement has plummeted in recent years.

Researchers also found that the fixation on theory and cultural ideologies was on the rise. There was a clear preoccupation with postmodern theory and "race, gender, and class"—issues that never existed in the early sixties.

The influence of gender and race have altered literature curricula in startling ways. For example, based on the number of times her name was cited in course descriptions, African-American novelist Toni Morrison is now the sixth most important author in the English language. But this was not the only high rating to give the researchers pause. Zora Neale Hurston, a writer of the Harlem Literary Renaissance, now ranks ahead of Twain, Fielding, Poe, Dryden, Pope, and Swift; and obscure seventeenth-century female dramatist, Aphra Behn, who wrote about the slave trade in Suriname, ranks ahead of Shaw, Pound, Scott, Auden, Beckett, Nabokov, and Kipling.

Finally, the NAS analysts observed a dramatic rise in "Film and Television Studies" in literature departments over the past forty years. In 1964 catalogs, there were only seven mentions of film or television distributed among three course descriptions. One course explored "the contemporary press," including approaches to reporting, interviewing, and writing. Another focused on production methods and federal regulation in television and radio programming. A third taught dramatic writing for television, film, radio, and the stage. By 1989, some fifty-three courses dealt with film or television, and by 1997, there were ninety-five courses in this category. Apparently, as researchers observed, film studies are a growth industry in today's English departments.

The result of such changes is that graduates of these programs possess "only the most rudimentary knowledge of English literature's longer history, or of its greatest writers and works." Rather than a comprehensive knowledge of the field, they've been pushed into premature specialization, normally reserved for graduate schools, and exposure to dubious "theoretical insights" about trendy, politically correct authors soon to be forgotten. And of even greater concern, the next generation of writers, scholars, and teachers will likely come from the ranks of these ill-served students. As the NAS team concluded, "Anyone concerned about preserving our rich and creative literary culture has good reason to be alarmed."[9]

EXACTING A PRICE

Whether it's the transformation of the traditional curriculum or the deterioration of academic standards, there is truly ample cause for alarm. In his assessment of the failure of higher education, Ed Feulner, president of the Heritage Foundation, argues that America's most prestigious colleges and universities have failed in the basic responsibility: to teach students something about history, literature, mathematics, the natural sciences, foreign language, philosophy, and English.

"The reason most 'Generation Xers' don't come away from college with such a 'bottom-line' education is simple," Feulner says, "It's no longer required of them." The vast majority of colleges in this country have eliminated core requirements once considered essential for a liberal-arts education. At the fifty top colleges and universities identified in the annual *U.S. News & World Report* guide to America's best, he says, commitment to a structured general education has largely vanished over the past thirty years. In short, as reported in a separate study by the NAS, there has been "a purging from the curriculum of many of the required basic survey courses that used to familiarize students with the historical, cultural, political, and scientific foundations of their society."[10]

What's left, as Russell Kirk once described it, is "lax institutions at which every lad and lass can succeed, because all standards for entrance or graduation have been swept away." Judgment is eliminated, hurt feelings are assuaged, self-esteem is ameliorated, and the result is a generation of semiliterate college graduates who are "able to ascertain the price of everything — but the value of nothing."[11] Any parent spending upwards of twenty-five thousand dollars a year in tuition and related expenses surely deserves more than the kind of superficial knowledge, narrow vision, and unrealistic expectations provided by today's university. High self-esteem and a blissful sense of accomplishment won't take graduates very far in a highly competitive marketplace, particularly when better educated men and women from Third World nations are vying for top jobs in business and industry.

In its assessment of some of the dangerous compromises being made by students and their families, the *New York Times* reported in 2003 that rising tuition and mounting debts are a major problem. "In their trek through college and beyond, student borrowers now amass an average of $27,600 in educational debt," according to the *Times*, "almost three and a half times what they compiled a decade ago in unadjusted dollars, according to a new survey by Nellie Mae, the student loan company." As costs continue to climb, so has the number of students who take out loans to help pay for tuition. Ten years ago, only 46 percent of graduating seniors had taken educational loans in their undergraduate careers. By the year 2000, however, according to the National Center for Education Statistics, approximately 70 percent of seniors had done so.

PRESTIGE-HUNGRY PREDATORS

In his article, "Cheers for No-Name U," Jacob Neusner says, "A generation ago no one doubted the value of education among 'the best and the brightest.' The elite schools today lie in shambles and disgrace. Who wants to emulate them? Stanford has turned its curriculum into an engine of propaganda . . . a Brown degree certifies nothing. The English department at Georgetown has repealed literature. Berkeley is a zoo, Harvard a jungle with prestige-hungry predators. . . ." Neusner, a professor and rabbi who has taught in both the Ivy League and a state college, suggests looking to lesser known colleges, but unfortunately the PC disease has overtaken many of these too.

—*American Enterprise,* September 1996

An economics professor at Skidmore College who has followed the trend of student debt over the last fifteen years asked the obvious question: "What will happen when people decide it's not worth it and won't go to college at all?" It's a question many parents are asking as well, as they find themselves doing without basic necessities—from home and auto repairs to vacations and dining out—so that their kids can earn a college degree that, in the end, really means almost nothing. But the *Times* continues:

> Still, for many students, loans have become an inescapable reality. Even after adjusting for inflation, tuition and fees at private and public universities

have more than doubled in the last twenty years, and though grants have increased as well, they have not nearly kept pace with the cost of higher education. The outcome is that loans have essentially swapped places with grants on the seesaw of educational finance. As recently as ten years ago, for example, loans accounted for a little more than 45 percent of all financial aid in the nation, according to the College Board. Today, they make up 54 percent, and few experts expect any sudden changes in the equation.[12]

Further, says the *Times*, family background plays a part in determining how students respond to higher debt levels. According to the Nellie Mae survey, 62 percent of low-income borrowers said they regretted taking out so much in loans. On the other hand, about half of those in the upper income levels—those who were too well off to qualify for federal grants—said it was probably worth it. Similarly, just 54 percent of low-income students said the debt actually paid off in attaining their career goals, but 63 percent of the wealthier students said it did.

A Devil's Bargain

As statistics regarding the rising cost of college tuition and the declining quality of the education students receive continue to accelerate in opposite directions, perceptive commentators are asking a hard question: Why indenture yourself for so little gain? "With very few exceptions," says columnist Dennis Prager, "any tuition over ten thousand dollars is rarely worth it. This is especially so for students in what is variously called the humanities, the social sciences (a term that is even more deceptive than the tuition), or the liberal arts."[13]

For students majoring in English, political science, or sociology, and particularly in politically charged programs such as women's studies and African-American studies, parents are often paying enormous sums for their children to be politicized by overpaid and underworked faculty members who are products of the sixties counterculture. If only half of what we've learned from Allan Bloom's *Closing of the American Mind* and Kors and

Silverglate's *Shadow University* is true, entrusting our children's future to this sort of radical indoctrination makes very little sense, ethically, emotionally, or financially.

The colleges are dominated by postmodernists and other nihilists for whom the pursuit of truth is considered reactionary and unrealistic. "For these professors, deans, and presidents," says Prager, "the primary purpose of the university is to mold students in their images—people alienated from America and from God." This is hardly the combination that would justify such a heavy accumulation of debt. Traditionally, parents have been glad to foot the bill for their children's education because they had the security of knowing that they were contributing to their future success and their fitness for productive work. But that is no longer something that can be taken for granted.

As parents and supporters of the university system are beginning to rethink the devil's bargain they've made, many are discovering that the idea that it makes a difference what college their child attends is a false assumption. As Prager concludes:

> For the most part, what college you go to doesn't amount to a hill of beans. If you find that hard to believe, answer these questions: Do you know what college your most trusted physician or lawyer attended? Do you know what college the writers or clergy you most admire attended? Do you care? Did you choose your spouse or any of your friends on the basis of what college they attended? In other words, can you name one area of life where the prestige of a person's alma mater has mattered to you?[14]

Even if the answer to the pundit's questions is not necessarily an unequivocal no, his point is nevertheless clear. Many of the most prestigious universities in America, where the cost of a four-year education can top a hundred and fifty thousand dollars, are not only overpriced for what they deliver but are precisely the same institutions that are doing the greatest damage to the emotional, physical, and mental health of American youth. Unfortunately, alumni, foundations, granting organizations, corporate sponsors, and the federal government are still heedless to what is transpiring on the university campuses, so that each year the endowments of the major universities continue to soar. The number of outrageous programs continues to multiply, and more and more students are being indoctrinated with dangerous ideas that will handicap them for years to come.

Why is this happening? Because no one who knows the truth has been willing to take the first step and put a stop to the madness. And because university administrators are counting on the apathy and ignorance of the American public to work in their favor. In light of all this, James Bowman, who is the American editor of the *Times Literary Supplement*, offers this startling assessment:

> By the time that colleges began to realize in the 1970s that their students were willing to incur almost ruinous levels of debt not necessarily to learn anything in particular but just to be able to say that they had successfully spent four years in their charge, the whole enterprise of higher education had become a scandalous racket. Universities answerable to no one but a kind of trade-guild system of accreditation and tenure became centers for the employment of otherwise unemployable adepts of the reigning ideology of the guild, which was neo-Marxist in character and would have been dangerously subversive if anyone outside the universities had taken it seriously.

But that is precisely what needs to happen, Bowman says. If there is to be any hope of turning things around, the whole equation must change, and the racketeers must be stopped. At such a juncture, a radical proposal is in order:

> If they were simply shut down, the high schools would no longer be able to salve their conscience that their failure to educate those in their charge could be made up for later. And if all the money now spent on higher education were returned to the people in the form of vouchers, so that they could make their own choices about how best to educate their children, I believe that in no time at all it would be routine for children to graduate

from high school with a level of accomplishment as good or better than that of college graduates today. The graduate and professional schools could be allowed to continue, then, and our newly competent high school graduates could apply to them directly if they felt the need for further, more specialized training.[15]

Bowman offers a remarkable assessment of our current malaise and the potential for changing the status quo on campus. For more than forty years, no major university has been seriously challenged for its failure to deliver on the promise of a quality education. The promise of a diploma from a top university has convinced too many students and their parents to remain silent in the face of what can only be interpreted as academic fraud. Others don't know what to expect, or they simply assume that tenured faculty and supercilious administrators know best. But that's hardly the case, as my interview with one brave young woman illustrates very well.

GRADE INFLATION

"Grade inflation penalizes the superior, the talented, and the hard working, and rewards the mediocre, incompetent, and lazy. . . . It teaches America's brightest young people that there is no particular merit attached to hard work. It is a measure of the deterioration of our institutions of higher education."

—Paul Copperman, *The Literacy Hoax*

A VOICE IN THE WILDERNESS

I arranged to meet Ashley at Harvard Square a couple of hours before her seminar with Professor Samuel Huntington, author of the celebrated 1996 book, *The Clash of Civilizations*. She had recently transferred from a small

New England college, she said, where the liberal mind-block was stifling. Since making the move to Boston she had become more active in politics, and she was happy to be surrounded by new friends who shared her conservative views, her faith in America, and her strong code of ethics. "I'm impressed, Ashley," I said to her, "that as a junior at the oldest and best-known Ivy League school in the country, you've found your own voice, and you're willing to take a stand for what you believe in. How did this happen?"

"I think it's probably genetic," she said with a big smile. "My dad was an undergrad at a small college back in the seventies, and he attended an assembly one day where a speaker was brought in to address the entire student body. It was the Vietnam era, of course, and this guy was saying that America was corrupt and that our government was the enemy of freedom, and he just went on and on, and my dad was getting pretty sick of it. So at one point he stood up, right in the middle of the auditorium, and he said he'd heard about all of that he wanted to hear. He looked around at his classmates and said, 'We don't have to listen to this radical. Whaddaya say? Let's get out of here! We can just walk out.' So that's what he did. He turned and headed for the door, but when he looked around nobody was coming with him. He was the only one with the guts to speak up, so he walked out by himself."

"Were there any repercussions from that?" I asked.

"I don't think so," she said. "He went on to graduate and earn his law degree, and now my dad's a politician, and a little tougher than I am! But that story has always been a source of inspiration for me."

"Now that you're at Harvard," I said, "what's it like for you on this campus?"

"Probably the biggest surprise has been the upsurge in people expressing their views when President Bush sent the military into Iraq," she said. "There were marches, sit-ins, and a lot of debate about that, but I was surprised to see that there were actually two sides to the debates. The antiwar crowd was more vocal, but a surprising number of students actually supported the president and refused to take part in the demonstrations."

"Is that different from what you had experienced at your previous school?" I asked.

"Absolutely," she said. "There was only one point of view at my other school, and it was very liberal. During the buildup to the war in Iraq, I wrote a letter to the editor of the campus newspaper stating my support for the troops. Basically, I said that whether or not we supported the war, we ought to support the troops, you know? I thought that was fairly obvious, but the next week the entire editorial section of the school newspaper was filled with letters attacking me, saying how insane I was. One person said I obviously loved genocide. And what surprised me was that one girl came up to me and said, 'You know, Ashley, I really worry about you! Saying all those things and supporting the war like that. This is a caring, compassionate campus,' she said, 'but what's going to happen to you when you go out into the real world and say things like that? You know, you really need to be more careful!' Well, I was just flabbergasted!"

"She was living in a bubble," I said, "and had no idea that in the real world most people are behind the president. Did you get any positive feedback from your letter?"

"Actually," she said, "a couple of professors sent me a note saying they admired my courage for speaking out. They said they knew about four or five professors who were closet conservatives, but they try to keep it quiet because it's not accepted on that campus."

"What about students?" I asked. "Were there any groups or individuals willing to stand with you on those kinds of issues?"

"Well," she hesitated a moment. "We had about sixty students who signed up for the Republican Club on campus, but most of the time only four or five would actually show up for meetings or rallies, or help us pass out flyers and things like that."

"So once again," I said, "you were pretty much out there on your own."

"Yes," she said, "I really realized how alone I was one time when I agreed to write a point-counterpoint column for the college newspaper. I was writing on behalf of the College Republicans, and someone else was writing for the Democrats. Well, I dared to write about affirmative action, and as a result they called a meeting of the newspaper staff and student government to discuss what to do about what I'd said. Everybody agreed they had to make up for the newspaper's having published my article; saying that affirmative action might not be the right answer was just intolerable in their view. The African American Alliance was really outraged and demanded that the student government explain how such an article could have been published, and that was all anybody talked about for weeks."

"They don't understand free speech up there, do they?" I said.

"Well, they certainly exercised theirs," she said. "They called me a racist and a bigot, and I'm really just the opposite. If we're all equal, and I sincerely believe we are, then affirmative action is the last thing we need. To insist on one race being given more rights than another, or more privileges, is about as racist as it gets, and that was my point. Anyway, over the next few weeks I got dozens of e-mails harassing me. Even friends wrote and said they were really worried about me. But I'm no radical. There were people on campus going around wearing NRA hats and all sorts of things, and I didn't do that. But from where the liberals on that campus were coming from, a mainstream point of view like mine looked radical. They couldn't deal with the fact that I might actually be a conservative."

"So how did that change campus life for you?" I asked.

"A couple of times when I went to the ladies room, girls would come up to me and say, 'Hey, aren't you the girl who wrote that article?' I'd say, 'Yep, that's me.' And they'd say, 'Did you do that just to make everybody mad? Is that why you did it?' I said, 'Of course not. It's a valid opinion. These issues wouldn't be so hotly debated, you know, if there weren't two sides to the issue.' But no one seemed to notice that there was only one side on campus, and that maybe something was wrong with that."

TAKING IT TO HEART

"As you told me earlier," I said, "you eventually decided to leave there and come to Harvard. How is your situation different now?"

"I have a seminar with Dr. Samuel Huntington in a couple of hours," Ashley said, "and it's one of the best things I'm doing. His book about the clash of civilizations is a classic, and he really understands the issues. There are about twenty of us in the seminar, and the first day of class he came right out and told us who he is, how old he is, and he said, 'I'm an old-school liberal, but a lot of times these days I end up voting conservative.' That really shocked me; not that he said he voted conservative but that he was brave enough to say it. He was the first professor I've ever had who was honest enough to tell us where he stood, and I really appreciated that. He was honest. He told us what he stood for, and we could take it at face value."

For several minutes we talked about the political environment at Harvard, the number of conservative organizations and conservative students she'd met, and the general atmosphere of liberalism that influences most things on campus. But I wanted to know what other factors had an influence on students. So I said, "What about parents, Ashley? Do they care what's happening on campus, or do they just want their kids to get an Ivy League degree, regardless of what happens in the classrooms or the dorm?"

"Honestly, I don't think they believe it," she said. "A lot of kids here understand that the campus is liberal, but they think that's okay. They just think that's the way the world is. And parents, from what I've seen, don't really know enough about it to say or do very much."

"But survey after survey shows that most Americans are not liberal," I said. "The universities are very liberal, but the culture is not. Doesn't that ever occur to any of these people?"

"You know," Ashley said, shaking her head, "this has been going on so long that it's just the way it is. It reminds me of Bernard Goldberg's book, *Bias*, about loss of objectivity in the media. He says they're not really trying to be liberal; that's just who they are, so they think that's normal. It's their worldview. I think that's the way it is here, too. The liberals have been in charge so long that nobody questions it anymore."

"The problem with liberalism on campus," I said, "is that there's a kind of mind control that comes with it. It's what you described earlier about ethnic groups denying your free-speech rights, and for the campus newspapers to forbid certain kinds of articles from being published because they just don't want to hear the other side. It's the absolute opposite of free speech, and it's intellectually dishonest. The people who are screaming loudest about diversity and tolerance are totally non-diverse and intolerant."

"Exactly," she said. "I agree, and there's a 'blame America first' attitude in practically everything on the campus. When we had our support-the-troops rally, the posters we made were totally non-partisan. They just said 'Support Our Troops.' There was an American flag, and it said, 'Come to the rally,' and gave the time and place. Well, someone went around campus that night and stapled a poster on top of ours that said, 'Feel free to bring flags that are not American to this rally.' They were saying that, because there's freedom of speech, people should have the right to bring any flag they wanted to, and to be openly anti-American in their views. That just didn't make sense to me."

"It doesn't make sense to most people," I said, "except on the college campus or in places like 'The People's Republic of Cambridge,' as they call it, where we're seated now!"

"If someone was advertising a gay-pride rally," Ashley continued, "what would happen if I went around and put up a sign that said, 'Feel free to bring flags that aren't rainbow flags.' I would be standing in front of the dean tomorrow morning, for sure. I would have been accosted and maybe even physically harmed. But when it comes to being patriotic and supporting our troops, they're absolutely biased and intolerant. That scares me."

"You would think that after 9/11," I said, "people would understand what's at stake here. Don't you think any of your fellow students have made the connection?"

"Some of them have," she said. "One of my best friends is in Afghanistan right now, in the military, and he sent me an e-mail saying, 'It's not so bad over here. The war's going okay, but what troubles me is knowing that nobody at home supports what we're doing.' And I thought that was really awful. But when I mentioned this to one of our critics on campus, he said he didn't support the troops because they chose to be in the military and be part of all that."

"What did you say to that?" I said.

"This is probably the most extreme position I have," she said, "but I said, 'Love it or leave it!' If you can't support your country and the people who are brave enough to stand up for us in the military, then you don't need to be here. And you don't have any right to be here. This country gives us so much, and so many people just take it for granted."

"Most of the faculty," I said, "have been co-opted by the Left. In fact, as so many studies have shown, it's almost impossible for conservatives to be hired to teach at most universities. But I would like to think that at least the students are more open-minded, and at least willing to consider other options."

"I haven't seen much of that," she said. "As just one example, we had a speaker who came in and complained about the conservative bias in the news media. He said it was impossible to get the truth out of the major media, so you need to go to these certain Web sites or subscribe to these certain magazines to find out what's really going on. And some of my friends left the meeting saying, 'Wow, I never knew the media was so biased! I didn't know they lied about all those things.' They were just totally taken in by that. So I asked them, 'If I brought in Bernard Goldberg who says it's really just the opposite, would you suddenly say, 'Wow! I never knew the media was so liberal'? They hadn't even thought about that. In fact, they hadn't thought about very much. Whatever the professor or the lecturer says to them, they just take it right to heart."

THE COURAGE OF CONVICTION

Dr. Harvey Mansfield, who is the most distinguished and outspoken conservative on the Harvard faculty, told me that a disturbingly large number of his students no longer seem to have critical thinking skills. In fact, one of my greatest concerns about what's happening in high schools and colleges today is that many teachers have apparently taken pains to chisel away the students' ability to ask questions, to express doubts, or to challenge obvious logical fallacies. So I asked Ashley if she had seen any signs of that in her classes, at either of the colleges she'd attended.

"Yes and no," she said. "Students don't challenge what they hear very often, but I don't know if it isn't that they're just taught to believe that these professors are the voice of wisdom. We see these distinguished professors and think, *Wow, they've got to be right!* Especially when you have a class with someone who is a famous author or who is really well known in their field. You have to think that they know what they're talking about. They wouldn't be teaching at Harvard if they didn't know their stuff, would they?"

"There's a big difference between courtesy and gullibility," I said. "In an honest academic environment, students ought to be willing to speak up if they don't follow a particular line of thinking, or particularly if the professor has stepped over the line. And any professor worth his salt should be more than willing to deal with questions or objections."

"I agree," she said, "but I haven't seen much of that. I don't know what it is. Most of my friends are smart; they wouldn't be here if they weren't. But they're so easily swayed. I have some friends who don't care about politics, and that's fine. But when a professor says Democrats are good and Republicans are bad, they can't just say, 'Okay, I'll remember that!' And I really think that's all some of them know how to do, because they don't really want to go any deeper than that. Whatever information they get from their professors, they just accept it as truth."

"When I was teaching in college," I said, "I found that many of my students weren't prepared to think for themselves. They'd been trained since kindergarten not to think but to just listen and then spit it all back at exam time. Even with affluent kids from very good private schools, it was clear that they didn't have any critical thinking skills. They hadn't been taught to think for themselves or to have opinions, unless it was about clothes or music or things like that. They knew everything about the latest fashions and pop culture, but they didn't have a clue about what was going on in the world."

"It's not encouraged," she said. "Teachers don't really want their students to know what's happening outside the classroom, and that's what makes people like Professor Huntington so special. He loves it when someone disagrees with him. He's a funny guy. He wrote a book several years ago called

American Politics and the Promise of Disharmony, and one day he said, 'Oh, yeah, I've changed my mind on some of that.' I thought, *Wow! How refreshing!* That was so honest, and I appreciated that. He's an honest liberal."

"Unfortunately," I said, "not all liberals are so open-minded."

"I think they're liberal for the sake of being liberal," she said. "I'm a conservative, but there are some issues on which I have what some people call liberal views. Some of my friends laugh at me and call me a tree-hugging conservative. They don't know that just because most of my ideas lean toward the conservative point of view, I'm not in lockstep. I'm an open-minded person, and I think that surprises them. Unfortunately, I have friends who are closed-minded liberals. They say they hate George Bush and they hate everything he stands for, and they never stop to consider the issues on their own merit. They say, 'This is how I define myself. I'm a liberal who hates George Bush.' And that's it."

"Ashley," I said, "if there were just one thing you'd want parents and prospective students to know about what's happening on the Harvard campus today, what would it be?"

"First of all," she said without hesitation, "I think they need to make sure that when they're growing up, and long before they go away to college, that they're prepared to think on their own, and not to take everything they hear at face value. That's difficult because parents want their kids to agree with them, and I can't imagine my nice conservative parents saying to me, 'Okay, Ashley, now here's what liberals think, and their view is just as good as ours.' But they've never discouraged me from thinking for myself, and they would never stop loving me even if I took a different political position from theirs. They want me to think for myself. Kids need to know that they can form their own opinions, and their professors aren't the end-all be-all of what's good and right on any issue. It was really hard for me at my other school because of all the accusations and bitterness I had to endure as a result of speaking up, but I would do it again in a heartbeat, because to do anything less would be dishonest."

"Ashley, I think you're a hero," I said, "because you've forced some people, probably for the first time in their lives, to realize that there's more than one side to the issues. Even if they hated it, at least they got to hear another opinion, and you stood your ground."

"That's exactly it," she said. "It was terrible, and I spent a lot of time in tears. For a time I even began to question myself: *Did I really say something racist in there?* And then I began to think that all those people who claimed to be my friends really hated me. But I realized that: *You know what? I provoked thought in people who had never done that before.* In the whole two years that I was on that other campus, no one else had ever provoked people to think about an issue like that. So now when I think about all that, I'm proud of myself. Easier said than done," she said with a laugh, "because at the time I was an emotional wreck! But it was the right thing for me to do, and I'm glad I did it. So if you ask me what advice I'd give to kids coming to college, I'd say, 'Don't be afraid. Say what you believe, and be prepared for the reaction.'"

3

The Agenda Is Reeducation

At universities that have embraced speech codes and sensitivity training, every element of the college experience has been designed to turn the student into a perfect little soldier of the Left. Like some Orwellian boot camp or Maoist reeducation compound, nothing is too small or too insignificant to be overlooked. This is one reason why policy handbooks at many of these universities are tomes, hundreds of pages in length in some cases, covering every attitude and behavior, regulating every aspect of the student's daily life.

Freshman orientation begins the process of change; lecturers and discussion-group leaders maintain discipline and conformity; student activities directors and student government leaders reward favored groups with privileges and university funds—deciding who's in and who's out; and residence advisors (RAs) make sure that students conform to the campus code, even in their most intimate moments.

Charles, a young man who recently completed a masters in political science and has now gone on to law school, observed this heavy-handed liberal regimentation for six straight years during his undergraduate and graduate studies at Washington University in St. Louis. "In my experience," he told me, "residential life is the most aggressively PC element in the university. RAs are used as agents of 'sensitivity' training, and they can be ruthless if somebody doesn't toe the line. At one point," he said, "I actually applied for a position as an RA, but I was rejected because of my views, which were libertarian but not liberal. They wanted somebody who wouldn't question but would walk the party line, and that's exactly what they got.

"The focus of leftist radicalism on that campus," Charles told me, "is something called the Social Justice Center and its 'isms' campaign. The details of the approved 'isms' are always posted on the RA's bulletin board in the dorms. The Social Justice Center itself is an outgrowth of the Residential Life Administration and is closely tied in with RA training. The training that RAs undergo, in some cases, resembles Maoist reeducation. One ex-RA told me they have a 'Wall of Shame' that blames white people in general, and particularly males and Westerners, for most of the world's problems. Apparently it was quite an intense experience, literally reducing some of the girls in the training program to tears."

I wanted to know if the students are turned into little zombies, or if any of them actually escape with their self-respect in tact. So I asked Charles, "Does anyone ever object?"

"They can't afford to object," he said, "but I don't think most students take the propagandizing that goes on in residential life very seriously. Most people go along with it, but I don't think they're really convinced of the evils of 'ageism' or 'classism' or all the other stuff put out by the Social Justice Center. To most people I know, the SJC crowd was an object of ridicule and probably did more to incite conservative reactions than to encourage Leftism. The real purpose, I suspect, was to announce to the world what the politically correct line was at Washington University—that capitalism is bad, for example, and white Anglo Saxons aren't respected. It lets people on campus know, from day one, whose views will be in charge in the dormitories. In a way, they're harmless and counterproductive, but they're a nuisance, and I think they may have subtle effects you don't always see at first."

An Intellectual Gulag

East, west, north, south: it doesn't matter where you are. The PC mindset has become the dominant orthodoxy on virtually every college campus in this country. I taught for ten years on a Christian college campus, and I have colleagues and friends on conservative and Christian campuses all over the country. The PC drill is a bit different in those places, but it's there in many subtle ways. It exists most of all among younger faculty members who grew up in this PC environment, but it also exists in officials and administrators who, in their efforts to emulate the major secular institutions, have bought into the jargon and ideologies of the professional and academic associations. It's a sort of secondhand PC that can be even worse than the original.

Before entering this world of extremes, students need to be prepared for the jargon and have some knowledge of what they're about to run into. The PC environment on campus shows up in course content, textbooks, lectures, discussion groups, in the professor's choice of visiting guest lecturers and speakers, and in the authorized organizations and events that may receive university funds.

Eagle Forum's newsletter, *Education Reporter*, published a list of the principal tenets of the PC dogma: From day one, said the editors, the new student learns that everything on campus is political. From the classroom to the dorm room, everything comes down to gender and racial oppression. Democratic institutions are denigrated while socialist and globalist institutions like the United Nations are praised. Pride of country, or nationalism, is scorned as fascism and jingoism, while anti-American and unpatriotic attitudes are considered noble and enlightened.

Since the humanities and social sciences are the real strongholds of the PC agenda on campus, most students run headlong into it in their first English class. Works by "dead white European males" are out, and works by little-known ethnic, homosexual, or feminist writers are suddenly in. It's not just that professors favor this material but the textbooks and reading lists offer little else. Students in humanities also get a stiff dose of "oppression studies," which trivialize and ridicule traditional American values and Judeo-Christian morality while exalting the isms of "tolerance, diversity, and multiculturalism."

Victimology, as Professor Charles Sykes eloquently warned in his 1992 work, *A Nation of Victims*, is central to virtually everything. Every group, with the exception of white males and conservative Christians, is entitled to claim victim status and receive preferential treatment. Multiculturalism, as the *Education Reporter* explains, is "a code word for the false notion that Western civilization is bad and every other group, whether civilized or not, is superior."[1] At a time when most universities have eliminated required courses, the State University of New York requires that all students take a prescribed class in multiculturalism—in fact, it's the only required course on all of SUNY's sixteen campuses.

Radical feminism on campus demands that the entire world be seen as a conspiracy against women. Women's studies programs, and the obligatory women's centers, preach that all men are guilty, individually and collectively, of oppression. Even sex within marriage is referred to as rape, and male students are often forbidden from enrolling or attending women's studies classes, lectures, or events. Joking about these ludicrous doctrines is absolutely forbidden and can lead to disciplinary action or even expulsion from the university. Students discover quickly that campus feminists, like most of the PC crowd, have no visible sense of humor.

Education Reporter also noted that the *University of California at Davis Law Review* has decided that the female pronoun will be used as standard in all their publications and articles, except when referring to a criminal defendant, for which the male pronoun is preferred. Equally humorless are the supporters of affirmative action on campus. Racial preferences for blacks and Hispanics, which are actually a form of reverse discrimination in admissions, grading, and employment, only benefit those groups that proclaim their "victim status." But affirmative action is sacrosanct on university campuses, even at the Universities of Texas and California where the courts ruled it unconstitutional. And as the University of Michigan case proved most recently, equality before the law is actually a meaningless phrase for the universities, the media, and the courts, at least when it comes to affirmative action.

Christianity, in particular, is always politically incorrect. At some colleges, students are not permitted to turn in papers with the dates B.C. (Before Christ) or A.D. (Anno Domini). Instead, they must use the secularized alternatives, B.C.E. (Before Common Era) and C.E. (Common Era).

"Tolerance" is really a code word for the acceptance of all behaviors except those that comport with the Ten Commandments.

Most shocking of all for many new students is the fact that sex, with anyone, anytime, is not only condoned on campus, but is positively encouraged. As the young woman from the University of Massachusetts (discussed in Chapter One) discovered, there are virtually no limits to how, when, and with whom students may engage in sexual activities. Dating is out; "hooking up" is in. Premarital and homosexual sex are not debatable and may not be criticized.

Students discover quickly that tolerance cuts just one way. Perverse, vulgar, and anti-American behaviors are tolerated, while chastity and moral restraint are not. Vandalism and arson by ethnic and liberal groups who are "offended" by the behavior or words of Americans who hold traditional or conservative values is tolerated, but *criticism* of vandalism and arson by ethnic and liberal groups is not.*

SENSITIVITY TRAINING

The Massachusetts Institute of Technology (MIT) campus is located just across the Charles River from Boston, in Cambridge, Massachusetts, and in very close proximity to the sprawling 192-acre Harvard complex. Unlike Harvard, which maintains the architectural styles and character of its roots as America's oldest university, MIT is more modern and less attractive, but is nevertheless renowned as a center of scientific inquiry. In my interview there with a bright young woman I will call Madison, I was told that the hypersexualization of the campus was one of the biggest surprises she encountered.

I admit, I was surprised, too, assuming that a student body made up primarily of math prodigies and computer nerds would have other things on their minds. But sexuality wasn't the only surprise she experienced. Madison grew up in the Northwest where she graduated from a prestigious private

---

* At the Universities of Arizona, Massachusetts, and Indiana, as well as private universities such as Brown and Amherst, among others, student publications that spoke honestly about contested social issues have been confiscated and burned by angry minority groups, and no reprimand or restitution was required by administrators.

school. She was a gifted student and won a scholarship to MIT. Like most of the young women I interviewed at these elite schools, Madison was gracious and self-assured, and she didn't hesitate to tell me what she thought about campus life today.

"You're a bright, outspoken young woman," I said, "and not afraid to say what you think, even when it's not politically correct. But before you tell me about what's happening on the MIT campus, I'd be curious to know what shaped your values and beliefs."

"My family had a lot to do with it," she said, "but I've always been willing to say what I believe is right. I grew up going to Catholic schools, so I have pretty traditional values. When I was in high school my mom for some reason listened to talk radio every day in the car. I pretty much tuned it out until I was in the tenth grade. I was a bit of a liberal back then. I believed in traditional constitutional values, and since liberals always talked about that, I assumed that's what they believed. But I began to notice that they only talked about it and never actually lived by it. So I started tuning in to what my mom was listening to in the car, and before long I found myself really out of step with the Democrats, and I started seeing what was happening at school in a different way. I eventually realized I was really more in tune with Bush and the Republicans, especially after all the stuff that happened after the 2000 elections, and that's when I changed."

"You told me earlier that your high school was fairly liberal." I said. "Did you lose a lot of friends when your views started to change?"

"Actually, I found that people respected me more because I had an opinion and I spoke out about it," she said. "Most people wouldn't speak up—I think they thought it would probably hurt their grades, or whatever—but I wasn't worried about that."

"You had ideas and you were willing to express them," I said. "That's great. But how have things changed since you've been at MIT?"

"When I first got here," she said, "it was orientation week, and I was really shocked by what I saw. The first thing was that MIT has segregated housing. Chocolate City, for example, is solely for black men. That's not a joke," Madison assured me. "That's the name of it. I mean, who would think that in this day and age you could have a residence house that's solely for one race? But that's common here, and they have separate programs for different groups and genders. If you're a minority, you come to campus three months early, with other minorities, to get a leg up on the competition. They assume that if you're a minority you come from bad schools, which isn't necessarily the case. But a lot of kids go through those programs. By the time everyone else arrived on campus, those kids had already made friends with other minority students and pretty much stuck with those friends and didn't welcome anybody else.

"Then during orientation," Madison said, "there are 'welcome festivals' and 'fruit fests'—if you're gay you got a fruit fest—and if you're a minority you got your dances and lunches. Most of us were shocked to see all this; it was so racist and discriminatory, just the opposite of the 'equality' they kept talking about. One freshman wrote an op-ed in the campus newspaper questioning the equality of all this stuff, and he was really shot down by people in the minority community. He was given a really hard time; in fact, he had to have a 'discussion' about it and deal with people's hurt feelings."

"Sensitivity training—a little cultural reeducation to sober him up," I said. "Educators learned that little trick from the Chinese Cultural Revolution. So did he mend his ways after that?"

"Actually, no," she said. "He never apologized. I think there were quite a few people who agreed with him; I certainly did. I have several friends on campus who are minorities, and they didn't want to be labeled in that way, either, or to be forced to go to the minority orientation. They didn't see themselves that way."

"Did they say anything?" I asked.

"I think we were all too intimidated as freshmen to come out and say anything," she said.

ASSESSING THE DAMAGE

"I'd be interested to know what the political environment is like on campus," I said.

"Well, there's no conservative paper here like on other campuses," she said. "There's an alternative paper called *The Thistle*, which is pro-Palestinian, but they only publish it when they have something to react to. The College Republicans are pretty active here, but it's hard to get people to come to meetings. Other than that, talk radio is big, and in addition to national shows like Sean Hannity or Rush Limbaugh or Michael Savage, there's a guy here in Boston named Jay Severin who has a big following on campus."

"What about activists?" I said. "Is there much of that?"

"There are quite a few," she said, "but there's one activist on campus who—I guess I shouldn't use her name, but that's a shame because she'll run for office one day, and this woman should never be elected for anything! She came here from Cal Tech and she's a rabid feminist. Very pro-Palestinian, rabid anti-American, and loves Noam Chomsky, who is probably the most outrageous leftist professor on campus. Right after 9/11 she started wearing a veil, to express solidarity with the Muslim people who were being oppressed in the United States because of 9/11. She's been involved in every controversy you can imagine."

"What kind of controversies?" I asked.

"For one thing," Madison said, "she loves to tear down other people's posters, especially frat-party posters. She's a feminist, and she's offended by female sexuality, so frat parties, being a bunch of guys whose posters usually have pictures of women on them, make her crazy. One of the residence halls had a jungle party, and they had a picture of Tarzan and Jane on their posters, and she was terribly offended and wrote e-mails attacking those students and saying that everybody ought to be tearing down their posters. Then she made her own posters with pictures of men, and she took scissors and basically castrated them, and she spent five hours lecturing the entire student body, saying that all men are rapists, and reciting some bizarre research that said one in four have actually acted on their impulses."

"I hope she's not a math major!" I said.

"No, she's actually a grad student," she said, "a teaching assistant in material sciences and engineering. She's supposed to run a lecture for a class that all freshman have to take, but she's so unpopular that no one will attend her section because she spends the entire time justifying what happened on September 11th instead of dealing with the course material. Then one time, on World International Women's Day, instead of talking about what the students came to hear, about the course, she used the whole class as a soapbox for her political views."

"Can't she be stopped?" I said.

"Actually," Madison said with a bemused smile on her face, "I think they've already cancelled her contract because she was spending too much time being a radical and not enough time doing science. She wasn't writing her thesis, and students didn't want to come to her classes anymore. I don't know if that will stop her, but I hope so. Unfortunately, there's also another group on campus called Refuse & Resist. Their issue is supposed to be date-rape, but I've never seen them do anything related to that. When they set up a booth on campus they didn't give out information on the condition of women around the world. Instead, they had Twinkies and donut holes and you can probably guess what they did with them.

"On another occasion," she said, "they made a papier-mâché phallus, and they used it as a piñata in front of the student center to smash the patriarchy. They ended up painting the phallus red, white, and blue and putting a picture of President Bush's face on it before they smashed it."

"What about the antiwar protests?" I asked. "Is there much of that here?"

"I'm ashamed of what happened here," she said. "There was a national campus walk-out, you know. They advertised it in advance, and I decided to set up a booth and hand out yellow ribbons, giving them some information about what the war was really about and why it was needed. So some friends and I went around at three o'clock in the morning and put up posters saying things like, 'War has never solved anything, except slavery, genocide, dictatorships, etc.' Others said, 'Free Iraq,' or 'Blessed are the Peace-Keepers.' They were inoffensive posters, all around campus.

"But as I was putting them up," she said, "I saw that the antiwar people had plastered posters at eye-level, every single inch of the ethnic corridor, maybe a thousand sheets of paper, advertising the walk-outs so that every-one would know it was happening. There's also a war memorial in the lobby of Building 10, and students aren't allowed to put posters there, but they did it anyway. Some of them said 'Remember Rachel Cory'—she's the peace protester who was run over by a bulldozer in Israel—and there were all sorts of anti-military slogans. When I saw what they were doing, I politely explained to them that not only was it against the rules to put posters on the war memorial but it was really bad taste to put anti-military slogans on a memorial to honor the former MIT students who died in the service of their country. But they said their cause was too important to worry about rules."

"The ends justify the means," I said. "It was Karl Marx who came up with that one."

SOMETHING FOR EVERYBODY

A survey conducted by the New York Civil Rights Coalition, "The Stigma of Inclusion: Racial Paternalism in Higher Education," ex-amined policies at fifty prominent universities. One area of special concern was the trend toward racially-segregated dorms. At Cornell, minority students have three choices: Ujamaa, for black students, the Latino Living Center for Hispanics, and Akwe:kon, for Native Americans. At MIT, African-American men can choose to live in Chocolate City, and minorities at Oberlin can live in Third World House. At Stanford, Muwekma-tah-ruk is for Native Americans, Ujamaa for African Americans, Casa Zapata is for Chicano/Latinos, and the Asian-American house is called Okada, named for the author of a book about the treatment of Japanese Americans during World War II.

KEEPING A RECORD

"Later that morning," she said, "at about 10:00 A.M. while I was on my way to class, I discovered that it wasn't enough for there to be a thousand pieces of paper advertising their walk-out, but they'd covered up my posters as well—every single one of them."

"Did they leave the posters on the war memorial?" I asked.

"Yes," she said, "but I took them down."

"Students need to be taking pictures of these things," I said. "Get them out to people and post them on the Internet so the rest of America can see what freedom looks like on the university campus." As I reflected on all this I had to wonder how many moms and dads would be pleased to see pictures of the piñata party at the MIT Student Center. At Middlebury College and UC Berkeley, as I was told, there are naked men who run around the campus, sometimes in the middle of the day, and the administration does nothing to stop it. You have to wonder how alumni would react to that kind of news? A digital camera might be just what's needed.

"Justice Brandeis once said that 'sunlight is the best disinfectant,'" I said. "We could use a little more of that. But how many of these radicals do you think there are?" I asked her. "Are there a lot of students at MIT who feel this way?"

"Well, let me give you an example," Madison said. "The people behind the antiwar demonstrations advertised that two million students would walk out of class all across America on that day. 'The war will stop, and everything will be good again!' That's what they said. So they had a combined rally for MIT and Harvard at lunchtime when students like me wanted to eat lunch. And at 11:30, right in the middle of classes, they were going to walk out and make a big scene. In my class of eighty people, two walked out. Of the thousand or so people who actually showed up at Harvard Square to watch what was going on, only about a hundred were MIT students, and the rest were from Harvard or Boston University, or people they'd brought in from outside."

"That's amazing," I said. I don't know many college students who wouldn't like any excuse to cut class for a day. But even with that temptation, apparently not many of Madison's classmates wanted to be part of the protests, preferring to stay in class. The protest organizers must have thought a walk-out would be like saying, "Wear blue jeans on gay day!" when most students are wearing jeans anyway. But, in this case, they stayed away in droves.

"Most MIT students didn't agree with the walk-out, even though a lot of the faculty was pushing it. But the radicals get away with that stuff," Madison said, "because the administration supports it. And the student senate rubber stamps most of what the Left does on campus."

"What's the conservative-liberal balance on the student senate?" I asked.

"Mostly liberal, but with a fair number of conservatives," she said. "The senate is basically nonpartisan and doesn't deal with politics, but there's a vocal minority of liberals who unfortunately get a lot of support from the administration. The student newspaper is liberal; most of the professors and TAs are liberal. However, in most cases I'd say they're respectful and open to people with different ideas. I've taken a lot of political-science classes, and most of my TAs and professors have appreciated my comments, and they've been respectful.

"But once in a while," she added quickly, "you meet a TA like the one I'll be seeing in an hour. He's a black Muslim, and he hates America. In our first lecture he told us that if we toe the Reagan line, we've been brainwashed, and our papers will get an automatic F. So I asked him, 'What if we haven't been brainwashed, and we want to argue from a conservative perspective?' And he said, 'Don't even think about it.' If we didn't toe the Thomas Friedman line, he said, we wouldn't pass the course."

"Thomas Friedman?" I said. "As in the writer for the *New York Times* opinion page, that bastion of unbiased thinking? Friedman is very liberal! Is that the standard you're expected to adopt?"

"That's right," she said. "All this TA can talk about is how dumb conservatives are, how dumb Fox News is, and how Americans don't care about starving people. After listening to all this trash, I finally said I wanted to switch recitation classes, and he said, 'Forget it!' So I decided I would go to the professor and tell him I wanted to change sections. Unfortunately, this professor is also very liberal. He loves to talk about sodomy. I don't think he's interested in anything but sodomy."

"What's the subject of the class?" I asked.

"It deals with liberty, equality, and what's the best combination in a democratic society."

"Wow! Great course," I said. "Too bad you have to get it from a slanted perspective."

SILENCE OF THE LAMBS

"The first two weeks of class we talked about utilitarianism," Madison continued, "and at some point morality laws came up, and both the TA and the professor are intellectually dishonest because they frame morality laws solely in the context of sodomy. They said conservatives want to ban sodomy, and in Massachusetts on a college campus, if you think sodomy laws are a good thing, then you hate gays. That's the way they think. So at recitation they always want to argue sodomy laws, and here's me sitting there, groaning, biting my tongue.

"But one day somebody said something so dumb I just couldn't sit still. Specifically," she said, "the student said that the only people who support sodomy laws are religious bigots who enjoy oppressing gay people. So I did my take on the whole discussion and informed people that these opinions were merely an assertion and not based on any facts, and the TA suddenly jumped in and started saying I was wrong. He said, 'You just don't get it, do you? Do you know how many gay people have been oppressed by people like you?' And then he asked if I'd read the *Bowers v. Hardwick* decision by the Supreme Court, assuming I hadn't so he could pull a fast one on me.

"I, of course, had read it," Madison said. "I'm very interested in common law; so he was taken aback since I actually knew more about that case than he did. But he went on for at least ten minutes, and he kept telling me I was wrong, and giving me all these sophist arguments, trying to make a fool out of me in front of the class.

"*So, that's it*, I thought. *I'm switching recitations.* I couldn't take any more weeks like that discussing sodomy the whole time; what a waste! My ideas weren't being respected, so I informed the professor that I wanted to switch recitations, and he said he was disappointed I felt that way. I said I was disappointed in the TA and didn't think he was a very good teacher. Well, the professor defended the TA and said he'd make sure he's more open next time."

"I hope you're keeping a record of this," I said. "Every conservative student should keep a journal. There are so many things that happen inside and outside of class that need to be journaled, just in case, because you never know. If you have to go to the administration, then you've got a record, and those people will gang up on you if they think you're vulnerable. So you have to be prepared in advance.

"On another note," I said, "how many conservatives do you know on the MIT faculty?"

"We used to have one," she said. "He was upset by the Marxist attitudes on campus. You may have noticed that on the road between here and Harvard Square there's a Center for Marxist Education; it's right by the T-stop, beside the Marxist bookstore. This professor would make jokes about it, and he would talk about how no one really believes in communism anymore except here in Cambridge. People call this place 'Moscow on the Charles' and 'The People's Republic of Cambridge,' it's so leftist. But this professor, Thomas Christensen, was a specialist in Asia studies and pro-military, and he had a lot of insights that many of us were happy to hear."

"Is he still here?" I asked.

"No, he went to Princeton," she said.

"Aha, that makes two conservatives at Princeton!" I said. "The other is my friend Robert George, who is a professor of jurisprudence and head of the James Madison Program."

"There may be others here, too," she added, "but I don't know who they are."

"Part of the problem," I said, "is that faculty members who are more conservative tend not to speak up very much, because they have to live with these people, so they don't always let their views be heard." What I didn't say was that most of these professors will go out of their way to avoid controversy. By and large, students are more courageous than the faculty when it comes to standing up for their beliefs. Their sense of honor, unfortunately, puts them in harm's way with no one to stand up for them when the vigilantes come after them.

But there was something else I wanted to know, so I asked Madison, "Do you have any idea how many students at MIT are here on scholarships, fellowships, or some kind of tuition support other than mom and dad paying the bills?"

"Well, this is MIT," she said. "It's very competitive to get in, so I'm guessing that at least three-fourths of the students are on some type of scholarship. There are a lot of National Merit Scholars, of course, and quite a few who received Intel Science scholarships, Westinghouse scholarships, Robert C. Byrd scholarships, or minority scholarships. It would certainly be the majority on campus."

"That's about what I expected," I said, "which puts a lot of the onus for changing things back on those who are paying the bills. They're the ones paying for the socialist indoctrination on campus. They're funding a system that undermines everything this country stands for, but they're also some of the people I want to reach with this book. I want to ask them, 'Do you know what you're paying for? You're sending these great, bright kids who want to do something to save lives and change the world off to colleges where they're being insulted, humiliated, brainwashed, and indoctrinated! You've got to take action and do something about that! If nothing else, cut off the funds until these places drop the mind games and get back to education.' There are some strong young people on the campus," I said, "people like you, Madison. But there are a lot who aren't so strong, and they just say, 'I don't want to argue, so I'll go along.' And that really gets my goat!"

DEVELOPING SURVIVAL SKILLS

After a moment of reflection, I asked Madison, "Do you think the PC types convince many people at MIT?"

"Yes, I think they do," she said. "I'm sure there are others like me who disagree with the sophists on campus, but they keep quiet and try to avoid controversy. But I also know some people who came here straight as an arrow, and now they're lesbian activists."

"What concerns me," I said, "is that people's whole lives are being tampered with in this environment. Some students say they're not political or they don't want to talk about it, but if they've been swayed by their professors they will generally go into the voting booth and pick the liberal candidates because that's what they've been taught to do. Even in New York City," I said, "if you talk to people on the street about the issues, they'll agree with you on things like immigration, the economy, or the war. But when they go to the polls on election day, they're going to pull the Democrat lever because they think that's what they're supposed to do. It's a total disconnect, but that's precisely what this kind of leftist brainwashing is designed to do.

"One last thing," I said as I was preparing to leave. "I hope you'll document what you're seeing, Madison, because that's how you keep a record of what's happening. You need to let people know." She nodded and said, "I will."

One of the greatest ironies of the PC university is that students, their parents, and these various funding agencies (from the government to the scholarship providers) are paying for what's happening on campus. They pay the tuition that subjects our brightest young men and women to mind-control, speech codes, sexual intimidation, and anti-American indoctrination; and despite the thousands of articles, news stories, and books that have documented what's going on, they keep paying, and doing nothing to change the equation. It's sad, if not a crime.

The most vulnerable ones are the youngest students and those who come from inner-city public schools or other low-demand environments who don't have the academic or moral resources to resist the indoctrination. As my interview with Madison made clear, many of these young people are easy prey for the reeducation czars. They're not academically inclined in many cases and will soak up the rhetoric of leftist professors and TAs as gospel, often with wide-eyed credulity.

Until all these things begin to change, parents ought to consider keeping their sons and daughters out of college for a couple of years, at least until they have the maturity and enough work experience to help them withstand the kinds of pressure they will encounter. Others may want to consider local campuses that allow students to live at home and stay away from the coercive and invasive politics of dorm life. Not least, parents ought to be concerned about the outrageous rise of STDs on campus, where one recent survey indicates that at least one student in fifteen hundred is already HIV-positive, and life-threatening diseases are out of control.

Those who do enroll in one of the PC universities should be careful not to waste their education dollars on non-academic courses. Don't waste your time on what John Leo calls the "junk courses" that are trivial and trashy, and often profane. Besides the satisfaction of trivial curiosity, what possible intellectual value is there in courses on horror movies, pornography, pop music, witchcraft, or "Queer Studies"?

Students should try to avoid courses taught by TAs who don't even speak intelligible English, which is one of the biggest complaints on most campuses. Even though international students are often bright and well educated, they are not conversant enough with American life or the American idiom to be able to communicate information that American students need. The best way to decide which courses to take is to read the course descriptions carefully and be on the watch for PC code words and leftist objectives. Also, get to know the faculty members by their reputations on campus or by a little Internet research if possible. Talk to other students about specific courses and professors and find out what's being said about them; and be prepared to drop a course or transfer to another section if it turns out that the material, the approach, or the ideology of the instructor is skewed to the left.

Some other suggestions from Eagle Forum's *Education Reporter* are worth considering as well:

1. Don't expect to get into a first-rate college just because you're smart. Michele Hernandez, dean of admissions at Dartmouth, says that

students have a better chance of being admitted if they're from a ghetto, a barrio, or a reservation, or if they're from an identified "victim group," even if their academic qualifications are lower.

2. Try to avoid colleges with speech codes that are evidence of political correctness run amok.

3. Stay away from credit cards as much as possible. Tuition debt has reached astronomical levels in recent years, but students are still being lured into dangerous levels of debt. Most colleges are paid by credit card companies for the names and addresses of students so they can snag new customers before they even have enough income to pay their debts.

4. Grade inflation is another insidious system designed to make students and parents feel good about the exorbitant tuition they're paying. Sadly, grades are no longer a realistic appraisal of a student's actual performance.

5. And perhaps most important of all, students should immediately seek out companions who share their beliefs and values. Check out the conservative student groups on campus and join those that have worthy goals and objectives, and that will help give the student a buffer and a support group to fend off the radicals and their ideas.[2]

Conservative students need to consider running for student government where they can be a voice for change. They should write articles, op-eds, and letters to the editor of the campus newspaper and consider getting involved in the alternative newspaper on campus, if there's one available, where they can help shine the light on what's taking place within the university community. Even in the best schools and best situations, there will be many obstacles to overcome during the typical college career. But "forewarned *is* forearmed," and parents, students, and their supporters need to work together to resist the reeducation that poses as education on campus.

SOPHISTS AND GNOSTICS, UNITE!

Conservative students at Ivy League universities seldom refer to the leftists in their midst as "cultural elites." After all, they have as much claim to "elite" status as anyone. Instead, they often use terms like "Gnostics," associating the pagan Left with the ancients who claimed to possess occult wisdom available only to the anointed, and "Sophists," Greek philosophers who specialized in clever arguments based on dubious and misleading facts. Apparently those expensive history books were good for something.

VESTED INTERESTS

The silence of parents about what's happening on campus, due primarily to the fact that they don't know what's happening and their sons and daughters aren't telling them (often because of their embarrassment to talk to parents about such things), is a big part of the problem. Faculty complicity is an even greater problem. But there are other factors that work against the ability to expose campus corruption, not the least of these being the enormous amounts of money that universities receive from foundations, granting agencies, and government subsidies. In addition to tuition grants and other types of government-sponsored financial aid, government pours billions into many of these institutions. Here's a small sampling of what some major colleges receive from the federal government:

Johns Hopkins—$793 million
Stanford University—$391 million
Harvard University—$349 million
Washington University (St. Louis)—$347 million

Massachusetts Institute of Technology (MIT)—$301 million
Yale University—$300 million
Emory University—$248 million
Cornell University—$247 million
Duke University—$218 million
Northwestern University—$204 million.[3]

Such large contributions of taxpayer funds ought to ensure equal opportunity for all points of view on campus, but that's not the case. The polling firm of Luntz Research surveyed liberal arts and social science faculties at Ivy League universities on behalf of the Center for the Study of Popular Culture (CSPC) to find out the political and ideological orientation of faculty members. See if this tells you which way the wind is blowing:

- Only 3 percent identified themselves as Republican, while 57 percent said they are Democrats.

- 64 percent identified themselves as liberal, 23 percent as moderate, and only 6 percent as conservative.

- In the 2000 election, 61 percent voted for Al Gore, 5 percent for Ralph Nader, 6 percent for George W. Bush, and 28 percent either did not vote or refused to answer.

- When asked, "Who do you think has been the best president in the past forty years?" 26 percent said Bill Clinton, 17 percent John F. Kennedy, 15 percent Lyndon Johnson, 13 percent Jimmy Carter, and Ronald Reagan came in at 4 percent.

- 79 percent said George W. Bush's political views are "too conservative."

- 71 percent disagree that "news coverage of political and social issues reflects a liberal bias in the news media."

- 74 percent said that we "should not spend the money that would be required for research and possible development of a missile defense system."

- 61 percent believe "the federal government should do more to solve our country's problems" rather than individuals, communities, or private enterprise.

- 80 percent disagree that "if the federal budget has a surplus in any a given year, this money should be returned to taxpayers in the form of a tax cut."

- 40 percent agree that "the federal government owes American blacks some form of reparations for the harms caused by slavery and discrimination."

In announcing the results of this study, CSPC founder David Horowitz described the findings as clear evidence of the "institutional leftism" of today's university faculty. It is inherently unfair for institutions that receive hundreds of millions of dollars in government subsidies to represent predominantly only one political point of view—particularly when it is the anti-American and Marxist worldview of the extreme Left—and then, at the same time, to make it almost impossible for conservative and Christian scholars to be hired. Horowitz asks, "How can students get a good education if they're only being told one-half of the story?"[4]

But withholding information is only part of the equation; the other part is that these same leftist academics and administrators are filling students with overt bias and animosity toward the United States of America and advocating a type of insurgency unknown even in the darkest days of the sixties counter-cultural rebellion. Dr. Daniel Pipes, director of the Middle East Forum and one of America's most distinguished conservative scholars, points out that such radical views are routine in the academy today, which helps to explain why most Americans feel alienated from the university culture.

Of course, says Pipes, professors have every right to express their opinions, however cranky and mistaken. But fanatical opposition to their own government is very troubling, particularly in light of the funding these institutions receive from government. All of which, says Pipes, raises questions. For example:

- Why do American academics so often despise their own country while finding excuses for repressive and dangerous regimes?

- Why have university specialists proven so inept at understanding the great contemporary issues of war and peace, starting with Vietnam, then the Cold War, the Kuwait War, and now the War on Terror?

- Why do professors of linguistics, chemistry, American history, genetics, and business present themselves in public as authorities on the Middle East?

- What is the long-term effect of an extremist, intolerant, and anti-American environment on university students?

Pipes then says, "The time has come for adult supervision of the faculty and administrators at many American campuses. Especially as we are at war, the goal must be for universities to resume their civic responsibilities."[5] But a return to sanity cannot happen, I believe, until parents, alumni, legislatures, non-university specialists, scholarship providers, and other funding agencies make up their minds to put on the brakes and help create a more balanced atmosphere for all students. And the media, which is fighting its own battle for credibility, could gain a great deal of respect if reporters would simply focus their energies on these issues. If writers and investigative reports would report fairly and demand balance and equity in the classroom, real change would be possible.

COLLECTING EVIDENCE

A couple of hours after my meeting with Madison, I returned to the coffee shop at Harvard Square for a meeting with David Carl, a senior at Boston University who is the campus organizer for Massachusetts College Republicans. In addition to his activities at BU, Dave travels regularly to more than a hundred colleges around the state, encouraging student involvement and helping to coordinate multi-campus events.

"Dave," I said, "from all the mischief-making I've seen on these campuses, I could easily get the impression that there are thousands of activists and dozens of faculty sponsors keeping things in turmoil. But something tells me that may not be the case. I'd be curious to know how many students are really active in the liberal movements here in Massachusetts."

BLACKBALLING THE BARD

Are parents getting what they're paying for? A study of sixty-seven leading universities showed that only twenty-three required English majors to take even a single course in Shakespeare. In most cases such foundational courses have been replaced by offerings that are trivial, trashy, and profane. Harvard offers more than eighteen hundred courses each semester; for the Fall 2003 semester, only one of them was Shakespeare. Jerry Martin of the American Council of Trustees and Alumni says, "The survey confirms our worst fears. Dropping Shakespeare is not just a trend, it is the norm. Prestigious colleges and universities are contributing to the dumbing down of America." Boston University professor Roger Shattuck says, "Shoddy propaganda is replacing the study of great literature. In fact," he adds, "parents should sue for breach of contract."

"You're right," he said. "It's not a lot of people. At Harvard, maybe a hundred; at Hampshire College, which is small but very liberal, about the same; and at Boston University, only about thirty people do most of the damage. But here's the trick: they actually have a kind of sneaky strategy. Each of the people in the core group get themselves elected as officers in different liberal clubs. The members are all basically the same people, but the officers in one club will be members in another club, and vice versa. All the clubs have different names. There are groups like BUYAH, the Boston University Youth Alliance for

Housing, which is basically a group that pushes for rent-control. There's SMAC, or Students Making a Change, and several others.

"All of these groups," he said, "have university funding under these different names, but they're really all part of the same group—they just split up and spread themselves thin in order to get more money from the university. If one of them gets a radical speaker to come in and talk about some socialist issue, all the other clubs pool their resources. So rather than just having the money for one or two groups, they have six or seven groups pitching in, and all of it comes from tuition dollars."

Dave showed me the enormous file of posters, flyers, newspaper clippings, and leaflets that he had collected over his entire college career. They were mostly attacks on the government, the university, or conservative organizations and individuals, published by the various groups on campus or the socialist organizations that sponsor them. One article from the campus newspaper in Dave's freshman year described how student government was basically supporting the left-wing underground on campus.

"What we found," Dave said, "is that the same people who run student government run all these radical organizations, so they're not just using group funds, but they combine that with the even bigger funding of student government. They use student government offices to hold their club meetings; they use student government facilities to publish their alternative newspapers and flyers; and all the other things they do, they're doing it using school facilities to promote their leftist agenda.

"When you consider that this is the same group that determines who gets school funds," he said, "you have to wonder who's keeping tabs on these people. The answer is, nobody."

"Does the administration know about this?" I said.

"Believe me," he said, "they know exactly what's happening. They're totally behind it and would never pull the plug, unless somebody stepped in and put a stop to it. You wonder where all the money is going, and how these left-wing organizations can afford to hold so many leftist events? Follow the money," he said, "and suddenly it makes perfect sense."

"What about 9/11?" I said. "On most campuses students say they really had their eyes opened after the attacks on New York and Washington. Did that happen here?"

"You know," Dave said, "I think that initially there was a sense of reality that hit some of these kids. They were shocked by it, and they didn't say much at first. But within a few weeks they were back up and running again, so nothing really changed. I'd have to say that 9/11 sobered some people up, and I think some of these people started seeing how silly they were, but ultimately, we're still not out of the woods."

"I've talked to a lot of young people who were politically inactive before 9/11," I said, "but they suddenly realized that they really do love their country and, for the first time, they realized they wanted to do something to support it."

"I saw that, too," he said. "I think 9/11 had two effects. Certain groups, the middle-of-the-road kids who were pretty sure about their political stance, tended to move more to the right. We certainly saw more people signing up for College Republicans at that time. Not so much, though, with the war in Iraq, which was different. On the one hand, those on the extreme Left—the socialists, Maoists, Marxists, and all that crowd—they got even worse, if that's possible. They became even more vocal and outrageous."

As Dave thumbed through the flyers on the table, he showed me promotional pieces for events with Ralph Nader, MIT professor Noam Chomsky, and BU Professor Howard Zinn. "We have the Young Democratic Socialists on campus, the Spartacus Youth League, and just about any radical group you can think of," he said. "All these groups combine their efforts to promote the international Maoist movement—here's a copy of their publication, *NIM Notes*. See the hammer and sickle in the corner?" he said. "The organizers of these groups spend all their time, 24/7, devoted to defeating the American capitalist regime. That's their whole purpose and motivation."

"Since they believe public events are so important, I'm sure they're equally respectful of the speakers you and your friends bring in," I said with a smile. "Right?"

Dave laughed. "Right!" he said. "When we brought David Horowitz to speak at BU, we were picketed and screamed at by the Progressive Labor Party. They didn't have a lot of people show up, but it created a controversy. What they were saying was that Horowitz shouldn't have free speech because he's a conservative. They called him a racist since he opposes reparations for slavery. But, fortunately, since the approach they took was an attack on freedom of speech, a lot of the moderate groups kept their distance. They don't want to be associated with that, particularly when they're standing there with microphones protesting freely outside our event."

CONVICTIONS WITHOUT COURAGE

"A lot of people—especially parents—think this stuff is harmless," I said. "Do you think there's any long-term damage from this stuff, or is it just harmless college pranks?"

"No, it's not harmless," he said. "This much I can tell you: a whole group of people who were running student government and publishing the underground newspaper when I came here graduated last year, and, without exception, they all went on to become full-time organizers and anti-American activists. A group called Boston Mobilization, which is a consortium of radical groups here in the Boston area, put together a publication recently, and the names of the people who run it are the same ones who were student radicals on these campuses. I know a lot of them from BU, and they published this rag urging students to take grassroots action for 'peace, justice, and democracy.'"

"Sounds Orwellian," I said.

"The picture on the back is of a professor here at BU, Howard Zinn, who wrote *The People's History of the United States*. It's basically a far-left view of this country and an attack on everything the United States stands for. It's the most biased account of our history, which he actually admits in the last part of the book. He said he doesn't regret his bias because all history is biased and therefore he has chosen to do it his way. He leaves out all the good that the United States has done and focuses entirely on the negative.

"This so-called history," Dave said, "starts out by claiming that Columbus was a murderer, and it only gets worse from there. There's absolutely nothing about this country that Zinn approves of, and his whole aim is to overthrow our capitalist regime and install a socialist welfare state. Oddly enough, this book is required reading on campuses all over the United States. It has sold over a million copies, and people outside the university don't even know it exists. But every parent with a child in college ought to get a copy. And when they do, they need to be sure and read Dan Flynn's brilliant critique of the book in *FrontPage* magazine.[6]

"But I also have to say that, with the exception of professors like Zinn," Dave said, "I've found most of my classes at BU to be fairly well balanced. In some cases there was a left-of-center slant, but in most cases it was minimal, and that's because of the influence of John Silber, who was president here until the fall of 2003. Silber was here for thirty years and was replaced in November 2003 by Dan Golden, the former head of NASA."

"I've often cited Silber's book *Straight Shooting* in my writing," I said, "and I've heard the same comment from many others. I only hope the new president is as good."

"As you can imagine," Dave said, "the leftists on campus didn't like Silber, and the reason is obvious. He was socially conservative, and he didn't apologize for that.

"Groups like the Progressive Labor Party are communist front organizations," Dave told me. "They don't believe in elections because they want to create a Marxist government, and they support the overthrow of the government. We also have the Vegetarian Society, Students United for Peace, the Women's Center, and they're rabidly pro-choice. We have the National Zappatista Student Alliance, the Environmental Students Organization, Students Against Sweatshops, and the NAACP. Even though the NAACP supports a lot of the leftist issues, the president at BU is very strong on family values, and she's strongly pro-life. She's against gay marriage and things like that. Except for their position on race issues, the NAACP here would be considered socially conservative. But we also have Amnesty International, Law School Democrats, and the Green Party."

"With so much dissent," I said, "do you think the views of these groups are in the majority?"

"In reality," he said, "most of the students on campus today are more conservative than their parents, especially when it comes to economic issues. But since most of the kids on this campus are from urban northeastern cities, they tend to base their opinions on emotion, not logic, and they're not very knowledgeable on most of the issues. So they're more likely to be socially liberal. In terms of homosexuality, abortion, gun control, and things like that, they're generally liberal. Economically, they're conservative, and a lot of them are in favor of a strong national defense."

"Along with John Silber and Howard Zinn," I said, "you also have professors like Peter Wood, whose new book, *Diversity: The Invention of a Concept*, is one of the best assessments of the problem ever written. But what about faculty in general? Do they speak up about political and social issues?"

"The liberal professors on campus are all fairly outspoken," he said, "but while the conservative professors may mention their beliefs occasionally, they don't really make an issue of it. That's what I've seen. Conservative professors stay in their classrooms and offices during the day, and at the end of the day they go home. They're not involved with the students. They're not walking around campus or being exposed to what's happening. On the other hand, the leftist professors are almost always actively involved with their students. You don't have to wonder where they stand," Dave said. "They'll tell you."

4

Dumbing Down

I n order for typical young Americans to submit to intellectual or sociological indoctrination, they must first be deprived of knowledge, stripped
of basic beliefs, and made to question the family and community values that
would otherwise enable them to resist radical changes. Prior to 1960, this
probably could not have happened. The level of general knowledge and the
self-assurance of the typical high-schooler was simply too great, and no
amount of manipulation could have transformed his or her thinking to such
an extent. Furthermore, the horrors of war and the menace of communism
were still fresh enough in the minds of most Americans that attempts to subvert the popular ethos would have been sniffed out quickly.

There were, however, sufficient numbers of true believers among intellectuals, recent immigrants, and the avant-garde to populate the halls of academia with like-minded faculty who were determined to change curricula
and rewrite the basic tenets of public education. The goal was to free the next
generation of their objectionable beliefs and prejudices, a process that called
for the transformation of public education at all levels. In time, all these
things did happen, and revolutionary changes have been taking place for the
last forty years, so that today it's undeniable that there has been a "dumbing
down" of public education that has led, in turn, to a collapse of social, cultural, and moral standards in America's schools and colleges.

In one of the most eye-opening works of the past decade, *The Deliberate
Dumbing Down of America*, Charlotte Thomson Iserbyt examines the stages
of this transformation and provides many details that help to connect the

dots, revealing just how insidious the plans of "educators" have been. As a former staff member of the U.S. Department of Education, Iserbyt discovered research reports, documents, interdepartmental memos, and directives that laid out in shocking detail a comprehensive strategy for the takeover of America's classrooms by Washington educrats and their allies.

THE MYTH OF THE IVY LEAGUE

"[D]espite its watered-down required curriculum and almost absent academic discipline, the myth of Harvard as a great undergraduate institution carries on. Why? Because, like Yale, it rests on the native intelligence of its students and surely not on its vacuous 'core' curriculum. . . . Princeton? Much the same . . . students are required to take eleven different courses in four major areas. . . . Sounds great, but again there's a rub. They can choose whatever they want from a full catalogue of over one thousand courses." Yale? "Because students design their own education, no one can any longer be sure a that a Yale degree is the sign of an educated person."

—Martin Gross, *The End of Sanity*

As early as 1960, Iserbyt says, the United Nations Educational, Scientific, and Cultural Organization (UNESCO) adopted a statement called the Convention Against Discrimination. This document, she writes, "laid the groundwork for control of American education, both public and private, by UN agencies and agents."[1] That same year, by no coincidence, the Department of Health, Education, and Welfare published a report entitled Soviet Education Programs: Foundations, Curriculums, Teacher Preparation, that was to be a blueprint for school-to-work programs all across America. Instead of teaching by traditional methods, as it had been done for at least two hundred years, teachers were told to implement Pavlovian conditioned reflex theory, which was a form of mind control developed by psychologist B.F. Skinner, whose book, *Beyond Freedom and Dignity*, published in 1971, stirred controversy by introducing the theory of radical behaviorism. In this case, America's children were to be the subjects of experiments in thought reform.

CHANGING DIRECTIONS

John Dewey's *School and Society* (1899) had already laid the groundwork for this transformation of the schools. Dewey was an honorary president of the National Education Association in 1932 and a co-author of the *Humanist Manifesto*. He later served as president of the League for Industrial Democracy, also known as the Intercollegiate Socialist Society. While his socialist credentials were no secret, he was the most renowned education theorist of his day. Today educators still refer to him as "the father of modern education" and praise his ideals. In that earlier work, Dewey had said:

> I believe the true center of correlation on the school subjects is not science, nor literature, nor history, nor geography, but the child's social activities. . . .
> I believe that the school is primarily a social institution. . . . The teacher's business is simply to determine, on the basis of larger experience and riper wisdom, how the discipline of life shall come to the child. . . . All the questions of the grading of the child and his promotion should be determined by reference to the same standard. Examinations are of use only so far as they test the child's fitness for social life.[2]

Even as Dewey and friends were plotting enormous changes, he was busily rewriting textbooks and course materials from the perspective of "naturalistic theory," which omitted any reference to God or religion in American culture. Thus progressive education reform was, from the start, a frontal assault on the fundamental beliefs of average Americans and a system for revising the goals and practices of traditional education.

By the sixties, the progressives had ensconced themselves in the system at all levels, and from this power base, writes Charlotte Iserbyt, "American education would henceforth concern itself with the importance of the group rather than with the importance of the individual." Public education would no longer focus primarily on the acquisition of knowledge about history, language, or science, but on the student's emotional health and socialization. In 1965 two major initiatives were introduced, this time with congressional funding under the Elementary and Secondary Education Act. The first was the Behavioral Science Teacher Education Program; the second, a government-sponsored sourcebook entitled *Pacesetters in Innovation*, whose mission was to transform classrooms into social-science laboratories. Overnight the role of public school teachers, as mandated by the new 584-page catalog of behavior modification techniques, was to shape the way pupils learn, act, and think.

When Catherine Barrett, then president of the National Education Association, addressed the union's membership in 1975, she stressed the importance of continued indoctrination and transformation, saying, "First, we will help all of our people understand that school is a concept and not a place. We will not confuse 'schooling' with education. The school will be the community, the community the school." She went on to say:

> We will need to recognize that so-called basic skills, which currently represent nearly the total effort in elementary schools, will be taught in one quarter of the present school day. The remaining time will be devoted to what is truly fundamental and basic—time for academic inquiry, time for students to develop their own interests, time for a dialogue between students and teachers; more than a dispenser of information, the teacher will be a conveyor of values, a philosopher. Students will learn to write love letters and lab notes.[3]

The NEA, the nation's largest teacher union, was making it clear that "reading, writing, and arithmetic" was yesterday's terminology. From now on America's public schools were to serve as "agents of change."

Rooting out the American spirit of independence, however, would take time and persistence, since American culture was grounded in patrio-tism, individualism, and reverence. In a 1972 keynote address to members of the Association of Childhood Education, Harvard psychiatrist Chester M. Pierce challenged public school teachers to lead the way in transform-ing the next generation: "Every child in America entering school at the age of five is mentally ill," he said, "because he comes to school with certain allegiances to our Founding Fathers, toward our elected officials, toward his parents, toward a belief in a supernatural being, and toward the sover-eignty of this nation as a separate entity. It's up to you as teachers to make all these sick children well—by creating the international child of the future."[4]

In his extensive review of Charlotte Iserbyt's book, columnist Alan Caruba condemns the reasoning behind this type of thinking. He writes:

> This is a formula for degrading patriotism and loyalty to everything for which this nation stands in favor of creating citizens of the "global gov-ernment" being pursued by the United Nations and the environmental-ism that preaches against the use of the earth's natural resources. All throughout the 1970's, the federal government funded these goals. Local educational systems were taken over by programs designed to destroy local control.[5]

Year by year and semester by semester, however, both public and private schools have been churning out graduates successfully transformed by pro-gressive education. Each year, in turn, scores of high school students score miserably on Scholastic Aptitude Tests. As education secretary William J. Bennett has pointed out in the *Index of Leading Cultural Indicators*, in just over thirty years the average scores of U.S. students on the SAT dropped nearly eighty points. And performance on exams such as the National Assessment of Educational Progress (NAEP) shows that knowledge and rea-soning skills continue to decline proportionally with each year of education, so that elementary school children score better on standardized exams than those in the higher grades. Bennett writes:

In 1992, 72 percent of fourth-grade students could do third-grade math (addition, subtraction, and simple problem-solving with whole numbers). Twenty percent of eighth-graders could do seventh-grade math (fractions, decimals, percents, and elementary concepts in geometry, statistics, and algebra), and only 6 percent of twelfth-grade students grasped the reasoning and problem-solving involving geometric relationships, algebra, and fractions that prepare them for college-level math.[6]

Analysis of performance in California's public schools in 2003 showed that 26 percent of that state's elementary school students, 14 percent of middle school students, and just 7 percent of high school students scored in the "excellent" range. The obvious correlation is that the longer students remain in school, the further they fall behind, and the less they benefit from prior knowledge or their own native intelligence. These are just some of the pernicious effects of dumbing down.

EDUCATIONAL ROT

Theodore Sizer, former dean of the Harvard Graduate School of Education and one of the designers of Goals 2000, summarized the aims of Outcome Based Education (OBE): "We want to move away from nationalism toward the concept of world family." Love of country, he said, was to be replaced by love of mankind, the United Nations, and Mother Earth. Under the Goals 2000 program introduced during the Clinton administration, three federal bureaucracies would be created: the National Education Goals Panel, the National Education Standards and Improvement Council, and the National Skills Board. They were to be the principal agents of indoctrination and enforcement.

By federal mandate, local school boards would no longer determine curriculum, testing standards, or graduation requirements for their schools. It would be done for them by bureaucrats who apply the principles of "progressive education" and the globalist agenda. And since public education would no longer be required to meet conventional academic achievement standards, the educrats decided that high school diplomas should be replaced with certificates of attendance.

Under these new programs, the federal government would also maintain electronic surveillance of student attainment, and each student was to have a computer record detailing participation and fulfillment of social objectives in the classroom. What the designers of the new curricula wanted to know was not what students had actually learned or how well they understood the principles of math, science, language, or history, but whether or not they demonstrated compliance with instructions, honesty, and suitable character traits. And students' academic records would then follow them into the workplace and throughout their adult lives.

The program would not stop with children but was to include parents as well. Parents needed to be reeducated in areas such as the principles of child development, parent-child learning objectives, child rearing, social and personal responsibility, tolerance, multicultural and world perspectives, and sensitivity to ethnic, racial, and biological diversity. William Spady, principal author of the Goals 2000 standards and the man who coined the term OBE in 1980, expressed the view that, "School is an instrument of socialization. It is supposed to teach civic values. Call it flat political indoctrination if you want. That's basically what it is." Fortunately, however, when the details of these programs became public, the public reacted with alarm.[7]

But contrast the view of the social programmers who conceived Goals 2000 with the statements of John Taylor Gatto in his book, *Dumbing Us Down: The Hidden Curriculum of Compulsory Schooling.* "Whatever education is," Gatto writes, "it should make you a unique individual, not a conformist; it should furnish you with an original spirit with which to allow you to find values which will be your road map through life; it should make you spiritually rich, a person who enjoys whatever they are doing, wherever you are, whomever you are with; it should teach you what is important, how to live, and how to die." Gatto's remarks may apply as easily to New Age spirituality as any other, but the vision he offers is light years beyond the kinds of social regimentation prescribed by the progressives' model.

Gatto goes on to say, "There is abundant evidence that less than a hundred hours is sufficient for a person to become totally literate and a self-teacher. Don't be panicked by scare tactics into surrendering your children to experts."[8] The perspective of this former "Teacher of the Year" for the state of New York brings a needed dash of realism to the debate. Reading, writing, arithmetic, and a basic grasp of American history are essential for success in life.

So why does the public school mafia deride these foundational elements of a well-rounded education, forcing their agenda of social engineering down America's throat? Brooks Alexander provides the answer: "In the ideological contest for cultural supremacy, education is the prime target; it influences the most people in the most pervasive way at the most impressionable age. No other social institution has anything close to the same potential for mass indoctrination."[9]

Another outspoken critic of the educationist agenda is George Mason University professor and syndicated columnist Walter Williams, who says, "The best thing we can do for American education is to abolish university education departments, abolish the U.S. Department of Education, and fire education 'experts.'" Over the last thirty years, scores on achievement tests have been in freefall, as documented both by SAT scores and the NAEP. Williams writes:

On a recent test, one-third of high school seniors couldn't identify Abraham Lincoln nor the countries we fought during WWII. Only 6 percent could solve the following math problem: "Christine borrows $850 for one year and pays a simple interest rate of 12 percent. What will be the total amount of money she repays?" A major insurance company reports that 44 percent of its applicants couldn't read at the ninth grade level. Eighty percent of a major manufacturer's applicants flunked its fifth-grade math and seventh-grade English competency tests. Few Americans need more proof that our education system is in shambles but why it's in shambles is important for the cure.[10]

Writing for the *American Enterprise* magazine, Karl Zinsmeister described a high school textbook called *Secondary Math: An Integrated Approach* that allocated a large portion of its pages to color photos and essays about the Dogon tribe of Africa, to pictures of the African-American poet Maya Angelou, and to former president Bill Clinton, who asked students to think about, "What role should zoos play in today's society?" In kindergarten, Zinsmeister says, kids spend weeks "exploring gender bias," while elementary texts are designed to teach kids about "a variety of family structures, emphasizing families with gay and lesbian parents." In a rare moment of candor, the *Los Angeles Times* described classes in baseball-card collecting, jigsaw puzzles, and crocheting at a Northridge, California, middle school.[11]

The reason for the rot is the fact that sixties radicals have taken over the colleges of education and today they dominate the education establishment. "For them," says Williams, "schooling is for building habits of social cooperation and equality rather than rigorous training of the mind. For many teachers, schooling must undermine parents and traditional values." Jay Parini, a professor at Middlebury College in Vermont, offered perhaps the most candid assessment of this infiltration of the academy when he confessed:

> After the Vietnam War, a lot of us didn't just crawl back into our literary cubicles; we stepped into academic positions. With the war over, our visibility was lost, and it seemed for a while—to the unobservant—that we had disappeared. Now we have tenure, and the work of reshaping the universities has begun in earnest.[12]

Since the sixties the radical vision of what a college education should be has "percolated throughout entire college curricula." And, says Williams, "Nowhere are half-witted education ideas given greater currency than in education departments, and for good reason. By and large education departments represent the academic slums of any university. Education majors tend to have the lowest SAT scores, and their professors tend to have the least academic respectability, making both easy prey to fads and half-baked ideas."[13]

INFILTRATING THE UNIVERSITIES

As we have seen in previous chapters, the pattern of transformation that wrecked the public schools entered the world of higher education, naturally and predictably, as at least two generations of high-school graduates who were products of this educational conspiracy began the journey through America's colleges and universities. Had the universities made it their mission to remedy the shortcomings of new students by demanding higher standards and elevating entrance requirements, rather than merely lowering them, the effect might have been to force secondary schools to revise their plans. The pressure generated by parents and employers when universities began turning away record numbers of applicants who were unprepared for the rigors of higher education could easily have short-circuited the progressive agenda.

But this did not happen. Rather, universities that had been turning out operatives for the public schools through their departments of education, as noted by Walter Williams, proceeded to scrap the traditional curricula, to eliminate obligatory and long-standing degree requirements along with foundational and survey courses of every kind, and to lower standards, much as the public schools had already done. Consequently, rather than losing students or tuition income, which was a matter of no small concern, enrollment soared to record levels even as academic standards were collapsing all around them.

The implications of these changes have been monumental. Among the most disturbing was not only that admissions standards were being lowered but that, thanks to surging enrollment and affirmative action policies that granted favored status to candidates who would never have qualified for university admission under any previous model, record numbers of men and women were graduating from America's universities who were in many ways illiterate and intellectually unformed. Paradoxically, the grades these students were earning began to rise, not because they had suddenly acquired exceptional habits of scholarship but because the universities discovered that parents would gladly agree to pay exorbitant tuition and residence fees so long as Johnny and Susie were earning A's and B's at college.

Dr. Harvey C. Mansfield, a distinguished professor of government at Harvard, and also a graduate of Harvard College in the fifties, is a serious scholar who demands a lot of his students, a fact that earned him the nickname Harvey "C-minus" Mansfield. The push for "grade inflation" from both the faculty and the administration provoked him to propose a new system that would surely satisfy everyone: namely, that each student should receive two course grades. The first grade would build the ego and satisfy Mom and Dad, and the second, somewhat lower no doubt, would be an honest assessment of the student's accomplishments.

In a column for the *Wall Street Journal*, Mansfield discussed the problem of grade inflation in detail. "Having at last awakened to the scandal of giving its students 51 percent A's and A-minuses and graduating 91 percent of them with honors," he said, "Harvard is now ready—let's be optimistic—to claim the honor of being the first university to do something about it." The dual-grade proposal was facetious, of course, but he didn't hesitate to pinpoint the real source of the problem. "In the 1960s, when grade inflation got started," he says, "some people on the Left believed that grading was done to subjugate students. Almost nobody believes that now. Grade inflation is an unintended situation in which individual professors routinely overgrade their students almost as thoughtlessly as parents might spoil their children. If they do think about it, they see that they (and the students) are trapped in a system that nobody can change by himself."

Students certainly don't object, and parents are pleased, Mansfield says. Likewise, professors get fewer complaints, and administrators can point to rising GPAs and boast of their brilliance. But there's more to it than that. "Grade inflation," says Mansfield, "is not a policy but it is an unintended consequence of policies, in which the liberals running our universities have lost their own authority." And he adds:

Liberal policies, however, have transferred authority from professor to student. More and more the university curriculum offers choice to students, implying that they are sovereign consumers free to pick what they want. Even core requirements can be fulfilled in several ways. In keeping with the philosophy of multiculturalism it is thought wrong to "privilege" courses on Western civilization by requiring them, despite the facts that it is our civilization, and that, because it is the only self-critical civilization, it is better than the others. This reluctance to require diminishes the authority of professors. It shows that they forswear the right to insist that students study specific things. The professors' experienced judgment is held to be no better than that of their students.

ANTI-AMERICAN INFLUENCE

Use of taxpayer funds to support international studies programs at universities is under fire for contributing to anti-American bias. In testimony before the House Subcommittee on Select Education, Stanley Kurtz of the Hoover Institution reported that support for area studies by the Department of Education exceeds a hundred million dollars. After 9/11 the Bush administration increased funding by 26 percent. Kurtz said later: "Our universities have gone to Congress with the claim that their programs of Middle East and other area studies contribute to national security and therefore deserve a special subsidy. Yet these subsidized programs have a one-sided bias against American foreign policy and discourage students from serving their country in a national-security capacity."

—Stanley Kurtz, "Reforming the Campus,"
National Review, 14 October 2003

Complicating matters even further, Mansfield says that course evaluations which allow students to rate their professors' performances are another gift of liberal policies with unwanted consequences. "Here is a direct connection to grade inflation," he writes, "as it has been shown that young professors or part-time faculty without tenure make sure to give high grades so as to get high ratings. In most universities student course evaluations are the sole measure of competence in teaching, in part because they are the only thing you can count. So the wise are judged according to how well they charm the unwise."[14]

In the end, grade inflation is yet another indication that liberals have mismanaged the universities. Professors have not been true to themselves but have treated students as spoiled, wealthy brats, which were the very ones the sixties radicals set out to displace. The longer range problem, however, is that elite universities like Harvard, Yale, Stanford, and MIT have lowered standards to such an extent that they are now graduating students who lack the competencies upon which the reputations of these institutions were built. Who knows what the impact of such changes may be?

ON SHAKY GROUND

When I met with Dr. Mansfield at his office in Littauer Hall, on the Harvard campus, I asked him what the fallout of his modest proposal for double-grading had been.

"Well, it was essentially a publicity stunt," he said, "and it worked. It was intended to draw attention to grading practices, and despite the fact that this overgrading has been going on for decades, it's true that a lot of professors and students didn't realize the extent to which we were compromised by it. We have been giving about half A's and A-minuses. It's incredible!"

I said, "It would probably be more noticeable at another university where the SAT score of the average student is somewhat lower."

"That's one of the excuses we hear," he said, "but when I first came to Harvard as a seventeen-year-old freshman, I realized I was suddenly in the big leagues. It wasn't going to be like high school anymore. But nowadays, it's more like a continuation of high school, because you still get the same high grades you got before."

"The trick is getting in," I said.

"That's right. The trick is getting in," he said.

"What about the level of general knowledge among entering freshman," I said. "How does it compare to when you came here as an undergraduate?"

"Oh, that's very shaky," he said. "They're better in math and science than in my time, but they don't know much history, and they haven't had much practice in writing. The effect of that is compensated somewhat by the fact that many of them have natural talent—they're smart kids and they catch on quickly—but they have large gaps in their knowledge. They catch on quickly if they take the right courses, but since there are few requirements and no mandatory survey courses, a lot of them don't."

"The course catalog is enormous," I said. "I don't know how students manage it."

"That's true," he said. "There's such a variety of courses; they're scattered all over the place, and there's a vast range of choice despite the fact that we have a core curriculum, which amounts to about a year's worth of courses. Nonetheless, there are so many ways of satisfying the requirements that you don't have to take anything important or significant. The core isn't really a core; it's really just an approach at one."

"There are required English courses, I understand, but they're nothing like the survey courses you and I had to take as undergraduates," I said.

"That's exactly right," he said, "and the students really miss that. On the other hand, they like taking all these odd things; they're struck by this or that course title, so they end up with transcripts that are a hodgepodge, with no coherence."

"Unless they're coming back for graduate school," I said, "students don't understand that they haven't actually learned very much in the course of a four-year education."

"I think they know," he said. "They know the easy courses, and they know they could have taken something more challenging. I don't think they're really satisfied with what they've got. These are smart people so they know when they've had it easy."

I said, "Recently I spoke to a colleague at a major university who told me he sees some students with SAT scores as low as three hundred to four hundred, far below the typical entrance requirement, but because they're from one of the preferred minorities they get in. They take mostly junk courses for four years, learn next to nothing, and then graduate along with everybody else. Any way you look at that," I said, "it's unfair to everyone concerned, and not least to the student who knows he hasn't acquired the knowledge he'll be expected to demonstrate on the job."

"The shocking thing," Mansfield said, "is that even Harvard students, who have much higher SAT scores than that, also end up with very imperfect educations. I think that's why the university president, Larry Summers, is talking about restoring some of those survey courses that have been greatly missed. He's working on a revision of the undergraduate curriculum, including the core curriculum. And one of the things he mentioned was the lack of survey courses in the humanities."

"Since you've been here as a student, grad student, and a faculty member for, gosh, over fifty years," I said, "you're certainly in the best position to tell me what's up with the curriculum. What's the impact of the dumbing down that's been going on over the past thirty or forty years?"

"Requirements have diminished, very much," he said, "and the number of courses given has increased. The coherence has been lost. There always was a good deal of choice at Harvard. We had a president in the nineteenth century, Charles W. Eliot, who set up the so-called elective system, but it's out of control now. When I came here there were a few easy courses—we called them 'gut courses'—athletes and 'Gentleman's C' students took them. But most people looked down on those courses and regarded them with amused contempt. But now the gut courses have proliferated, and they're regarded as more legitimate than they used to be. It was only with a certain amount of embarrassment that you'd tell someone that you were taking one of those, and everybody would know you were taking it easy. But now the attitude toward those courses has changed."

LOSING THEIR PASSION

"How do the courses you took as an undergraduate compare to the courses being offered at Harvard today?" I said.

"They're a lot easier now," he said. "Math and science are still done well, and languages are done well, but the social science and humanities courses are much easier and don't require either as much reading or writing as they used to; and this whole core (which amounts to about a quarter of the student's entire requirement) is not respected by the students, or the faculty either. Those are often courses where the professor tries to make a difficult thing seem simpler, in order to attract more students, or to please undergraduates who are being asked to take something they might not ordinarily take. There's been a whole change toward a more consumerist attitude, and I think students are looked on now as consumers whom you have to please. It's not for them to please us, but we're to please them."

"I assume professors are doing this for their own careers," I said. "If they have students clamoring for their courses, they're going to be considered more important, and this means of course that the student evaluations are more important than ever."

"Yes, of course," he said. "Course evaluations from the students are very important in getting promoted, and all this has contributed greatly to grade inflation."

"Is it pressure from the students that forces professors to try to please them?" I asked.

"It isn't so much pressure from the students but the view of the faculty," he said. "The faculty think they ought to please students. And the students get used to this and naturally complain when it doesn't happen. It began in the late sixties when the professors didn't lose but actively surrendered their authority."

"Another thing that concerns me," I said, "is the future of the professor, and if there's going to be anyone qualified to carry on the great tradition. Thirty or forty years of grinding down standards and curriculum have had a visible impact on the caliber of scholars and scholarship, and instead of having real core knowledge a lot of professors today have theories *about* knowledge, and that's troubling. Do you think we'll have men and women capable of stepping into your shoes when the time comes?"

"I think so," he said. "There are some good graduate students. This is a place where political correctness reigns supreme and conservatives have a lot more trouble getting jobs than those who aren't conservatives. That reflects the power of liberal faculties around the United States, and that's what hurts me most, to see students who've spent years getting their Ph.D. degrees, becoming quite learned and doing good work, but not being able to get a job. In a way, however, it has helped conservatism politically because a lot of them, therefore, went to Washington instead of into the teaching professions. If only the liberals had known! They could have prevented that by giving them jobs in small backwater colleges where they would have been safe and out of the way!"

"Will it get to the point where there aren't any more conservative professors on campus?" I asked.

"No, I'm more optimistic than that," he said. "I see a lot more conservatives among undergraduates these days, and especially among those going into the professions. I think things may be getting better, partly because I'm impressed with our new president, Larry Summers, who's been heard to say he wants more conservatives on this faculty."

"How did he get hired?!" I said with a laugh. "But let me follow up on what you just said: You're optimistic? Is that right? I'd like to know how you can be optimistic in light of the chaos of cultural and moral values on campus, not to mention the lack of a solid curriculum."

"I can't really give any evidence why I should be optimistic," he said, "but I don't think this can continue much longer. There's such a contradiction between the constant talk of diversity and the failure to practice it. I think this is being picked up by the students, and the time will come when the Left will be forced to concede some positions. I would cite this evidence, as I said before, that those on the Left lack conviction. They're push-overs.

"I can tell you," he added, "that they were stunned by the attitude of the American people after 9/11. It was an affront to their multiculturalism.

There are people who hate us, who want to kill us: how do you explain that? I thought it was so wonderful when President Bush used the four-letter word, Evil! They might not admit it, but the liberals in our midst have to confront the fact of evil."

"It's sad to think it had to take a major disaster to make people wake up," I said. "I wonder if it's going to take another one, or something even worse, before some people will get the picture. I wouldn't be surprised, seeing the way things are going at the moment, that we very well may see something else in the future."

"Oh, yes! If we don't prevent it, we'll see it," he said.

"And the Left's position plays right into that. If you read the *New York Times*," I said, "you get the idea that they'd be perfectly happy if American diplomacy would just stop where it is right now, if America would get out of the Middle East and just let nature take its course. But that would be a terrible disaster; only, they can't see it."

"Here's another piece of evidence," Mansfield said. "That kind of thinking has much less effect here on this campus than it did ten or twenty years ago, to say nothing of the sixties."

"Really? That's the most amazing thing you've said!" I said. "Is it because they've lost their passion? One thing I know about political action, going back to my own graduate studies in the seventies, is that the one thing the Left always had was plenty of passion. They were shockingly ignorant on most issues, but they had a great deal of passion."

"Yes, that's changed," he said. "They had ideas but they haven't worked. They were able to set an agenda for government, the media, the universities, but didn't see any fruit from it."

THE BEST ADVICE

"On that note," I said, "what's your advice to the mothers and fathers of America who are preparing their children to apply to places like Harvard? Is there anything they should know before they go through this process?"

"Oh, for sure!" he said. "They should know that most of the choices their children will be confronted with when they come to Harvard are bad or misleading, and that they need to get some good advice. In the first place, to use common sense, but to get good advice from students with conservative opinions, from the faculty, or from their parents as to the choice of courses as well as the way to live.

"I haven't talked much about this," he continued, "and I don't really get into the moral or sexual climate all that much, but there are a lot of bad things going on, including the so-called 'hook-ups' between students and others on campus. I've been looking into this, doing some research in the area of 'manliness' for a course I taught last year. We had a report from a committee dealing with sexual assault in which it was said that many young adults want to engage in 'experimentation with sexual intimacy.' That's what they said. It wasn't recommended, but it also wasn't discouraged; and nobody said that many young adults really *don't* want to do that.

"So when you send your child to Harvard," Dr. Mansfield said, "you need to know there are all sorts of temptations of this sort, so you have to speak in a way that you think is going to be most effective, using the Bible or using common sense, or both. But bad things can happen to you here if you take up with that kind of 'experimentation.' If you're going to find out something new in a laboratory, let it be about science and not something you'll regret the rest of your life."

"I've been seeing some of the new statistics of STDs, HIV, rape, suicide, and all those things," I said, " and the way these figures have skyrocketed on the university campus is really frightening. You can ruin your life that way, very easily."

"Yes, that's right," he said. "There's a notion that you can have sex quickly and without love—it won't hurt you—especially for the women. They think this is a new thing, but that would have to be a major concern for a parent. And it's not just Harvard. I'm sure it's a problem at any of the bigger schools, but in today's climate it's a concern at practically any college in the country, except one or two where there's a deliberate and pervasive moral climate."

"What about academics?" I said. "What are your concerns in that regard?"

"The lack of core courses that reflect some deliberation by the faculty about what's important for an educated person to know," he said. "I would say that's the number one thing."

"Does the politically correct view of 'dead white European male' militate against that?" I asked.

"Yes, it militates against it ever happening so long as the professors now in charge remain in charge. But, as I say, I believe that their beliefs are being shaken, and they will be shaken even further. Consequently, I think they can be led—or maybe in some cases coerced—into a more disciplined education. On the other hand, political correctness isn't retreating yet, even though it's not believed as fervently as it used to be."

"I'm glad to hear that there are going to be changes to the core curriculum," I said, "and that it may soon become more comprehensive and rigorous, but the current core is pretty fluffy, seems to me."

"It is," he said. "It's a core that consists of approaches. So students learn the historical approach, for example, or the social-science approach; they don't learn what's the most important history or which literary works, for example, are considered to be the greatest books and authors."

"Who's to say?" I said with a laugh. "That's what students say to me when I bring up the subject of 'great literature.' I asked one young man if he had been exposed to the great books, and he reacted almost in shock. 'Oh, no!' he said. 'We don't talk about great anything!' You have to wonder what students are learning when their professors refuse to say that anything is great or a classic; the view is that all works of literature are of essentially equal value. Frankly, I'm shocked to know that my degree field of comparative literature is one of the worst."

"Yes, it is. It's one of the worst," Dr. Mansfield said. "And the romance languages are about the same, along with sociology. Government, on the whole, is one of the better ones. Economics is also one of the better ones at Harvard. But the humanities—especially comparative literature, English, and languages—those are all pretty bad."

"What else?" I asked. "Any final thoughts?"

"Yes," he said, "I think it's important not to lose hope altogether. The knowledge is still there to be had, and there are teachers who are still authentic and dedicated to the profession. I would say that to the parents of children who are coming to college. It's still possible to get an education; there are a few mavericks around, especially at the larger schools. There are still a few decent and honest professors. In the smaller colleges I think the situation may be worse, because there the faculty all know each other and hiring is done more on the basis of potential friendships or sharing of opinions than it is here. But you have to look for those things, and you have to make your wishes clear. Parents have a lot more power than they realize, if they will only use it to get people to listen to their concerns."

MAKING THE SYSTEM WORK

For education to work at any level, as Harvey Mansfield makes clear, there must be standards. At the elementary and secondary school levels, students have to develop skills in the fundamentals that will allow them to acquire the kinds of knowledge they'll need, not just for successful university careers but to become good citizens. For those who are headed for the job market, there must be sufficient mastery of the language and computational skills they'll need to hold a job. And those admitted to colleges have to be able to perform at a reasonably high level of academic competency if the term "higher education" is to have any meaning.

Unfortunately, the generation that gave us Woodstock has also given us a dumbed down view of education that has stranded millions of young people in a limbo of academic mediocrity and unmet expectations. As Christopher Lasch attests, the idea that forcing universities to open their doors to all comers and to rig the numbers so that certain groups could break down the barriers of class and privilege was ultimately a false faith. Lasch writes:

> The democratization of education has accomplished little to justify this faith. It has neither improved popular understanding of modern society,

raised the quality of popular culture, nor reduced the gap between wealth and poverty, which remains as wide as ever. On the other hand, it has contributed to the decline of critical thought and the erosion of intellectual standards, forcing us to consider the possibility that mass education, as conservatives have argued all along, is intrinsically incompatible with the maintenance of educational quality.[15]

Rudolf Flesch warned in his 1955 bestseller, *Why Johnny Can't Read*, that experiments with "whole language" reading and classroom novelties such as the "look-say" method were threatening literacy and would inevitably have a long-term pernicious effect on learning. Today, fifty years later, every American university has to offer remedial programs in reading, writing, and mathematics. A survey published in 2003 revealed that at least 29 percent of freshmen at our major universities are enrolled in at least one of these remedial programs. The figure jumps to 41 percent at community colleges, and it may actually be much higher than researchers will say.

Problems with basic literacy are behind most of the declines in academic achievement. Scores on the verbal portion of the SAT, for example, reached historic lows in the mid-nineties, and educators decided that the tests had to be redesigned to give the impression that student skills weren't actually falling, which, of course, they were. But the problem goes beyond the classroom, particularly when we see government research that puts the number of functionally illiterate Americans at over forty million. A 1994 report by the Educational Testing Service found that "half of the nation's college graduates could not read a bus schedule, and only 42 percent could summarize an argument presented in a newspaper article or contrast the views in two editorials about fuel efficiency."

A study that divided students into five levels of literacy, as Charles Sykes reports, found that just 11 percent of graduates of four-year colleges, and 2 percent of graduates of two-year colleges, ranked in the top level. Only 35 percent of four-year college graduates were able to write a coherent letter describing a billing error. And in another study, it was reported that American business loses more than forty billion dollars in revenue each year because of the low level of employee literacy and the time needed to retrain workers who are unable to deal with the new technologies. To illustrate the importance of this problem, the report said that one company, the Stone Savannah River Pulp & Paper Corporation, had spent more than two hundred thousand dollars to train workers to use computers when supervisors discovered that employees lacked the basic reading and language skills necessary to operate the equipment.[16]

In his analysis of the changes in America's colleges and universities over the past forty years, Martin L. Gross writes,

> This dumbing down of the American college serves the motives of the New Establishment, which now finds it easy to indoctrinate its under-educated students into its own biases and bigotries. Since college graduates, especially those from the Ivy League, inevitably end up as the nation's leaders, what does this say about the present and future of the American culture—its politics, literature, economics, journalism, films, and especially its philosophical direction?[17]

Ultimately, this is the greatest risk of the deliberate dumbing down of America: not just that the colleges are taking in poorly prepared undergraduates or turning out graduates with diplomas that are little more than certificates of attendance, but that the caliber of men and women who will lead this nation in coming years has sunk to unprecedented levels, and those who end up in leadership roles in government, business, and other areas of society will do so with the immodest assumption that they are suitably educated for the task, when, truthfully, this is seldom the case.

A DANGEROUS CREED

Make no mistake, the dumbing down of education is a crisis that threatens the survival of the American Republic. While educrats, school officials, and university administrators try to deny this fact, it is now common knowledge. The truth is undeniable, and every measure of standardized academic achievement has made this point in incontrovertible terms. Men and women who lack the basic skills to hold a job are living proof. Employers whose profits are siphoned off by the need to retrain and educate their workers are material witnesses. Universities certainly offer corroboration as they continually lower standards and make exceptions for new categories of students and then sentence them to months in remedial programs to try and bring them up to speed.

Hoover Institution scholar Thomas Sowell makes the connection between dumbing down in the schools and reprogramming in the universities as poignantly as anyone. "Creating mindless followers is one of the most dangerous things that our public schools are doing," Sowell writes. "Young people who know only how to vent their emotions, and not how to weigh opposing arguments through logic and evidence, are sitting ducks for the next talented demagogue who comes along in some cult or movement, including movements like those that put the Nazis in power in Germany." But then he adds with even greater portent that, "At one time, the educator's creed was: 'We are here to teach you how to think, not what to think.' Today, schools across the country are teaching students what to think—whether about the environment, the war, social policy, or whatever."[18]

For many years, public education taught America's children that learning was a minor annoyance on the road to unlimited self-indulgence and higher self-esteem. Students were allowed to coast through twelve years of school with only the most superficial intellectual exertion and, at the same time, they were assured that they were the "best and brightest." They were praised for unquestioning acceptance of the socialization they had endured since kindergarten. More recently, however, there's a new sense that most of the messages our children are receiving are countercultural and preoccupied with a liberal social agenda.

While there are signs of restlessness in the academy, most visibly in the attempt to return to a core curriculum and to restore survey courses in history, government, and the humanities that offer students a broad general knowledge, the majority of professors and administrators strongly resist changes that would draw attention to the importance of character, personal behavior, national pride, or morality. The idea of an Academic Bill of Rights to protect freedom of thought and intellectual diversity on campus has created a strongly unfavorable reaction on the Left. Faculty members say they want to elevate the level of academic discourse but are unwilling to make the kinds of demands on students that might actually achieve that end.

At one point in my conversation with Harvey Mansfield, I mentioned my concerns about this imbalance in the curriculum. "For weeks now as I've been traveling around the country," I said, "I've heard complaints about the bias on campus. The liberals say their goal is 'tolerance' and 'diversity,' but they're not very diverse, and they're incredibly intolerant. They don't allow conservatives on the faculty, and they won't permit any consideration of the ideas that might actually extend academic freedom."

"This happens," Dr. Mansfield said, "not because they sit down and say 'Let's not have any conservatives,' but because they don't appreciate the good work that conservatives do in the subjects in which they're interested. I see that very much with my students," he said. "If they write on honor or patriotism, in favor of morality, or against feminism, or if they write on anything to do with religion, the professor says, 'This work is not interesting to me.' They won't read it. They say, 'That isn't what we need. We need someone just like me, only a little bit different.' And what makes it worse is this notion of academic and social-science objectivity. They say, 'I have my values over here and my work over there, so my values are separate from my work.' The fact that fifty people in our department are liberals doesn't matter. Yes, they're liberals, they say, but they're all neutral when it comes to the way they study their subject."

"It's like the argument from the media," I said. "They insist there's no liberal bias in the media—they're just reporting the facts. But anyone with the least bit of common sense can see that there's an obvious bias in most of what's reported these days."

"That's right," he said. "That's why they think that diversity doesn't apply to them."

At the root of all these problems, I believe, is an attitude of disdain for traditional values and the historical moral framework of American culture.

Very much like the village churches of the seventeenth and eighteenth centuries, local schools were originally designed as places where character and personal integrity were instilled in children from their earliest years. Just as all of the first universities in this country were founded as seminaries or schools of religion, common schools and colleges were places where reading, writing, history, science, and math were taught in a moral setting that was designed for molding men and women of character. Rather than stripping them of knowledge and values, teachers sought to build on the traits their pupils had learned at home and in the churches. Thus, they multiplied the effect of teaching by relying on the civilizing influence of religion.

Throughout Western history, morality, education, and religious instruction have inspired the greatest works of art, literature, poetry, music, sculpture, and architecture. From the earliest times, religious teachings combined with lessons in reading and writing were the vehicles for preserving civilization and passing on the finest aspects of culture to posterity. These are the values that inspire compassion and public service and the framework that permits societies to remain optimistic and resilient in the face of war, pestilence, famine, or other threats to the common good.

Charles Francis Potter, whose pamphlet *Humanism: A New Religion* was a major influence in the early days of the public school movement, believed that public education would one day be seen not as a molder of character and morality but as "the most powerful ally of humanism." In that work, Potter asks the rhetorical question, "What can the theistic Sunday Schools, meeting for an hour once a week, and teaching only a fraction of the children, do to stem the tide of a five-day program of humanistic teaching?"[19]

By all appearances, Potter's gamble was successful. Commonly held views and moral values have been largely eradicated from America's classrooms and university lecture halls, and the new humanistic credo has taken its place. This, after all, is where the dumbing down of education was meant to take us all along; but whether a nation can survive such an assault on its foundational beliefs is a matter of grave concern.

Part II
DISCOVERY

5

The New Orthodoxy

The Supreme Court ruling in the case of *Regents of the University of California v. Bakke* found that the use of quotas and set-asides in university admissions was unconstitutional. While the justices in that 1978 case questioned the way race-based admissions were conducted, they nevertheless indicated that universities could employ policies that offered "competitive consideration of race and ethnic origin." So while the *Bakke* case appeared to take one side of the issue, it didn't actually close the door on affirmative action admissions.

Thus, twenty-five years later, the cases of *Gratz v. Bollinger* involving University of Michigan undergraduate admissions and *Grutter v. Bollinger* involving the law school gave the court yet another opportunity to address the issue of discriminatory admissions policies. This time, white students who had been denied admission to the university claimed they were excluded because of their race. Attorneys argued that the plaintiffs were essentially denied the right of equal protection under the Fourteenth Amendment to the Constitution.

The students asked the court to stop the university from employing such practices and, by implication, to overrule *Bakke*. When the court finally spoke in 2003, they said the university could continue using affirmative action policies in the law school because of the non-specific way in which the program was structured but that the "point system" being used for undergraduate admissions would have to be scrapped. Both cases were argued aggressively, and dozens of amicus briefs were filed on both sides of the debate. Those concerned about reverse discrimination supported the plaintiffs while those who saw no problem with admissions based on race took the other side. Most striking, perhaps, was the fact that the U.S. Army submitted a brief supporting the university's right to consider race as a factor in admissions.

But what do such rulings really mean, and what do Americans think about the issues? A Marist Poll conducted in January 2003, several months before the Michigan ruling, suggests that most Americans believe that equal opportunity for students of all racial and ethnic backgrounds is an important concern. Some 85 percent of those polled, as researchers reported, believe that "living and learning among people of different interests, abilities, gender, and racial backgrounds better prepares college students to live and work in society." This view was held by individuals of all racial, gender, age, educational, political, geographic, and economic backgrounds.

However most respondents did not like the idea of using race as a factor in deciding whether or not to admit students to college. Fully 80 percent of all those surveyed, and 64 percent of minorities, said they oppose "race-conscious admissions policies." And respondents also disapproved of admissions policies that consider the wealth, fame, gender, athletic ability, or legacy status—that is, whether an applicant's parents or other relatives had attended the school.

When asked what should be the primary concern of college admissions, respondents to the Marist survey favored a combination of "quantitative and qualitative factors." High school grades topped the list, at 88 percent; scores on standardized exams was second, at 85 percent. Qualitative factors included recommendations from principals, teachers, or counselors, selected by 85 percent of respondents; the student's leadership or service to the community, at 80 percent; leadership or service in school came in at 77 percent; and artistic, musical, or theatrical talent was chosen by 73 percent. And the researchers also noted that 78 percent said admissions officers should take economic hardship into consideration as a factor as well.[1]

BETTER CHECK UNDER THE HOOD

You wouldn't buy a used car without looking under the hood, and you shouldn't send your son or daughter to college without looking a little deeper. Most published ratings are based on a school's endowment, faculty, or other resources, which may have little or no relationship to what students will see. Many colleges boast about their faculty, but at elite schools the majority of classes are taught by graduate teaching assistants. Before heading off to college, check it out.

THE ADMISSIONS GAME

A book recently published by Harvard Press, entitled *Increasing Faculty Diversity: The Occupational Choices of High-Achieving Minority Students*, reports that about 10 percent of black and Hispanic college seniors say they want to become college professors, which is roughly the same percentage as whites. Unfortunately, few of these students actually earn high enough grades to get into graduate school. Ironically, as reported by columnist John Leo, the authors of the book (and the study it contains) say that affirmative action is a big part of the problem, by granting admission to poorly qualified minority students at elite colleges where they're much less likely to earn high marks. Not only does this keep them out of graduate school, but it erodes self-confidence and often discourages any further interest in pursuing academic careers.

The idea that affirmative action changes the natural order in college admissions is an argument that has long been made by scholars such as Thomas Sowell, a Hoover Institution economist and columnist who earned admission to Harvard as a young black man the old-fashioned way: he earned it. But the anxiety of admissions officers to "play with the numbers" has long-term implications. To meet their quotas for "underprivileged" applicants, schools that normally look for applicants with top SATs, around 1400, frequently take minorities with scores of 1200 or less. Colleges that require 1200 scores then end up taking minorities with scores of 1000 or less, and at each level, minority students end up in competition with white and Asian students with higher academic qualifications. The university may score points for sensitivity, but these minority students suffer the consequences of disappointment and failure.

Of the minority students in the survey who were enrolled in elite universities, only 12 percent of those with the highest SAT scores (over 1300) had GPAs of A-minus or better. At state universities, however, 44 percent had averages of A-minus or better. It would seem fairly obvious that giving low-scoring minority students preferential admission to elite universities where they're more likely to fail would come to be seen as counterproductive; but then, that's a conclusion based on logic, which has very little to do with the way admissions decisions are actually made these days.[2]

According to some who have participated in faculty admissions panels that review student qualifications, high scores, good grades, and exceptional extracurriculars aren't even the first things these committees look for. So what does it take to be accepted at the university of your dreams? As my principal researcher, Connee Robertson Black, discovered in a review of the subject, you might be surprised. "Study hard, right?" she asks. "Really work on those SAT scores, even spending a thousand dollars on a cram course to up your score, and just be yourself? Not necessarily. Colleges have actually turned down applicants with perfect SATs. 'Too much of a grind,' they say, 'not well rounded.'

"Are you lucky enough to come from a stable home with sufficient money and parents who are college graduates? Points off for that! You have way too many advantages. Did you only take six advanced placement courses? Slacker! Your A's do not impress—someone with even C's and D's, low SAT scores, and an unstable background can beat you out. You're compared to your peers. Colleges expect only the very best from those with 'advantages.'

"Did you go to the best prep school or high school your parents could afford? If too many from your school want to go to the same big-name college, forget it: colleges only take limited numbers from each school, no matter how great the applicant may be. Places are held for the 'disadvantaged'—lots of places. Because women and minorities were left out a generation ago, colleges try to rectify that by overkill, punishing many of today's majority population applicants. Merit, or choosing the very best students for admittance, isn't always the criterion.

"Quota systems rule. Your skin color or ethnicity may be the thing that gets you into your dream college—or that holds you back. There are just so many places for blacks, so many for Hispanics and Asian Americans, and if you're from a very small minority—Pacific Islander or Native American, for example—it's your lucky day! Slack and more slack will be cut on grades, scores, essays, and everything else. A white male has to be exceptional—and not just academically—to make the cut.

"Gender plays a serious part as well. Most colleges try to make it exactly even: 50 percent male, 50 percent female. Or maybe you're from the wrong place. Colleges want broad diversity. Maybe they have too many East Coast students and want applicants from the South. Those from obscure or rural locations have a leg up. You have to wonder if Einstein would be selected if he were an incoming freshman today. He's white and male, European background, and even though he's scientifically gifted, he has poor social skills and is not a leader or even well rounded. Definitely a 'Maybe.'

"Who makes these life-changing decisions for college applicants and either admits them to the realms of educational greatness or condemns them to a lesser life? You'd be surprised by the answer. If you're envisioning wise, tweedy eggheads making lofty decisions from their wealth of experience in knowing just who should be admitted to their sacred circle, think again. That's not necessarily the case. Some colleges have faculty members deciding admissions; some have a combination of faculty and admissions officers; and others have just admissions officers. And what are their qualifications? There are none.

"Those who make such decisions can be highly qualified and knowledgeable about who would do well at their college, or they may be recent graduates themselves. Their previous jobs may have been in a college admissions office, the Peace Corps, animal control, or a ski lodge. Frequently the choosers of students are ethnic minorities who are hired to select others of their own race or group. There is a pretense of scientific method and number-crunching, but it's far from rocket science. Picking suitable students when a pool of thousands is left over is largely subjective. These all-too-human selectors frequently choose students they can relate to, someone who is, in ideas and background, most like them.

"The SAT is being changed. It has already been dumbed down by eliminating the analogies section and adding a hundred points of padding so today's low scores won't compare so poorly with those of yesteryear. Some colleges intend to eliminate SAT scores entirely, ridding themselves of the last and truest comparison of students' academic skills. An essay section is being added without regard for spelling or punctuation! What, you have to wonder, will it measure?

"To please those who guard the gates, students should stop to consider who will be reading their essays. Anything favorable about multiculturalism and the environment will be appreciated. They may not want to hear you rave about Mom, apple pie, or the good old USA. And this applies to application essays, as well.

"If your grades are the pits, then give them a sob story. Tell them how hard your circumstances are. Very much like today's soft juries, the admissions people may just cut you some slack, especially if you tell them how you fight for the environment, globalism, and the disadvantaged. Volunteering at the women's shelter would go a long way, too. But don't be too disheartened if you don't get accepted to your first-choice college. It may not be that there was anything wrong with you at all, except the wrong skin color, gender, or hometown."[3]

BACK TO BASICS

In his own assessment of the admissions dilemma, Thomas Sowell starts where more admissions counselors ought to begin. "Why do universities exist in the first place?" he asks. "Is it to parcel out benefits to different racial or ethnic groups? If so, why not just give them money? Do universities exist to be fair—whatever that means? If fair means equal chances or proportional representation, then why not make admissions a lottery?"

The problem, Sowell says, is that too many admissions officers act as if their role is to hand out goodies to the most deserving. "In other words," he writes, "if student A went to a top-notch high school and scored 1500 on the SATs, while student B went to a mediocre high school and scored 1300, then student B may be admitted and student A denied admission if the little tin gods in the admissions office decide that B made better use of his opportunities." But only a university official would ever see it that way: "You couldn't make up anything as silly as this," Sowell writes. Universities aren't there to reward students for their past but to prepare them for the future. Taxpayers and donors who are paying the tab aren't doing so to try to remake society but to ensure that universities turn out graduates who are capable of participating as future leaders and citizens of a free republic.

To put it in terms anyone can understand, Sowell asks, "Do you want to fly in planes flown by the best qualified pilots available or in planes flown by quota pilots or by pilots whose life stories were most appealing to those on admissions committees? If you are going to have heart surgery, do you want the best surgeon you can get, or do you want a surgeon who had to overcome a lot of handicaps just to make it through medical school?" Further, he says, "Would you be offended to have your life saved by someone who had easily become the best surgeon because he was born in the lap of privilege and always had the finest education available, regardless of how much it cost? Would it bother you if he was Asian American or even—heaven help us—a WASP?"

Too often, those in the sensitivity crowd miss the point, however, which is that the most important thing is to make sure that the most qualified candidates end up in the most critical jobs. Whoever they are and whatever their race or background, it's those who prove themselves by achievement and perseverance who need to be doing the big jobs. "Anyone who is serious about wanting to help minority young people," writes Thomas Sowell, "must know that the place to start is at precisely the other end of the educational process. That means beginning in the earliest grades, teaching reading, math, and other mental skills on which their future depends."

With a decent education during their elementary and high school years, he concludes, the universities wouldn't need quotas to find the most qualified applicants. But as we've witnessed in the preceding chapter, that would mean clashing with the educrats and teachers' unions who are behind the dumbing down of our children, pushing an agenda of psychological manipulation in America's classrooms.[4]

What we eventually come to see is that getting in is just a small part of the problem. When a new student arrives on campus and makes it to the first day of class, he or she will have a whole new set of problems. And one of the most ominous of these on today's PC campus is the dreaded "Freshman Orientation." Orientation is no longer the benign introduction to college life it was back in the sixties.

Freshman Boot Camp

When I entered college (to say nothing of the freshman beanie I was required to wear), orientation only demanded about an hour a day for the first two weeks of school. In it I learned about recommended study habits, dorm rules, and library policies and fines for overdue books. We were given a perspective on each of the various colleges on campus and the major departments within them, with an eye to helping us nail down a major. Not least, we were told about intramural activities and coeducational concerns, the dangers of dating and drinking, and warned about what could happen if we didn't follow the rules.

Today, orientation is more like boot camp, or a socialist indoctrination center, complete with role-playing, sensitivity sessions, sexual propagandizing, and emotional manipulation of students on a host of politically correct issues. I spoke to one student at Tufts University in Boston who told me he simply skipped orientation, even though it was a required class, and suffered no repercussions. But students shouldn't count on that. As Alan Charles Kors related in a recent address, colleges today use shock tactics and mind-control games to invade the private spaces in students' minds, in order to change their natural reactions and transform them into perfectly obedient PC warriors. And no one gets a pass.

BIO-ETHICS AT PRINCETON

"Very often it is not wrong at all to kill a child once it has left the womb. Simply killing an infant is never equivalent to killing a person." Dr. Peter Singer, professor of Bioethics at Princeton University, was granted tenure *after* making these statements.

—*Whistleblower* magazine, December 2003

At Wake Forest University, Kors revealed, one of the few events designated as "mandatory" for freshman orientation was attendance at a film entitled *Blue Eyed*. Basically it is a workshop in which white students are emotionally abused, made fun of, made to fail, and taught helpless passivity so they can identify with "a person of color for a day."[5] In the dorms at exclusive Swarthmore College, first-year students were asked to line up by skin color, from lightest to darkest. Then they had to confess how they felt about their place in the line. It was as if Chairman Mao had designed the program to humiliate the privileged and exalt the "disadvantaged." Even if these are extreme examples, the fact is, practically all colleges today have some form of morally and politically coercive indoctrination built into their freshman orientation or dorm-life programs.

In the early nineties, the *New York Times* and the *Wall Street Journal* examined freshman orientation on America's campuses. The *Times* observed that "orientation has evolved into an intense . . . initiation." In these initiation rituals, student affairs officers and the "consultants" they often hire to administer them deal with everything from date rape and sexual orientation to race relations and how students are expected to deal with them. In recent years, as Kors says, public scrutiny of the problems associated with political correctness has caused some college administrators to back away from the more radical programs, but the problem hasn't gone away.

The director of Dartmouth's mandatory "Social Issues" orientation was quoted as saying that students need to address "the various forms of isms: sexism, racism, classism," that fester just beneath the skin. Oberlin College, in Ohio, "educated" its freshmen about "differences in race, ethnicity, sexuality, gender, and culture," and held separate orientations for blacks, Hispanics, gays and lesbians, and Asians. Columbia challenged white students to rid themselves of "their own social and personal beliefs that foster inequality." One assistant dean explained to the *Times* that "you can't bring all these people together . . . without some sort of training."[6]

The director of multicultural programs at Stanford volunteered that, "For the white heterosexual male who feels disconnected and marginalized by multiculturalism, we've got to do a lot of work here." And a member of the Cultural Diversity Project at Northwestern University, in Illinois, said his committee's goal was "changing the world, or at least the way [new students] perceive it." At the same time, Bryn Mawr College let it be known they were willing to share their "Building Pluralism" program with any school that asked for it. This orientation workshop delved into the most private experiences of first-year students, particularly those dealing with sexuality, race, and religion. By the end of the orientation, students were expected to have individual and collective "action plans" for "breaking free" of the cycle of oppression they had tolerated prior to college and for achieving "new meaning" as "change agents."

Professor Graham Walker, when he was a newly hired member of the faculty, volunteered to help with freshman orientation at the University of Pennsylvania, and he soon realized that he disagreed strongly with statements in the official orientation materials. He was expected to discuss a number of case studies with freshmen, but he immediately recognized that the scenarios were designed to produce predetermined responses. In one case involving a conservative, Bible Belt student who discovered that his roommate was gay, the approved response was supposed to be, "In my community we regard this behavior as wrong, but those are just our values. I embrace my roommate's values equally with embracing my own values, and therefore I am becoming tolerant and setting aside the dogmatic intolerant view with which I arrived here in Philadelphia." Understandably, Professor Walker found that approach more than a little disturbing.

Instead of following blindly the school's notion of "tolerance," Walker said, he read some of the orientation materials aloud to his discussion group and then analyzed what was being said. "I thought the freshmen needed some ability to resist the indoctrination that was going on," he said. But expressing a point of view that was not approved by the campus thought police was risky business and eventually cost Walker his job. "In the academic world," he said, "your colleagues sit down around a table, with you absent, and they vote on whether or not you keep your job. When Dr. Walker was denied tenure, he moved on, and eventually landed at Catholic University of America in Washington, DC, where he was free at last to say what he truly believed.[7]

Thor Halvorssen, the former executive director of the Foundation for Individual Rights in Education (FIRE), believes that orientation programs that attempt to manipulate student thought and behavior are especially troubling when students can't opt out. "These issues should be discussed in the classroom, openly and voluntarily," he says, "not in forums where there are no dissenting voices, and not as the first contact students have with their schools." Unfortunately, there's real pressure on freshmen to attend these sessions, even when the program literature suggests that orientation is not mandatory.[8]

The administrators who design these programs claim to be changing stereotypes and bias in the incoming students when, in fact, they're merely creating new biases. And it's happening on a grand scale. Nearly a third of the 278 schools surveyed by the National Orientation Directors Association (NODA) had separate orientation sessions for minority and homosexual students. At Yale, incoming minority students were told to meet with "ethnic counselors" and to participate in small-group discussions, followed by a separate minority reception. The agenda is clearly not to ensure harmony and compatibility on campus but to set racial and sexual boundaries, and to defy students to cross that line.[9]

DISSATISFIED CUSTOMERS

"You asked me, 'What's the impact of race- and gender-based freshman orientation on the students?'" a faculty friend at a large Midwestern university said recently. "I think what it does is, instead of achieving the goal of understanding among the races, it actually increases the awareness that we're different and creates tensions that might not otherwise be there. It basically segregates people by groups, and as a result there's probably more racism and class-hatred on campus now than there was thirty years ago. Now we have separate dorms, separate dining facilities, separate clubs, separate classes, separate yearbooks, separate graduation ceremonies, and a terrible sense of anger and division. The result of university diversity policies has only heightened the awareness of differences and made it more likely that there will be bitterness between people of different racial and ethnic backgrounds."

"There are hotheads, of course," I said to him, "but basically the American people like to get along. But it seems to me that these policies have made it impossible to do that. If you try to be nice to people in other racial groups they become suspicious, and they act as if you're kissing up for some ulterior motive."

"Yes, and this really troubles me," he said. "No one trusts anyone else's motives, and there's all this uncertainty: 'What did you mean by that?' they say. 'Can I trust what you say?' And that just increases the tension in the classroom."

"Orientation in general," I said, "seems to be designed to create doubt, fear, and resentment between the races. It's not about getting along but about increasing the amount of distrust and resentment among both students and faculty."

"Another thing about freshman orientation," he said, "is that they tend to engage in these sensitivity encounters that are basically forms of brainwashing. By all rights, that should have gone out in the seventies. There's a tremendous amount of group pressure put on students to think and behave in certain ways. It has very little to do with openness to certain ideas and very much to do with accepting a particular way of thinking."

"There are sensitivity training sessions in some of the orientation classes," I said, "that involve demonizing white Anglo Saxons and making them take on subservient roles. If they come near a person of color they have to bow their head and look down. They're not allowed to make eye contact; they have to role-play racist stereotypes and build these feelings and emotions that are, frankly I think, quite dangerous. Have you heard about the film *Blue Eyed* that's being shown on a lot of campuses? They force students to watch this film which characterizes whites as demons and anyone of color as a saint."

"It's a sort of pseudoscience that passes for sociology," he said. "I refer to it as *Blue Lagoon anthropology*—the notion that people in Third World countries live in harmony with nature and each other, and they're corrupted when they come into contact with Western civilization. Christopher Columbus, to these people, is like the serpent in the Garden. America was an Eden until Columbus came along and brought Western civilization into it, with all its restrictions and prohibitions and moral judgments."

"The NEA and their companions started out in the elementary schools, indoctrinating students in these liberal views," I said, "and they have been enormously successful in stripping at least two generations of young Americans not only of basic knowledge but of moral standards and beliefs, as well. Most of these kids have no knowledge of the past, but they're already fully propagandized like little robots, in lockstep with what their teachers have been telling them. Even in high school they have no critical thinking skills."

"Which doesn't mean they're not intelligent," he said, "it just means they're disengaged."

"As you know, I taught in a Christian university for a number of years," I said, "and most of my students were highly motivated and very bright. But when I would try to challenge them to think critically, for the most part they couldn't do it. What bothered me most was not that they *couldn't* do it, but that they didn't really care and didn't want to learn. If it wasn't on MTV, or if it wasn't something their friends were already into, then they didn't much care.

"But one good sign," I added, "is that in some places alumni are beginning to react to this stuff. I have a friend in Washington who served in the White House. He's a graduate of Amherst College and has been a generous donor for many years. But when he began seeing the news about what's going on at that very liberal campus, he wrote to the alumni association and said, 'I'm not sending you any more money until I see that the leftist bias on campus has changed.' I doubt there's much chance of that happening in his lifetime," I said, "but if enough alumni do that, and if scholarship providers and funding groups of all sorts begin speaking up, then maybe something can happen. It's only when you start hitting them in the pocketbook that they start to squeal."

"I recently read about one family foundation," my friend said, "that demanded their money back from one of the Eastern universities because they realized the money they'd given wasn't being used for what they intended."

"Yes, I saw the story," I said, "about the Robertson Foundation at Princeton.[10] But I also know the story of Fort Worth businessmen, Lee and Perry Bass, who gave twenty million dollars to Yale, their alma mater, to encourage them to design a program to teach Western civilization. After years of wrangling, both sides gave up on the idea, and Yale made it sound as if they'd refused to be compromised. But the fact is, the Bass family demanded their money back when the university took too long to get the job done. Even with an endowment the size of Yale's," I said, "twenty million dollars isn't something to joke about!"

HALF THE STORY

The more we discover about the messages being inculcated into students in the universities today, the more troubling it is. And the more we understand about the methods of deception, disinformation, and deconstruction being used, the more determined we should be to kick the impostors, as Martin Anderson put it, out of the temple.

Dr. Robert George, whom I got to know during my term as director of the Wilberforce Forum in Washington, is someone who understands the risks of what's happening on campus today and is taking steps to change it. As the Cyrus H. McCormick Professor of Jurisprudence at Princeton, Dr. George holds a prestigious chair from which he wields considerable intellectual clout. As founder and director of the James Madison Program, he has reached out to scores of bright young people who are able to challenge the PC doctrines of the Left; and as a man of robust Catholic faith, a father, and a frequent guest on Capitol Hill, he's having an influence on ethics and helping students come to terms with some of the most complex ethical issues of our time.

When I asked Dr. George for his thoughts on what's happening on campus, he said he's concerned, but we shouldn't lose hope. "The situation is mixed," he said. "There are certainly some good people who have emerged as professors at various institutions in recent years, scholars who are dedicated to the pursuit of truth. They're distributed across many fields, from the natural sciences to English literature and the humanities. Yet, we still see people who are being excluded from key faculty positions because their views don't conform to the campus orthodoxy, particularly if they subscribe to traditional Judeo-Christian ethics. The screen that excludes such people is imperfect, however, and some of us have broken through."

"The bias against conservatives is so strong," I said, "do those who get in have to dissemble in their résumés in order to be considered for faculty positions?"

"I can't speak for everyone," he said, "but it's not what happened in my case. My approach was not to hide my convictions but to express them very clearly and to put them in the form of a challenge to the people on the other side. I was fortunate enough that when it came to passing on my case, both hiring me and reviewing me for tenure, there were enough good old-fashioned liberals on the panel that I was able to get through."

"We used to call them 'honest liberals,'" I said.

"Exactly," he said. "And I think that in many cases the strategy of candor that I adopted really is the best strategy. To hide your beliefs doesn't work because you'll eventually be smoked out, and then you're going to look like your were dissembling, as you put it. My own judgment was that it would be much better to just be honest."

"In all fairness," I said, "I suspect it's a different story for those who may not have your distinguished credentials, and who are applying for teaching positions at mid-level colleges and universities. I'd be surprised if many of those who didn't earn top honors at Oxford and Harvard, as you've done, would be treated quite so fairly."

"Well, I'm not suggesting that every case will be just like my own," he said. "It's certainly true that there are too many people on the moral and cultural Left in the academy who are prepared to act on prejudice against us. Given that, it's really important for conservative and Christian scholars to go beyond the standards required for appointment to most academic positions. Your record has to be better. You have to remove any possible excuses that could be used as a cover for prejudice against you. So, yes, it was to my advantage that the credentials I was able to present were those that are esteemed in the academic world. I held degrees from the right sorts of institutions, earned the right sorts of honors and recognition."

I said, "In one of the letters Stephen Balch sent out from the National Association of Scholars last year, he said it looked like that, among a faculty of eight hundred or so at Princeton, you were about the only tenured conservative on the faculty. Was that the case then, and is it true now?"

"There's a small number of conservative members on the faculty," he said. "When he was here, John DiIulio was certainly an outspoken conservative. When he went to Penn, that left me as about the only outspoken conservative at Princeton. But there's a number of quiet conservatives."

"On the other side," I said, "you have outspoken liberals like Peter Singer, Paul Krugman, and Cornell West, who do their best to enflame the Left. But one of the issues that concerns me is the curriculum. Back in the sixties and seventies when I was in university, we assumed the core curriculum would always remain the same. But that's no longer the case. And most of the elite universities have very few required courses. Is the degeneration of the catalog still ongoing, and is it a major problem?"

"Given the governing ideology of many who are in control of departments and program in universities at the moment," he said, "you probably wouldn't want to go in the direction of required courses, because the courses that would be required would be courses designed to erode people's appreciation of the Western tradition. So I suspect it's often a good thing that we don't have required courses. But, still, it's a shame that people are able to graduate from elite colleges and universities, never having taken an American history course, and never having studied Shakespeare.

"These are the great treasures of our civilization," he said, "intellectual treasures that should be understood as the patrimony of all of us. Students should be exposed to them. It should be part of their standard education. Not only do many universities not require them, but in many cases students aren't even encouraged to take them. And in some cases they're not effectively available. To be effectively available, they have to be offered regularly, and in a format that is attractive to the students. But in too many cases that's not done."

"Students coming in from the typical high school," I said, "aren't inclined to do that. Too often the whole Western history thing has been expunged from the curriculum, even in lower school. So they don't know what they're missing."

"Yes, and now we're into a second generation," he said, "because the erosion that began with the collapse of academic standards and core curricula in the sixties means that students coming to college today are kids whose parents don't know what they're missing either. So it's not only the students who don't know what's missing, there are not parents in the background telling them what they're missing or encouraging them to rectify the situation. So unless the situation is turned around, it's just going to get worse and worse, because it won't be too long until there will be a third generation that doesn't know what they're missing, and there won't even be grandparents who know."

PRESENCE WITH A PRICE TAG

Saudi Arabia is contributing millions of dollars to establish Middle Eastern Studies programs and endowed chairs at our best colleges. Universities from Columbia to Stanford have come under fire for the anti-American bias of these programs. Money talks, and Muslim/Arabic views are getting a hearing all over the country: all these classes are taught by Arabs. Their influence in putting Arabs in a favorable light is pervasive. The University of North Carolina at Chapel Hill required all freshmen to read an expurgated version of the Koran, until public opinion forced a halt. It is politically correct on most campuses to criticize only two groups: Christians and Jews. The rise in anti-Semitism on American campuses parallels the increasing Arab presence.

SIGNS OF HOPE?

"I think the thing that most surprised me about 9/11 and the war in Afghanistan and Iraq," I said, "was that so many Americans turned out to be patriotic and care about their country. They reacted like people who believe in Western values. I thought all that had disappeared."

"It's interesting," he said, "at Princeton, and I'm told this is true at other places as well, but at Princeton a large percentage of the students support the war. Very few faculty, as you would expect. But the difference between student and faculty opinion with respect to the terrorist attacks of 9/11 is absolutely remarkable."

"That's encouraging," I said, "and I think you're right. I've seen much the same thing on other campuses. But, I must say, I got a surprising comment from a young man at Harvard who said, 'So what's the big deal about a liberal faculty? Everybody knows the faculty is liberal, and if we don't happen to hold those values we just don't bring it up.'"

Dr. George said, "No, that's unfortunate. That's mistaken. It's a bad way to look at it, because it's not just that students are being force-fed liberal dogma, it's that they don't have an appreciation for the alternative. I mean, what student today can give you the reasons for the traditional understanding of marriage? What student today can explain why fidelity, exclusivity, and monogamy are intrinsic to the idea of marriage? They may reject some crazy professor's advocacy of bestiality or group sex, or something of that sort, but what they aren't being given is an alternative understanding.

"They can reject it," he continued, "but they still don't know the other options. Take abortion, for example. You may have a student who rejects Peter Singer's views about infanticide, that the mother has the right to kill her child up to some point well after birth, but the student really doesn't know why he rejects it. It's just an emotional thing, or perhaps a matter of uncritical religious faith. But is anyone communicating to him the basic facts of human embryogenesis and intrauterine development and discussing their relevance to the determination of the moral status of the child in the womb? It really doesn't matter what the faculty member's personal opinion is; if he's honest he should be prepared to equip students with an understanding of why some well-informed people hold a pro-life view."

"Which makes last year's Zogby poll of college seniors all the more shocking," I said. "The survey showed that 75 percent of college seniors believe there's no objective standard of right and wrong. Only 25 percent said they believe there are absolute standards of right and wrong, which is especially scary when you realize that this 75 percent are going to become the leaders of the next generation."

"I heard something astonishing the other day," he said. "I don't recall the source, but I was told that even among Bible-believing evangelical Christians the position that there is an objective moral truth is a minority position."

"I think that was the Barna survey," I said, "and, yes, I believe it's true. They say one thing on Sunday and for the rest of the week they hold a diametrically opposite view."

"If Harvard seniors don't believe in objective truth," he said, "that's bad and worrying. But if evangelical Christians don't believe in objective truth, as Robert Bork would say, we're doomed."

For several minutes we talked about grade inflation, student evaluations, and the dumbing down of the curriculum, and Dr. George assured me that his classes were heavily subscribed, even though they're known to be very demanding and with no grade inflation. "I would think that the brighter, more disciplined students would gravitate toward courses that demand a little more of them," I said, "and where they feel there's some integrity."

"I think that's right," he said. "If you do get a reputation for teaching harder courses, there tends to be some self-selection among the students. Students who aren't serious just don't sign up for the course. And the courses that get a reputation for being easy—the so called 'gut courses'—students who aren't serious flock to them. With that in mind, even with the reputation of my courses and with the self-selection that's going on, I get a lot of very good students but I still get a broad range of grades."

"Are there any signs that students are beginning to see through the hegemony of the Left and are looking for other answers?" I asked. "And particularly, is there any indication that they're willing to stand up for their beliefs despite the risks they have to take to do it?"

"Absolutely," he said, "and I'm sure it's true at most of the major schools you've talked about. It's always a substantial minority of conservative students, many of them Christians or observant Jews, and increasingly from Asian families. It's a minority, but it's substantial and within that minority you have the more activist ones as well as those who aren't activists but nevertheless don't go along with the established orthodoxy."

"It's been surprising to see how many of the conservative students around the country are involved with the student newspapers," I said. "Is that a trend?"

"I've noticed that, too," he said. "Our main student newspaper actually editorialized against the University of Michigan's affirmative action policy. The university signed on to a brief supporting the university's position, but the newspaper rejected that. There's a problem, though, at the graduate level. This is very important because graduate students are the future professors, and I don't find the representation of conservatives among graduate students that you find among undergraduates."

"Graduate study involves mentoring relationships," I said, "and a professor who has a particular bias may look for students who mirror back to him what he wants to see. So as long as liberal professors are in the majority, they're often going to pick students who fit in with the orthodoxy."

"I'm afraid that's right," he said. "And that means that the hegemony of the Left is being institutionalized. But my fear is that the left-wing dominance we have now is being replicated in the next generation of graduate students."

TARGETED GIVING

"All of this raises the question I've been pursing throughout my research," I said. "Is there any sign we can break that dominance?"

"Money can help," said Dr. George. "This is an area where people can make a difference by marshaling financial resources. People who have wealth and care about the future of the academy, and want to do something about it, really can do something by contributing to programs that encourage and support graduate students and faculty. Organizations like the Earhart Foundation have identified and sponsored for many years outstanding graduate students who don't subscribe to the liberal orthodoxy, and they help fund their study."

"So that's something positive that people can do," I said. "Charitable giving for most of us, or actually funding grants of that type for those who have deeper pockets."

"Yes, indeed," he said. "Given all the factors that deter students from going to graduate school these days, what we need most is support. We need incentives for conservative students to go to graduate school, and we need support for them while they're here. Fellowships that provide the financial incentive to take on the challenge of doing a Ph.D., which under the best of circumstances is a strain, takes many years, and is very difficult. But also the prestige of a fellowship of that type means a lot.

"If a student is able to go to the admissions office and say, 'I've got a fully funded scholarship that will pay for four years toward a Ph.D. at Yale,'" he said, "that sometimes helps with the admissions process. Then, when a student knows the resources are there to support him through four or five years of graduate school, he doesn't have to play the game of conforming in order to get the support necessary to have his fellowship renewed each year. So here's a place where something very concrete can be done by people who aren't in the academy but who understand the importance of trying to reverse the trends and reform the academic institutions."

"It's a great idea, and it's the positive side of a two-sided coin," I said. "The other side is, of course, foundations and other organizations that support the universities—and, in particular, alumni—withholding their support so long as the policies that are critical of traditional culture remain in place. Does that have any impact?"

"Yes, it does," he said, "although the positive and negative need to be put together. Certainly people should be careful in their giving to universities to ensure that their resources aren't being used for purposes that violate their consciences."

I said, "That's why my friend who worked in the White House decided to say to his alma mater: "My gifts to this school are based on policy. So when your policies change, I'll give again."

"He's done half the job," Dr. George said, "but the positive and negative need to be combined. You certainly shouldn't give money that can be misused, and withholding gifts may help, but so many other people are going to give, no matter what, that the university just absorbs the loss. So here's what you can do. Universities have a hard time turning down money—they will, of course, as Yale famously rejected twenty million dollars from the Bass family—but that's an exception. So what you should do is target your gift. You say, 'I would like to make a significant capital gift to support a particular faculty member whose work I admire.' You give on the condition that the money goes to support that professor's research, graduate students, or institute and programs.

"The James Madison Program at Princeton, which I founded in 2000, has benefited from that sort of giving," he said. "Some people—including Steve Forbes who had stopped giving money to Princeton because of Peter Singer's appointment—now are giving money but are targeting their money for the exclusive use of our program. It's the difference between cursing the darkness and lighting a candle. Not giving money is cursing the darkness. By itself, it's not going to change anything. Lighting a candle changes things."[11]

"That's marvelous," I said. "What a great suggestion. I've said there are two basic problems: one is the group I call collaborators, and the other is the complacency of the Right. How many parents are there who don't really care what their children learn at Harvard or Princeton so long as they come home with that sheepskin that means they're going to have a secure future?"

"It happens," he said, "but it's a real failure of faith and trust. God put your children in your care as a kind of trust. Your task is to keep them true to him, not to make sure they're wealthy or that they can achieve success as the world sees it. Wealth and success are great when they're the result of true learning and good character; that's icing on the cake. But the cake is maintenance of good character and good faith."

"You know," I said, "I think everyone's finally realizing what a change it's been since the sixties when the counterculture was the Left. Today those who think the way you just described are the radicals: we're the counterculture!"

"There's something else worth mentioning here," he said. "People need to think of themselves not as alumni of Stanford or Columbia or Chicago anymore, but as alumni of the American university system. And they need to target their giving. They need to say, 'I'm willing to give my money wherever academic reform is taking place.' If it's not taking place at your own home institution, then look for another institution where they're doing things right."

MAKING A STATEMENT

The fact is, today's campus liberals don't want to hear the truth, and they want to make sure that no one else does either. That's the only conclusion we can draw from the speech codes and other manifestations of thought control in the universities. Speech codes have gone so far at Bucknell University in Pennsylvania that students were prohibited from listening to talk radio in the dorms. The student handbook says that any sort of "bias-related behavior" is forbidden, so the thought police on that campus decided to make sure that talkers like Rush Limbaugh, Sean Hannity, and Michael Savage were never heard.

The university campus is supposed to be a place for honest and unimpeded exploration of ideas; in fact, the whole idea behind tenure for professors is that, with a certain degree of job security, faculty members will be free to explore new approaches to problems without fear of political or ideological backlash. But the situation has changed over the last forty years, so that those who control the political and social climate on campus are now in a position to make the rules and to enforce their own leftist orthodoxies on the rest of us.

The radical social agenda that hit the universities in the sixties has now come full circle, and America's colleges are a closed society. Courses seldom focus on our common history but on narrow slices of American culture, narrowly interpreted, politically charged, and promoting a Balkanization of the campus and the university culture. For centuries men and women from every continent, race, and socio-economic background have come to this country to escape classification; but on today's campus, liberals have managed to keep the focus on group identity, racial differences, and group politics. The result has been to turn America into a nation divided into warring camps, and to break down the framework of social order.

Consider, as just one example, a film being shown to orientation classes and sensitivity seminars all over the country. Funded by the Ford Foundation, *Skin Deep* was first released in 1996 and portrays a sensitivity session for a group of college students from different parts of the country—the East

Coast, California, Texas. The first thing these students see is a series of news reports about racial incidents on campus, and those watching the film soon discover that all the white kids have either seen or participated in something of the kind. Their families and friends have all made racial slurs, and the non-whites have all been victimized. The point, of course, is that it's high time for the black, Hispanic, and Asian students to stand up for their rights.

At one point a Vietnamese student says, "As a person of color growing up in this society, I was taught to hate myself, and I did hate myself. If you're a white person, you were taught to love yourself!" One by one, the minority students vent their anger and outrage, but the white kids are never allowed to deny their own guilt—they're forced to admit it. Although some of the whites actually belong to groups that are fighting against racism, they're still forced to admit their racist heritage and to feel the pain they've inflicted on others, simply by being a part of the majority culture.

Such a film, especially with the imprimatur of the Ford Foundation, is going to have an impact on college students, although perhaps not the one the social programmers had in mind. White students, even when they acknowledge the importance of race relations, can't help but resent the types of bullying tactics used in such films, and also the strong-arm tactics used by the facilitators who force them to undergo hours of programming and indoctrination. And this is a big part of the problem: colleges and universities are now the primary promoters of racial resentment. At issue in the University of Michigan case was the practice of awarding twenty extra points to minority applicants purely on the basis of race, regardless of academic qualifications. And the court gave only an ambiguous answer. Nothing really changed, and the resentment continues to build on both sides.

Universities such as Vanderbilt, Stanford, MIT, the Universities of California, and others where I've visited and spoken with students and faculty, as well as Pennsylvania, Cornell, and Michigan, offer separate graduation exercises for blacks, Hispanics, and Asians. And many of these also have segregated dorms and cafeterias. You may wonder how this could happen when campus liberals have been demanding "free speech" and "inclusion" for decades. The answer is that the goal of the leftists was never racial harmony but to inculcate a view of society that is essentially anti-American and anti-capitalist, and the university is their ideal laboratory.

Yesteryear's flower children, as Walter Williams says, are today's academic elite, and they control the universities. When a student at California Polytechnical University posted a flyer announcing a visit by Mason Weaver, a conservative black author who wrote the book *It's OK To Leave the Plantation*, he was verbally assaulted by members of a minority group. Weaver's book demonstrates how dependence on government has kept inner-city blacks in virtual slavery for decades; but campus "progressives" demanded that the young man remove the flyer and write a letter of apology to the minority students, which he wisely refused to do. But the real reason for the complaint wasn't racism—they resented the fact that the author was black. They objected because Weaver's view was one they didn't want students to hear.

Of all places, the university is a place where students and faculty should anticipate and appreciate differing views. For hundreds of years universities have been forums for debate and discovery. Works of scholarship, in many cases, are meant to provoke emotional responses. New ideas are bound to be unsettling, to push students to think for themselves. But that's not what the new orthodoxy is all about. The ideal of today's campus radicals is to exchange a venerated history of liberty and justice for a discredited socialist nightmare. And I dare say there are examples of just this sort of thought control on every campus in America.

So how to deal with such situations? It's simple, says Walter Williams: "Close your pocketbook."[12] And, as Robert George recommends with customary brilliance, you can make a statement by making sure the campus Left knows you're giving your support to an institution "where they're doing things right."

6

Changing the Curriculum

I n the mid-eighties, the American Council on Education reported that students at 75 percent of America's universities could earn a bachelor's degree without ever having studied European history. Nearly as many colleges had no requirement for American literature or history, and fully 86 percent no longer required students to know anything about the classics or Greek and Roman civilization. And as the Modern Language Association reported more recently, foreign language is no longer required for graduation on most campuses.

Compare that to 1966 when at least a third of all colleges and universities required students to have studied at least one foreign language prior to admission. But as we've seen, by the early sixties changes were on the way, and by 1975 just 18 percent of schools required foreign language, and the trend was clearly downward. In 1966, 90 percent of American universities had required at least one foreign language for graduation, but the figure dropped to 53 percent by 1975 and 47 percent by the mid-eighties.

By and large, most American universities have lost touch with what a college education is supposed to be about. In today's multicultural environment, it hardly comes as a surprise when students have no respect for their cultural heritage and no knowledge of the sacrifices our patriots have made for more than three hundred years to protect our legacy of freedom and democracy. When the National Association of Scholars examined course offerings at the nation's top fifty universities in 1999, they found that only a third of them still require freshman English. Just 12 percent require math,

34 percent require students to study science, only 4 percent have a philosophy requirement. None of them require students to study great literature, but the most disturbing discovery was the fact that just one of the top fifty colleges in America requires students to take a course in American history. No wonder our young people don't know who they are.[1]

Even the school year has been shortened, from an average of 191 days in 1964 to only 156 classroom days in 1993. In assessing these results, researchers said, "To a considerable extent, the structured curriculum was dashed to pieces during the late 1960s and early 1970s when the rage in higher education was a radical libertarianism based on notions of 'relevance' and the assumption that a special insight belonged to youth." As a result they said, colleges today "can no longer guarantee that students acquire a basic knowledge of their civilization and its heritage."

Instead, students are being treated to a relativistic hodgepodge someone described as the "I'm OK, You're OK" school of American history. All cultures are equal, they're taught; there's nothing special about America. The sixties nostrum, "If it feels good, do it!" has become the philosophy of the guidance counselor and the easy answer of today's undergraduate advisors. Consider the following perspective from the Harvard handbook to its highly vaunted "core curriculum":

> The philosophy of the Core rests on the conviction that every Harvard graduate should be broadly educated, as well as trained in a particular academic specialty. It assumes that students need some guidance in achieving this goal, and that the faculty has an obligation to direct them toward the knowledge, intellectual skills, and habits of thought that are the distinguishing traits of what Harvard commencement ceremonies call "the company of educated men and women."

So much for the justification of a core. But what will it include? If you sense that something's missing here, you're right. Here comes the inevitable "but":

> But the Core differs from other programs of general education. It does not define intellectual breadth as the mastery of a set of Great Books, or the

digestion of a specific quantum of information, or the surveying of current knowledge in certain fields. Rather, the program seeks to introduce students to the major *approaches* to knowledge in areas that the faculty considers indispensable to undergraduate education. It aims to show what kinds of knowledge and *what forms of inquiry exist* in these areas, how different means of analysis are acquired, *how they are used*, and what their value is. The courses within each area of the program are equivalent in the sense that, while their subject matter may vary, *their emphasis on a particular way of thinking is the same*. (Emphasis added.)

Harvard's administration maintains that by requiring a core of approximately thirty semester hours, or a year's worth of courses, students are getting a good general education. "The Core," it says, "is, simply, an attempt to say what it means to be broadly educated today, and to translate that appraisal into courses that will capture the interest of students and faculty alike." Yet, by not requiring its graduates to examine the broad outlines of Western culture, literature, history, or even Philosophy 101, Harvard is telling its students they're well enough educated even without a knowledge of our culture's greatest achievements. And they're perfectly content with that.

SIXTIES THROWBACKS

So what are the subjects that really matter to America's prestigious universities? Literature students at Brown University may choose to study black homosexual men and lesbians. At Bowdoin College, in Maine, music appreciation recently included a class whose aim was to analyze Beethoven's ninth symphony as a metaphor for a rapist at work. And at Syracuse University, students won't be studying Shakespeare or Dante, but they can spend a semester on gay and lesbian literature in the Caribbean.

Meanwhile, at the University of Texas students can sign up for "Race and Sport in African American Life," which examines "how sports have been used to justify and promote . . . racist notions of blackness." At the University of Virginia, students who may have missed the collapse of the

Soviet Union in 1989 can enroll in a class called "Marxism: What is to be learned from it?" As researchers from Young America's Foundation point out, the catalog description for the course describes Marxism as "the standard against which all subsequent social thought must be judged."[2]

Unfortunately, political indoctrination in the academy is nothing new. It goes on in the majority of college classrooms as professors and TAs, either explicitly or implicitly, pass on their biases to their students. For some students, however, the bias is so obvious and offensive that the most logical reaction is to deny it, to ignore it, or occasionally to rebel against it. And on more and more campuses, students are beginning to speak up, refusing to be blackmailed by their leftist professors.

Near the end of our trip to New England, my wife and I decided to drive up for a long weekend in Maine where we planned to meet with a student at Bowdoin College, an old-line private university that boasts among its alumni such notables as Nathaniel Hawthorne, Henry Wadsworth Longfellow, President Franklin Pierce, and the Civil War general Joshua Chamberlain. With a student body of less than fifteen hundred, Bowdoin is one of a half dozen small, exclusive schools on the East Coast that attracts a few independent thinkers—which made our interview with the young man I'll refer to as Rick especially interesting.

"Rick," I said, "I got your name from some young friends in Washington who said you're interested in politics. I'd be curious to know how that interest got started, and why you're here in the hinterlands of Maine."

"I started to get interested in politics during my last year in high school," he said. "I had a great professor, Dr. Ansara, who taught political science. I didn't quite know where I stood politically, but I decided to register as a Republican so I could vote for John McCain. He was different, so I went along with that. I'm glad now that he didn't get elected, but that's how I got started."

"And how does that get you to Bowdoin?" I asked.

"I knew that I didn't want to go to a big school," he said. "I went to a small high school and I thought that if I went to someplace like Michigan I'd just get lost. I like the feel of a small school, and there's plenty of room here to express yourself. Bowdoin isn't very activist; no one's burning the American flag. They have things like 'Out Week,' which is 'gay pride week,' and there's all this obnoxious stuff chalked on the sidewalks. Basically, I'd have to say the school is liberal, but not activist."

I said, "What sort of things have tweaked your buttons since you've been here?"

"What hit me most," he said, "was the week of September 11. Just before the president gave his big speech that night, on the evening of the attacks, the college sponsored a faculty panel that included the dean of students and four faculty members who were going to discuss what was going on. They began talking about it but then we all stopped to watch the speech on a big screen TV in the auditorium. So we all watched it, and when it was over the panel went back to their seats, and I was thinking, 'Man, that was really a great speech!' And I wasn't alone.

"According to the polls on the Internet the next day," Rick said, "there was like a 95 percent approval rating for the speech. That was unheard-of. Bush was well prepared, it was well done, and he didn't fall into so many stereotypical things like he could have done. He didn't pat himself on the back the way Clinton would have done, and it was really inspiring. But when we got back to the panel, the first speaker said, 'Well, I'm terrified. That was scary!' He thought it was a terrible speech! And it just went that way the whole time, right across the board. And I thought, *Are you kidding me?*"

"Sounds like you watched two different speeches," I said.

"The difference between what I saw and what the panel saw was like night and day," he said. "But, on the other hand, the idea that the school had decided to put those five people on a panel was just ridiculous. I mean, there are professors on campus who would at least defend the idea of military retaliation for something like 9/11. We have a few professors who would say, 'This is an appropriate response, and here's why.' But no one on the panel said anything of the kind. I was absolutely livid. I thought, *These people have all concluded that we're the terrorists!* So I said, 'That's it. I've had enough,' and I walked out."

Connee asked Rick, "Did anyone else agree with you?"

"A couple of my friends walked out with me," he said, "but what blew my mind was that they couldn't find a single person on campus who would defend the president's position."

"How did the other students react to all this?" I asked.

"Okay, let me give you an example," he said. "Earlier that afternoon there had been this big meeting on campus. I decided to go down and see what it was all about—that was the first time I'd left the TV all day. I had seen the second plane hit the Trade Center and just kept watching to see what was happening; like everybody else, I was really feeling the emotion of all that. But when I got to the meeting, there was a lot of talk about what it meant, and at one point this Muslim girl stood up and said, 'You know, Islam is not the enemy,' and everybody in the crowd agreed with her, and there was this emotional scene and everybody got all choked up.

"So after a few minutes," Rick said, "a Christian guy stood up and invited everyone to come to a meeting where they were going to talk some more about some of these things, and suddenly all the students starting yelling and jeering at this guy, saying he had no right to bring his religion into it! And I thought, *What? She brings up religion and it's okay, but when a Christian does the same thing, it's not okay? What are they thinking?*

"That got my attention," he added. "And to make matters worse, at the end of the meeting they all stood up and started singing 'We shall overcome!' and I was just rolling my eyes and thinking, *What the hell is that? They think they're back in the sixties!*"

AN HONEST ASSESSMENT

"What about the curriculum on campus?" I said. "Does it also reflect this kind of bias?"

"We have a non-Eurocentric studies requirement," Rick told me. "We have to take two classes during our time here that are not Eurocentric: things like African-American literature, Middle East history, or something else that's not based on Western culture. But there's absolutely *no requirement* for an American history course. There's *no requirement* for Shakespeare, and I suppose the presumption is that people will get that anyway. But of course they don't, and nobody seems to care."

"Most Americans don't know what's happening on these campuses," I said. "They haven't read Dinesh D'Souza or Roger Kimball or any of the others, and probably wouldn't believe it if they did. What would you say to them about what you've seen on the university campus, to help them realize this is going on?"

"Get a subscription to the student newspaper," he said. "That's number one. Have it delivered, because these papers are always lacking for real news so they cover all these crazy events, and they don't even realize how outrageous this stuff looks to people outside the university."

"What a great idea!" I said "Some parents are spending as much as a hundred and fifty grand to send their kids to college for four years . . ."

"So spend forty bucks for the college newspaper!" Rick said. "If that doesn't open your eyes, nothing will."

"And if there's an alternative paper on campus?" I said.

"Get that too," he said. "Check it out online, for that matter. See what's going on, and see what's going on at other similar campuses. They're all a bit different, but the same basic things are going on at every one of them, I guarantee you."

"What percentage of students," Connee asked, "would you say are buying the liberal line?"

"It's hard to say," Rick said, "because as a student it's so much easier to be liberal than conservative. Liberals are the nice ones who care about the poor, the homeless, the minorities, and the gays. They care about the trees and stuff, and conservatives are the ones who want to cut down the trees and cut funding for Social Security and all that crap. That's what we hear all the time from the faculty, so which one do you want to be?"

"Unless you already have strong values," Connee said, "you need to be forewarned about what you're going to run into on campus. If you don't know what to expect, they'll just suck you in."

"The main thing," he said, "is that a lot of students are reluctant to challenge the professors on anything—political or otherwise. When a political issue does come up, they may question their classmates, as long as the professor stays out of it, but they're not really going to question the professor."

"And I suspect a big part of the problem," I said, "is that incoming students aren't prepared for this. The basics aren't there, and the quality of education in primary and secondary schools is so low that most students aren't prepared to think for themselves when they get here."

"Well, it's not much better when they do get here," Rick said. "From what I've seen, your professor may teach anthropology or English or whatever, but their actual expertise is so minute, so arcane, they don't have a clue. I mean, feminist Caribbean literature of the eighteenth century? What are you talking about? You're going to teach a course on that? There's a total of three books in the whole world on that subject, but that's what you're going to get at college, like it or not.

"You get down to these nitty-gritty subsets of knowledge," Rick added. "They're the expert in that, all right . . . they have to defend that . . . God help them if someone tries to discredit their theories on feminist literature from the Caribbean, because that basically invalidates everything they've ever done!"

"We've heard this before," Connee said. "Some people have told us that there are too many courses that focus on tiny little parts of a subject but never on the whole range of issues that people need to know about."

"When we were undergrads back in the sixties," I said, "the first two years were all survey. You got a broad perspective of literature, history, government, languages, art, and science. In your junior year you began to narrow it down to particular fields of interest, and in your senior year you specialized. Now you specialize in your freshman year and you never get the big picture."

"The biggest difference between now and then," Connee said, "is that we all shared a common body of knowledge. It may have been superficial, but we all had some knowledge of the great writers, world history, American history, and each of these other areas so that we could converse with some common knowledge of Western civilization."

"Well," Rick said, "that's gone! There's no Western Civ. at Bowdoin.

There might be a European history course but it's certainly not part of a larger curriculum based on that at all. But the way it is now, I'm actually glad there's no Western Civ. because I'm afraid of the way it might be taught. You'd be getting first-year teachers and these lecture-style courses and I don't know how they'd do it. They wouldn't be protected; they don't have tenure, so if they're really honest, they'd be attacked by the tenured faculty for being too traditional in their approach and their understanding of the Constitution. Again, their interests are so narrow, how are you going to study something like American history when the professor's area of academic focus is judicial review in the first decade of the nineteenth century, or something like that. The only thing worse than not having it at all, is having it done poorly, or done with a bias that distorts what really happened."

NO FREE SPEECH

Over two-thirds of public colleges and universities have adopted speech codes that censor free speech or limit it to a small area of campus. Those who attempt to express candid opinions that are not "politically correct" outside these "free speech zones" can be suspended, expelled, arrested, or required to attend sensitivity retraining sessions. The Foundation for Individual Rights in Education (FIRE) has declared war on such practices on the grounds that speech codes are unconstitutional. In some cases, the mere threat of litigation has brought about changes; in others, FIRE has been winning the battle in court.

"Do you think all your professors basically agree on these issues?" Connee asked.

"I'm not so jaded as to think there's a uniform thought-bloc here," he said, "but they all lean to the left. Some supported Gore, others supported

Nader, but it's still a very liberal view of the world. I read Bernard Goldberg's book, *Bias*, over the summer, and he said it's not that there's a left-wing conspiracy out there; these people actually think this is the way the world works. They don't even realize how far left they are. But I have to say, there are some great professors here, both liberal and conservative, and I've had a great experience. The problem isn't just that there are liberal professors; it's that there are some liberal professors who can't separate their politics from their teaching. Some of these guys think they have to indoctrinate students because they can't conceive of an enlightened thought that doesn't fit their worldview, and that's what causes the problems."

"I know of a professor at Columbia," I said, "who says to his students, 'I'm a Marxist, and this course will be taught from that perspective. If you have a problem with that, leave now.'"

"That's ridiculous," Rick said. "That's not teaching, that's indoctrination."

MULTICULTURALISM GONE MAD

Rick's input was refreshing. No excuses, he just didn't like some of the things that were happening in the classroom, and he didn't hesitate to say so. Sadly, that's not often the case, as students arrive on campus unsure of themselves, ignorant about most things except what's on at the movies and who's hot on MTV, and unwilling to stake out a position that may be unpopular. Critical thinking skills, as I've said before, are minimal, since they've been discouraged from the earliest years of school.

Students today are as bright as ever, but they've been raised in relative comfort in a country where life is easy, and the vast majority of students have simply never learned to question what they've been taught. All of which casts an interesting light on student reaction to a course at San Diego State University called "Education 451." As reported by Dr. Stan Ridgeley's report for the Intercollegiate Studies Institute (ISI), the course was designed as a compulsory introductory course for students in the education department. The course number 451 should ring a bell, says Ridgeley: whether intentional or merely a Freudian slip, it's straight out of Ray Bradbury's classic novel, *Fahrenheit 451*, and a perfect fit.

That novel concerns a fireman who burns books with missionary zeal. His crude philosophy is, "If you don't want a man unhappy politically, don't give him two sides to a question to worry him; give him one. Better yet, give him none." Strangely enough, the course description for Education 451, "Introduction to Multicultural Education," evokes the same mindset of censorship, coercion, and book-burning. Which is why, says Ridgeley, it won ISI's award for the wackiest anti-intellectual course on the college campus.

There are no textbooks in Education 451, no written tests, no syllabus, not even a clear description of course content. Instead, the course features Maoist-style "workshops" run by political pressure groups that require students, among other things, to stand in front of the class and proclaim their homosexuality: "I am gay" or "I am lesbian." Then they're instructed to discuss their feelings with the group, telling what it's like to be gay, lesbian, or bisexual. Afterwards, students go on "cultural plunges" to gay bars in the area. The shocking part is that none, or few, of the students are actually homosexual—but they have to act as if they were. Even more disturbing, the course is mandatory, and a graduation requirement for any student who wants to teach in the state of California.

Much to the surprise of administrators, not all students were thrilled by the course. "To mandate the course . . . that's sick and twisted," said the editor of the campus newspaper. "What does standing in the middle of a gay club have to do with reading, writing, and arithmetic?" Among the charges leveled at San Diego State and the course's organizers by ISI—along with the student groups that nominated it as the worst example of "multiculturalism gone mad"—are the following:

- Low academic standards: Questionable content aside, no serious coursework, and no written tests.

- Aimlessness: There's no syllabus, just an erratic lurching from class to class. The anonymous course designers seemed determined not to leave a paper trail that might come back to bite them.

- Trivial and politicized content: Some class sessions were "taught" by a student group called the Lesbian, Gay, Bisexual, and Transgender Association (LGBT), which runs "workshops." Why this student group would be providing material for an accredited graduate-level course is inconceivable.

- Indoctrination: Where have we heard this before? Soviet labor camps required workers to recite beliefs they did not hold and admit to sins they had not committed. The role-playing in Education 451 is little different.

- Finally, compulsory at taxpayer expense: Students seeking a teaching certificate from SDSU were at the mercy of SDSU's gay student group, all funded by California taxpayers.

Needless to say, the exposure that this course received was embarrassing for the university and changes were made, particularly after the school's dean was grilled before a nationwide audience on Fox News. But some lessons were learned. First, it's a pretty good bet that any course with "feminist," "diversity," "multicultural," "race," "gender," or "gay" in the title or catalog description, as Dr. Ridgeley points out, is going to be riddled with intellectual vacuity, lack of rigor, poorly qualified instructors, and trivial and politicized content.

But students are learning which classes to avoid. As Professor E. Christian Kopff from the University of Colorado points out, the word "multiculturalism" doesn't actually have anything to do with foreign languages, history, geography, economics, or particular cultures. Rather, it's a code word for lightweight courses taught by junior faculty presenting a leftist view of particular cultures. And courses like Education 451, which are not uncommon these days, are designed to break down students' attitudes about right and wrong, and good and evil. As Stanley Ridgeley puts it, "It's about substituting moral paralysis for critical judgment."[3] So, freshmen, be warned!

LUNCH WITH A LEGEND

During our visit to Yale University in New Haven, Connecticut, it was a special treat for Connee and me to have lunch with Dr. Donald Kagan, a legendary figure in his own right, at the legendary Mory's on the Yale campus. Memorialized in the Whiffenpoof Song of ancient fame and beloved of Yalies everywhere, the restaurant, which dates back to 1849, is now a private club, and without Kagan as our host we'd never have gotten in. On the walls were pictures of the famous and infamous who had dined there over many years, including the former President Bush in baseball attire. But our mission that day was not to reminisce but to learn about curriculum changes from a scholar who had seen it all.

"You know, of course, that Harvard's been trying to institute a new core curriculum," I said. "It's not clear how it will differ from what they've got now. The current one is pretty fluffy from what I can see, but I'd like to get your opinion on that."

"What a fraud that was!" he said. "They simply gave their imprimatur to a wildly disparate set of courses and called it a core curriculum. What nonsense!"

"There's no survey course of any sort in any department as far as I can tell," I said.

"And no course is required of everybody or for any group of people," he said, "and that makes a mockery of the whole idea of higher education."

"How do you do that in a subject like history?" I said. "How do you come into a place like Harvard or Yale without some type of structure, some way of knowing that there are certain history courses you must have before you even begin to do classical studies or any other specialization?"

Professor Kagan is an imminent historian, a renowned classics scholar, and the author of several very successful books on ancient civilizations and the history of warfare, including his newest, *The Peloponnesian War*. In matters of history, he is the expert. So I was anxious to hear what he would have to say.

"Long ago," he said, "the universities basically abandoned the responsibility of deciding what their students need to learn, and they invented the notion that the content of an education is irrelevant. What is important is to know the methods of acquiring knowledge. Learning various techniques is what counts. How a student might be able to make an intelligent choice among all the possible subjects, how he can discover what questions are important to ask, such issues are not considered. The tacit assumption is that nothing is more basic or important than anything else. The unintended implication, of course, is that students will assume that there may not be anything here you need to know.

"This retreat from educational responsibility seems to me to have arisen from the wishes of the faculty," he said, "more than from the needs of students. I began teaching college students in 1956. I had come to college as a student six years earlier, so that tells you the range. And that's been about the right time to see the total change on the university campuses. I've observed the scene for more than half a century and seen vast changes in the character of a college education during that time."

"Where did you begin your teaching career?" Connee asked.

"As a graduate student I taught at Ohio State. My first regular job was at Penn State, for a year; then I was at Cornell for nine years before coming to Yale in 1969. During that time I have seen many changes, but they all seem to me to have one thing in common—no change has come to the university in that period of time which has not had as one of its principal consequences making life easier and more pleasant for the faculty. Under the new dispensation faculty members are not required to teach anything they don't wish to teach. They are not required to think about what would be necessary for all students to learn. Rather, they're permitted to pursue their own interests without interference, and without much concern about what might be the common needs of the students or of the society in which they live. This, I fear, is a flight from the responsibilities of education as they've always been understood."

"Was it the student protests that caused that?" Connee asked.

"In was in part," he said. "The radical student agitation in the sixties set out to undermine all forms of authority, however legitimate and well-meaning they might be. Among the many targets of their complaints were required courses, especially of a traditional nature, and especially the more difficult ones in mathematics, science, and foreign languages. Since no one likes to teach unwilling students, especially in introductory or general courses, many in the faculty were delighted to go along with their demands. A few of us resisted what we saw as an abandonment of our professional responsibility, but ultimately to no avail."

"So no one paid attention to you?" Connee said.

"They paid attention, but voted for the changes anyway," he said.

"Were you the only one protesting the changes?" I asked.

"Oh, no," he said, "but I think you'd be stunned by how few there were. I was at Cornell during those terrible years, where I saw the revolution in full force. I must admit that I was very naïve up to that time. I chose this profession because I thought that scholarship and teaching college students was the most wonderful thing I could possibly do. As a student I had been taught by professors whom I admired greatly, and I came to think that professors were finer, more principled, and wiser than other people—and that the values inherent in being a professor were noble. I believed that right down to 1969 when Cornell exploded. Then, when I saw how most of my colleagues behaved, I was terribly disappointed.

"Look," he said, gesturing emphatically, "there were thousands, maybe two thousand on the faculty at Cornell at that time, but those of us who stood up publicly against what was happening and tried to fight it numbered fewer than twenty."

"If you look at most faculties today," I said, "the number of people who identify themselves as conservatives, let alone as Republicans, is in the single digits."

Dr. Kagan said, "From time to time I ask students 'Could you please tell me all the professors you know of that you'd call conservative?' Do you know what the number is?"

"I suspect we're looking at him," I said.

"That's almost right," he said with a laugh. "Actually, there is another conservative on the faculty in my department, Charley Hill.

He's a wonderful teacher and greatly admired by the students. But very few students could name a third."

HOW TO LOSE TWENTY MILLION DOLLARS

"I hope you're not going to retire any time soon," Connee said.

"No, I plan to continue as long as I can do a reasonably good job," he said.

Connee said, "I guess that makes you the token conservative on the history faculty!"

"Perhaps," he said, "but I don't believe any of my colleagues knew or cared about my politics when I was hired thirty-five years ago. Honestly, I don't know that my current colleagues think much about it now, either, although I suspect they probably don't like very many of the things I've done and said!"

"They can't argue with your performance," I said. "Your publications are absolutely wonderful, and they keep coming year after year. But, Dr. Kagan, there's one issue that really concerns me, and you're the perfect person to address it. It's an issue I'm passionate about, and that's the loss of the Western tradition and the loss to Western civilization as a whole. I know that's one of your passions, too, because you teach it. In fact, we live not too far from Lee Bass who was trying to get the Western civilization curriculum reestablished here at Yale. What a shocking and deplorable situation that was. I'd like to get your take on some of that, but I'd especially like to get your thoughts on the impact of the loss of any sort of substantial curriculum in Western civilization as a core focus."

Dr. Kagan reflected a moment and then said, "The terrible thing about the disappearance of a focused program of some kind that tries to teach you the heritage of Western civilization is that it hasn't been replaced by anything. A case might be made that we ought to focus on these things in a different way. But, in fact, the faculty has retreated from its educational responsibilities for producing citizens who live in a country that's part of the Western heritage. We no longer take it as our job to help them understand that civilization, to understand how it got that way, to understand what its merits and defects are, to understand how it has interacted with other cultures—all those things that you would need to be an intelligent, participating citizen. In my opinion the general departure from that in our major universities has helped to produce a much more ignorant and incompetent citizenry in general."

"Unfortunately, the academy doesn't seem worried," I said. "In fact, we were talking about this earlier: it's Nietzschean—nihilist skepticism gone rampant within the academy."

"Yes," Dr. Kagan said, "and the dominant thread to all this is that the university is telling students that ours is a terrible civilization, and the less they know about it the better. Except, of course, that they need to know that it's wicked, chauvinistic, racist, and all that."

"I would think that most of the courses that you personally teach would have some relationship to the foundations of Western culture," I said.

"Oh, sure," he said. "That's essential in history and classics."

Connee asked, "Didn't the university have more courses in Western history that were a lot more substantial than the ones you have now?"

"Before my time," he said, "they had a course at Yale called History 10, which was a history of Western civilization. Everybody at Yale had to take it. But even more important than the loss of a thoughtful program in Western civilization, I believe, is the loss of any course that is universally required. One splendid program, however, is left from the old days, Directed Studies. It began back in the late forties, and the latest version was created about twenty-five years ago."

"I'm generally familiar with it," I said, "but what's it all about?"

"There are three courses that run through the freshman year: literature, philosophy, and a third called History and Politics. A better name for it would be History of Political Thought. Most years we'll take in ninety to a hundred students."

"Is this going on now?" I asked.

"Oh, yes," he said with a smile. "It's one of the greatest things going on anywhere. They read Homer, Thucydides, Sophocles, Tacitus, and end up at the end of the nineteenth century with Nietzsche and several others."

"Wow, they're getting a real education!" I said.

Kagan laughed and said, "At least they're introduced, shall we say. The students in this program are elite. They have to apply and then are chosen through competition. They work their heads off. They write one paper every week all through the year. The classroom ratio is about fifteen to one, or something like that, and the professors grade the papers not just on content but on style. I've done that," he said, leaning forward and whispering enthusiastically. "It's the hardest teaching I've ever done in my life, but the payoff is fantastic!"

Settling back in his chair, Kagan said, "In this program you will find a hundred students reading, for example, Plato's *Republic*, all at the same time, which means that when they get together for lunch, and for bull sessions in the evening, they're not talking about the latest rock music or whatever, but they're arguing about history, literature, philosophy, and ideas. Now, that's what I call education!"

"Liberal or conservative, it really doesn't matter," I said, "because you have to come face-to-face with the ideas. That's all we've ever asked."

Dr. Kagan said, "If we had any courses that were universally required, where many students were reading the same books at the same time, whichever books that might be—the better the books, of course, the better the conversations—but the educational benefit would be enormous. And that's what is missing for almost all the students in the modern university. That, I believe, is the greatest loss by far."

Connee said, "Why would anyone ever want to do away with that?"

"It's the Nietzschean spirit," I said with a laugh. "The Raskolnikovs and Bazarovs of the world are at it again!" Whether it was the atmosphere at Mory's or the august company around us, my reference to those great anti-heroes of Russian literature raced forth unannounced. But, as always, Kagan brought things back to basics.

MOVING MOUNTAINS

"There are practical reasons why modern faculties would not install such programs," Kagan said. "When a new assistant professor arrives, fresh out of graduate school, he's asked, 'What would you like to teach next year?' That's not the way it was when I started teaching. It was more like, 'Your assignment next year will be three sections of The Ancient World, and you can have one elective.' But now it's, 'What would you like to teach?' And he says, 'Well, how about Transylvanian Trade from 1375 to 1400?' That was his dissertation topic, after all, and most of what he actually knows. You can't blame the new professor for wanting to teach what he knows, but is that what's best for the student—or the university?

COMIC BOOKS 101

"A good deal of the coursework available to students is both trivial and easy. How can anyone get anything but an A or B in a course on science fiction or comic books?" Many courses are now "relevant, student-oriented" courses. "A great many of the [post-sixties] faculty simply do not believe in the paramount values of intellectual accomplishment and hard work. Many of them promote a form of modern egalitarianism, which holds that the efforts of all individuals are inherently equal."

—Paul Copperman, *The Literacy Hoax*

"In a program like Directed Studies," he added, "there's discipline, not merely for students but the faculty as well. It requires breadth of learning, a willingness to cross disciplinary lines, to learn along with the students, to face the challenges of new and demanding books, and to deal with new ideas. It is not easy, but it's absolutely worth the effort. And it also means that the professor may be racing to stay ahead of his students, as well."

"Been there, done that!" I said.

"We all have," he said with a laugh. "And it did us a lot of good. Most of us were educated in the process of teaching. But it doesn't make life easier for the professor. It makes it harder."

"So is the real problem," Connee asked, "just that faculty members are lazy?"

Kagan paused and smiled. "What shall I say? You're given a choice between this easy, welcome, pleasant thing, or this excellent but very difficult thing: what are you going to do?"

"But why are they given a choice?" Connee asked.

"Aha," Kagan said with a flourish, "you've said it now! In the sixties the universities were already moving to a system that was faculty-dominated, where administrators either had no interest in the educational program or feared to challenge the faculty. Some good things came from the change and many bad ones, but the focus shifted from what educational program was best for the students to what the faculty chose to teach. Any desire administrators might have had to interfere were squelched by the revolutions of the sixties. And along the way, they learned that taking on the faculty is the best way to lose your job if you're a university president."

"But what about this new president at Harvard?" Connee asked. "If he wants to institute a new core curriculum, how's he going to do that? If he gives them too much to do they may go after him. But what you're doing with Directed Studies is apparently working."

"Oh, it's marvelous," he said.

"But the rub," I said, "is that students coming into the university, regardless where they studied, private or public, most of them haven't been broadly enough educated to know to choose a program like this that's rigorous and demanding."

"Yes," he said, "but we select the most promising candidates among the incoming freshman class and invite them to apply to the program. Descriptions of the program are sent to the entire freshman class. We always get many more applicants than we can take, and the program has turned out to be a great recruiting device that has increased our success in attracting the very best students in competition with our strongest competitors—like, for example, Harvard."

"That's great," I said. "But one more question: the Bass money. What happened?"

"It's a long story," he said, "and it doesn't need a lot more discussion. Most of what you read in the *Wall Street Journal* was basically correct." Over the next several minutes Dr. Kagan described the back-and-forth between the Yale history department and the president's office and how agreements to hire new faculty were made only to be later withdrawn, until all sides were exhausted by the delays and eventually Lee Bass demanded that his twenty million dollar gift be returned.

"Several stories I saw indicated that there was a group of liberal professors at the time who said, 'We're not having that stuff on our campus,'" I said, "and that was part of the reason for the delays. Was that actually the case?"

"Yes, that was part of it," he said. "And they were critical of it when Benno Schmidt was here and we were trying to put the program together."

"I'm sure they thought Bass would never take his money away," I said. "But he did. And they got twenty million dollars worth of bad press for the effort."

"The truth is," Kagan said, "you can't hurt Yale with twenty million dollars. It's just a drop in the bucket."

"I believe that," I said. "Thanks for the background on that. But I'd like to ask one last question. There was one particular comment that caught me off guard when I was talking to Harvey Mansfield. I asked him, 'Are you more optimistic or pessimistic about what's happening at these institutions?' and he said, 'This may sound crazy, but I'm optimistic.' So I asked him, 'On what basis?' And he said because the old Left has lost its passion. They're not defending their turf, and there's a crowd of young conservatives coming along."

Kagan smiled, then he shook his head and said, "Well, Harvey knows something I don't know."

"He said it's just a feeling," Connee responded. "I think he sees a lot of conservative students these days, as you probably do."

"They're wonderful," Kagan said, "and they lighten your day; but the truth of the matter, I think, is that the situation is likely to stay the same or get worse. Because there are certain institutional problems that go beyond any of these things. To change the academic world in any way is very difficult because of the inherent conservatism (with a lowercase 'c') of the system. To change it from good to bad took a revolution; to change it from bad to good is going to be even harder."

"Like moving a mountain," I said.

"Like moving a mountain," he said.

AN ACT OF CONGRESS

The fact that the universities are completely dominated by the academic Left is no longer a matter of debate. As gratifying as it is to know that Donald Kagan and a number of other strong conservatives are still holding their own, their numbers are growing progressively smaller every year and the hegemony of the Left only grows stronger. Hiding behind names such as "progressive" or "moderate," professors, residence hall advisers, student activities directors, and top-level administrators, at all but a very small percentage of the nation's institutions of higher education, are committed to a worldview and a liberal dogma that is antithetical to the traditions and values of most Americans. Yet, with little or no dissent from the rest of us, men and women who want to undermine the Republic have been hired, endowed, tenured, funded, and conspicuously rewarded for transforming the universities, and turning an entire generation of young Americans against their native land.

In time of war, such actions are seditious and treasonous, and they deserve the most onerous penalties of the law. But as we will see in later chapters, large numbers of faculty members are among the foremost defenders of Islamist terrorism and antagonists of both the government and the military of the United States. They repudiate our efforts to prevent future attacks. At any time, the factual distortions that are spread by American intellectuals—not to mention the thousands of foreign nationals who are teaching on our campuses—are a threat to the future well-being of the nation. Yet, except for the complaints of a few students, a few talk show hosts, the writers of exposés and the occasional op-ed piece, and a small but courageous handful of faithful faculty, there's been little or no attempt to end this travesty—at least, none large enough to make a difference.

A bill introduced by Rep. Tom Petri of Wisconsin in June 2003, called the Higher Education for Freedom Act, proposes a system of federal grants to colleges and universities to support the teaching of traditional American history, the American founding, the history and nature of free institutions, and the history and achievements of Western civilization. It's a start, perhaps, but the bill pours as much as six million dollars back into the very institutions that have created the problems without adequate guarantees of how the money will actually be spent. Subsequently, Rep. Jack Kingston of Georgia introduced a bill, in October 2003, to protect college students and faculty from the liberal propaganda on campus. By supporting an "Academic Bill of Rights," the congressman said, Congress would be helping to safeguard students' right to "get an education rather than an indoctrination."

In his remarks, Kingston said, "College is a time when you form your own opinions about the issues that affect our society. If our students are not shown the whole picture, they are being cheated out of a true education. University professors should be teaching our kids how to think, not what to think." Universities preach the importance of diversity but they don't even try to practice the most important kind of diversity—the diversity of ideas. He said, "At almost every American university, conservative professors are drastically outnumbered. And the number of liberal guest speakers outnumbers the number of conservative guest speakers by a margin greater than ten to one, limiting the opportunities for conservatives or anyone else who does not sing from the same liberal songbook."[4]

The number of registered Republicans and Democrats is about the same in the public at large, but as the Center for the Study of Popular Culture study of thirty-two colleges showed, there is no parity on the campus, and some colleges have no conservatives at all in their administrations. The Academic Bill of Rights calls for an end to unequal funding of student organizations and ideological neutrality in hiring and academic policies.

This is why David Horowitz is making a stir. As founder and chairman of the center and its exciting new spin-off, Students for Academic Freedom, Horowitz has brought together some of America's brightest minds to confront political correctness and intellectual bias on campus. In two bestselling books, *Destructive Generation* (1989), written with Peter Collier, and *Radical Son: A Generational Odyssey* (1997), Horowitz tells his own dramatic story, detailing his life as a foot-soldier of the Marxist underground and a supporter of the Black Panther movement in the sixties.

In those books, he describes the depth of passion of the Marxists and Maoists who manipulated the campus riots of that era. He describes the plots, lies, and tactics that were employed by Berkeley radicals to shut down the universities, to avoid the law, and to impede the democratic process by any means necessary. But, he also tells how, by some miracle, the blinders finally came off his own eyes and he came face-to-face with what his words, money, and influence were actually accomplishing.

AN IMPORTANT FIRST STEP

As editor of *Ramparts* magazine, the most outrageous and influential leftist periodical of the day, Horowitz saw it all first hand. He had inside information on the murder of Black Panther leader Bobby Seale, and he described the activities of many of the headline-grabbing thugs who had become darlings of the New Left and the liberal media. But when the brutality and duplicity of that movement became too much for his conscience to bear, Horowitz broke away, and has now become one of the most important voices in this country, warning all who will listen where the squishy liberalism of the university campus eventually leads.

The Academic Bill of Rights, which was drafted by Horowitz under the imprimatur of Students for Academic Freedom, is an effort to reform the academy. As described by Thomas C. Reeves, of the Wisconsin Policy Research Institute, the Academic Bill of Rights is "a document that seeks to secure intellectual independence on campus by opposing ideological or religious tests for faculty hiring and promotion, calls for balanced courses and reading lists in the humanities and social sciences, advocates free speech on campus, and seeks the restoration of research free of ideological restrictions."[5]

The beauty of the document is that it snares the Left in their own hypocrisy. As so-called liberals, these academic elites claim to believe in free speech, freedom of thought and conscience, and diversity of opinion. They demand that even the most outrageous behaviors and points-of-view be represented and respected on campus; yet, they don't hesitate to stifle traditional or conservative thinking, they deny faculty slots to those on the right, and refuse tenure to faculty members who fail to swear allegiance to the prevailing liberal orthodoxy.

The Academic Bill of Rights calls for those in the academy to abide by the principles they claim to believe in. Specifically, it expresses the university's commitment to fairness in hiring and granting of tenure, unbiased course offerings and grading procedures, a broad curriculum that presents the achievements of Western culture without prejudice, openness to a broad range of ideas in inviting speakers and lecturers to campus, respect for the opinions and beliefs of students, and establishing an environment of political and religious neutrality on campus.

The program is simple enough: Universities that adopt this Bill of Rights and actually take steps to live by it will be telling the world of their commitment to intellectual honesty and respect for differences of opinion, not merely the trendy versions of "tolerance" and "diversity" currently in vogue. Those who do not will be showing their disrespect for diversity. Predictably, the professors hate it, and they're fighting this proposal tooth and nail, because they perceive that they're being put on notice, and the goals of the Left are not at all benign. They have an agenda that brooks no competition.

In their lengthy response to the bill put forth by Rep. Kingston, the American Association of University Professors said, "The AAUP has consistently held that academic freedom can only be maintained so long as faculty remain autonomous and self-governing. We do not mean to imply, of course, that academic professionals never make mistakes or act in improper or unethical ways. But the AAUP has long stood for the proposition that violations of professional standards, like the principles of neutrality or non-indoctrination, are best remedied by the supervision of faculty peers."[6]

No matter how the academics may disguise their contempt for fairness and equality under a barrage of high-sounding rhetoric and obfuscation, it's perfectly clear why they will never consider actually implementing such policies. They are the privileged few, the anointed, and so long as they're protected by lifetime appointments and the safety of the herd, they bow to no one. In the end, however, they will not have the final say; when enough parents, alumni, and supporters of the university decide to stand up and speak out on behalf of real academic freedom, things will begin to change. The Academic Bill of Rights is certainly the best chance in a long time to do something that can be measured, and may actually change not just the curriculum but the entire political climate on the campus.

A copy of the Academic Bill of Rights is attached as Appendix I, in the back of the book, and I invite everyone who's concerned about what's happening in the colleges to make a copy of this document and pass it along to a university official near you. I assure you, it will make a difference.

7

Rewriting History

There is perhaps no more troubling aspect of the radicalization of the university campus than the revisionism that passes for history today. Several testing instruments, from the National Assessment of Educational Progress (NAEP) to the Scholastic Aptitude Test (SAT), reflect the degree to which students arriving on college campuses—not to mention those graduating from them—have been denied the most basic knowledge of history. And in place of legitimate facts about this nation's success as the world's longest surviving constitutional democracy, students have been fed a disingenuous and subversive concoction that heaps scorn on the achievements of America's pioneers and public figures, from the Founders to the current administration.

Even as liberal teachers attempt to discredit our greatest thinkers and inventors, they cast scorn on any who dare question their own corrupt practices. The spiritual and emotional damage to the Republic inflicted by this fraudulent retelling of history is incalculable. Not only are the educators attempting to rewrite history, but they are rewriting the tests, as they've done with the SAT, removing entire sections that examine students' ability to reason and make logical comparisons. After more than twenty years of declining SAT scores, test developers decided to give every student a hundred-point bonus to disguise the fact that young people preparing for college today are substantially less knowledgeable than their predecessors a generation ago.

But there's only so far this type of subterfuge can go. According to an article in the *Minneapolis Star Tribune*, most university students are woefully ignorant of the basic facts of American history. In a survey of fifty-five of America's highest-rated colleges and universities, researchers for the American Council of Trustees and Alumni (ACTA) found that 37 percent of college seniors thought that Ulysses S. Grant won the last battle of the Revolutionary War. Only 22 percent knew that the phrase "government of the people, by the people, and for the people" is from Abraham Lincoln's Gettysburg Address. And just 60 percent answered correctly that the Constitution established the division of powers between the states and the federal government. A fourth of those surveyed said the principle of states rights comes from the Articles of Confederation. But the researchers also found that 100 percent of the students surveyed were able to identify the cartoon figures Beavis and Butt-head, and gangsta-rapper Snoop Dogg.[1]

As we've already seen, there is a direct link between the dumbing down of America's public schools and the loss of standards in the university classrooms. When the Department of Education released its History Report Card, the results showed that 57 percent of high school seniors flunked even a basic knowledge of American history, and only 10 percent tested at grade level.[2] No one should be surprised by that. But what is surprising is that educators have no interest in correcting this failure. They simply shuffle students along with passing grades from high school to the universities where history, if studied at all, takes on a level of perversity and mockery that is beyond belief.

A NOT-SO-HIDDEN AGENDA

When Bradley Thompson, chairman of the history and political science department at Ashland University in Ohio, attended the annual meeting of the American Historical Association, he couldn't believe his eyes. The AHA is the nation's largest, most influential association of academic historians, but judging by the proceedings of their national conference, Thompson said, academics is not the main thing on the minds of most of America's history teachers.

In checking out the content of some two hundred panels, Thompson saw almost nothing dealing with subjects such as the American Revolution, the Civil War, America's involvement in two world wars, or even the War on Terror. Instead, there were dozens of papers on subjects ranging from the banal to the perverse. The real concern, he reported, is that "What goes on at this meeting will eventually make its way into your child's classroom." He was, frankly, shocked by what he saw and heard—as we all should be.

Some of the more benign papers dealt with "Meditations on a Coffee Pot: Visual Culture and Spanish America, 1520-1820," and "The Joys of Cooking: Ideologies of Housework in Early Modern England." Another presentation was called, "Body, Body, Burning Bright: Cremation in Victorian America." But these were merely the least offensive. "Without question," Thompson said, "the dominant theme of the conference was sex. Historians at America's best universities are obsessed with it." One scholar from an Ivy League university delivered a paper entitled, "Strong Hard Filth and the Aroma of Washington Square: Art, Homosexual Life, and Postal Service Censorship in the Ulysses Obscenity Trial of 1921." A scholar from UC Berkeley spoke on "Solitary Self/Solitary Sex." Another spoke on "Constructing Masculinity: Homosexual Sodomy, Ethnicity, and the Politics of Penetrative Manhood in Early Modern Spain."

A second tier of presentations dealt with the plight of the oppressed and downtrodden in American society and the anxieties of the "under-privileged," all combined with an unapologetic politicization of the historical and social issues involved. "Mainstream historians," said Thompson, "are driven by a pernicious political agenda that seeks to elevate 'group rights' over individual rights. By sanctifying the stories of oppressed and 'marginalized' groups, historians subtly indoctrinate students with the idea that justice and rights are synonymous with one's group identity, be it one's race, ethnicity, gender, or sexual orientation."

Ultimately, academic history, like most things in the academy, is driven by a hatred of America and its ideals. "It is common these days for students to be told that the colonization of North America represents an act of genocide; that the Founding Fathers were racist, sexist, 'classist,' 'homophobic,'

Euro-centric bigots; that the winning of the American West was an act of capitalist pillage; that the so-called 'Robber Barons' forced widows and orphans into the streets; that hidden in the closets of most white Americans is a robe and hood." To perpetrate such a hoax on their students, professional historians trivialize genuine history and emphasize their own mythical narratives about politically correct victim groups. In such an environment, students are actually better off not being subjected to history at all.

There was a time when American students knew in great detail the heroic story of the American Revolution and the tragedies of the Civil War. They could quote passages from the writings of George Washington and John Adams. They knew about the disputes between Thomas Jefferson and Alexander Hamilton, the duel between Hamilton and Burr, the genius of Ben Franklin, the courage of men like Sam Adams and Paul Revere, and the legendary frontier exploits of Daniel Boone, James Bowie, and the heroes of the Alamo.

This was certainly my own experience. In Mrs. Gann's fifth-grade class we memorized portions of the Declaration of Independence, the Constitution, and the Gettysburg Address. We were taught to be proud of our country. Yes, we were taught about Westward Expansion, American exceptionalism, the conquest of the American Indians, and the follies of slavery, but not with the aim of making us hate our country. Rather, we understood that "to err is human," and the lessons of history, properly understood, would help the nation to grow beyond its past mistakes. And the more events, dates, names, and accomplishments we knew, the more we cared.

But that has all changed now. As Bradley Thompson witnessed firsthand, teachers of history have little desire to relate history in that fashion. Instead, American youth are being taught to be ashamed of their country. They are taught that Third World countries with complex problems are, in most ways, superior to the United States; and further, they are taught that those countries suffer because of America. "By denigrating the principles and great deeds of America's past and dethroning its heroes," Thompson writes, "today's college professors are destroying in our youth the proper reverence for the ideals this nation stands for." And, in a fitting postscript, he adds, "a nation that hates itself cannot last."[3]

A Time To Remember

Very often when making comparisons between the state of the modern university and the way things used to be, writers and speakers will use the word *Orwellian*. Obviously, most of us understand the general meaning of that term, but what does it *really* mean? Most of the time the word *Orwellian* is used to describe a misuse of language or a deliberate obfuscation of the facts. Earlier I said that the kinds of social engineering used in schools today and the coercive tactics of university administrators were Orwellian, and that's true. But, for the sake of precision, I think it would be a good idea to take a moment to look back at George Orwell's fictional look-forward, to remember what sort of world it was that this English author had predicted so long ago.

Orwell's 1949 novel about the future, titled *1984*, describes a totalitarian world, a culture turned upside down. Whether from the effects of communism, fascism, or any of the isms that have plagued mankind—in which those in authority have all the rights and make the rules that the rest of society must obey—Orwell's fictional world is described as a place where black is white and "truth" is a lie. People's thoughts are controlled: they must be the "right" thoughts. There's no freedom, no democracy, and no one gets a vote. To say that "political correctness" is Orwellian is no exaggeration; the expression "politically correct," in fact, is straight out of the Chinese Communist Cultural Revolution, where everything was political and no contrary thoughts or behaviors were allowed. Nothing could impede the will of the Party, and that's very much in keeping with the worldview of *1984*.

As the third-person narrator, Orwell tells the story of a man who works for the Ministry of Truth. The protagonist, Winston Smith, is busily rewriting history as he's been ordered to do. Along with many others, he rewrites and reprints books, magazines, and newspapers to make the facts reported there suit whatever the totalitarian government—known as Big Brother—wishes to say. The original documents are then burned, leaving only today's "news" as history—at least until tomorrow. "Big Brother is watching you!" is the maxim used to remind the people to obey. Their "benevolent" leader's portrait is everywhere. And on everyone's wall is a telescreen, a two-way television that hears and sees everything that happens. They must be careful of every word and facial expression; people vanish daily, so they try to make sure that every word and look is neutral and pro-government, because the "Thought Police" can arrest them for "thoughtcrimes." No variation of the Party line is permitted—in thought, look, or deed.

Orwell describes how rewriting history insures that the Party's view is the official view:

> And if all others accepted the lie which the Party imposed—if all records told the same tale—then the lie passed into history and became truth. "Who controls the past," ran the Party slogan, "controls the future: who controls the present controls the past." And yet the past, though of its nature alterable, had never been altered. Whatever was true now was true from everlasting to everlasting. It was quite simple. All that was needed was an unending series of victories over your own memory. "Reality control," they called it in Newspeak, "doublethink."

Doublethink, the reader learns, is "to hold simultaneously two opinions which cancelled out . . . to use logic against logic, to repudiate morality while laying claim to it." Newspeak, in turn, is the new language created from Old Speak, which was once standard English. "The special function of certain Newspeak words," Orwell tells us, "was not so much to express meanings as to destroy them."

At one point in Orwell's narrative, a character named Syme, who also works at the Research Department with Winston Smith, describes the work he is doing, by saying, "We're destroying words—scores of them, hundreds of them every day. We're cutting the language down to the bone. . . . It's a beautiful thing, the destruction of words. . . . Don't you see that the whole aim of Newspeak is to narrow the range of thought? In the end, we shall make thoughtcrime literally impossible, because there will be no words in which to express it." In the future, Syme adds:

> The whole literature of the past will have been destroyed. Chaucer, Shakespeare, Milton, Byron—they'll exist only in Newspeak versions, not merely changed into something different but actually changed into something contradictory of what they used to be. . . . The whole climate of thought will be different. In fact, there will be no thought as we understand it now. Orthodoxy means not thinking—not needing to think. Orthodoxy is unconsciousness.

Reading these words, for anyone concerned about what's happening today in departments of English and comparative literature, is downright chilling. Some of the course descriptions listed in these pages make the point without further comment: if these are not Newspeak versions of the Western literary heritage, then what are they?

ADVANCE WARNING

At another point in the novel, Winston Smith is afraid he's being followed by the Thought Police. Considering the implications of his fears and what may have provoked this unwanted attention, the writer says, "It was terribly dangerous to let your thoughts wander in any public place or within reach of a telescreen. . . . The smallest thing could give you away. . . . In any case, to wear an improper expression on your face was itself a punishable offense." I cannot help but think of recent cases where "lookism" was cited as a racist or sexist act deserving punishment. Orwell had seen it coming a long way off.

Every moment of Winston's day was regulated by the state. Orwell says, "It was assumed that when he was not working, eating, or sleeping, he would be taking part in some kind of communal recreations; to do anything that suggested a taste for solitude . . . was always slightly dangerous. There was a word for it in Newspeak: *ownlife*, it was called, meaning individualism and eccentricity." The same idea, at the heart of conformist policies on the university campus, is called "group think," and it's practiced with passion on virtually every campus in the country. In most classrooms, individualism, original thinking, and free speech (that is, speech that does not conform to the liberal orthodoxy) are discouraged and often forbidden.

But does anyone believe this is what a college education is supposed to be? Does anyone on campus today want to hear about a time before the Sixties Revolution or the transitional years that followed, when things were different, when class warfare was not being forced down our throats, and when "tolerance" and "diversity" weren't code words for socialist indoctrination but were, in fact, natural byproducts of civilized behavior? Some students are beginning to question the campus orthodoxy; but this, too, was foreseen by Orwell. He writes:

> Within twenty years at the most, [Winston] reflected, the huge and simple question, "Was life better before the Revolution than it is now?" would have ceased once and for all to be answerable. . . . And when memory failed and records were falsified—when that happened, the claim of the Party to have improved the conditions of human life had got to be accepted, because there did not exist, and never again could exist, any standard against which it could be tested.

Winston wants out, but most of all, he wants to know the truth. He searches vainly for some old people who may still remember the past and can answer his nagging questions. Eventually he does find a few, but he finds that "the few scattered survivors from the ancient world were incapable of comparing one age with another." They remembered random events from their past lives, but very little else; they lost their connections with the world that used to be. They'd let it slip away, and truth had lost all meaning.

In the twisted world of the Orwellian future, "There is a need for unwavering, moment-to-moment flexibility in the treatment of the facts . . . this demands a continuous alteration of the past. . . ." Unfortunately, we don't need a very long memory of recent events to recall a time when such thinking was on public display. The people in Orwell's novel had become victims of *doublethink*, the author says, which is "a vast system of mental cheating." It is "to tell deliberate lies while genuinely believing in them, to forget any fact that becomes inconvenient . . . to deny the existence of objective reality." To forget, perhaps, what the meaning of "is" is.

Orwell informs the reader that, "Even the names of the four Ministries by which we are governed exhibit a sort of impudence in their deliberate reversal of the facts. The Ministry of Peace concerns itself with war, the Ministry of Truth with lies, the Ministry of Love with torture, and the Ministry of Plenty with starvation. . . . These are deliberate exercises in *doublethink*." Ultimately Winston is sentenced to be tortured at the Ministry of Love, where the following conversation with the representative of Big Brother, a man named O'Brien, takes place:

O'Brien asks him, "Where does the past exist, if at all?"

Winston answers, "In records. It is written down."

O'Brien says, "In records. And?"

"In the mind. In human memories," Winston responds.

O'Brien then says, "In memories. Very well, then. We, the Party, control all records, and we control all memories. Then we control the past, do we not?"

Winston is eventually told that his real crime was believing that reality is external and real, and not merely subjective. He dared to believe in a permanent and reliable standard of truth. But his torturer tells him, "Reality exists . . . only in the mind of the Party, which is collective and immortal. Whatever the Party holds to be truth *is* truth. It is impossible to see reality except by looking through the eyes of the Party. That is the fact that you have got to relearn, Winston. It needs an act of self-destruction, an effort of the will. You must humble yourself before you can become sane."

When Orwell penned this classic work in 1949, he clearly believed that such things could actually happen at some point, perhaps thirty-five or forty years in the future. The year 1984 was so far away that it must have seemed an eternity; yet, just twenty years after that date, we live in a society in which such things no longer seem extreme. Who could have imagined that historians would one day hide the great achievements of American culture from our own children? Who would expect them to dissemble the enormous debt we owe to Western culture? And, yet, teachers of history and "social studies" twist these things and reinterpret them daily. To be fair to Orwell, he warned us long ago that one day it would come to this.

LITERARY CORRECTNESS?

"Relativism is the key word today," says Harvard instructor Robert Cole. "There's a general conception in the literary-academic world that holding things to higher standards ... is patriarchal, Eurocentric, and conservative. If you say, 'This paper is no good because you don't support your argument,' that's almost like being racist and sexist."

WHERE IT ALL STARTED

An article in the conservative alternative magazine at the University of California at Berkeley, *The California Patriot*, reported recently that undergrads registering for the mandatory American Cultures class, which all students must do at least once in their time at Berkeley, hardly realize what they're in for. The truth is, the writer says, they've signed up for a class that fails to live up to its stated mission. "Too often students only learn that 'American culture' consists solely of white racism and oppression, liberal social policy, and the rejection and ridicule of any idea that challenges these notions."

The problem is that the typical faculty member has a distorted view of this country, and Berkeley's version of American culture is especially divisive, emphasizing differences and past harms, and promoting resentment

REWRITING HISTORY | 173

instead of tolerance or unity. The idea of *E Pluribus Unum*—that we are a nation of different peoples who have come together as one—is nowhere to be found on the Berkeley campus. A student taking History 7B, entitled "American History from the Civil War to the Present," reported that the professor spent weeks telling the class about the brutal conquest of Native Americans by white Europeans. A student in another section complained that people in his class were led to believe they were going to get an unbiased presentation, but what they actually got was: "U.S. History after the Civil War as interpreted by a one-sided man who wishes to overthrow capitalism."

The undergraduate catalog at Berkeley states that American Cultures courses are included in the curriculum to "provide students with the intellectual tools to understand better their own identity and the cultural identity of others." But any objective observer would have to wonder how being called a racist and an accomplice to war and murder is supposed to help students appreciate their culture, their nation, or their own race. "Attacking one's race as evil," the writer of the *Patriot* article says, "does not foster a better understanding of anything; it only assaults the values and intelligence of those who are forced to listen."[4]

I was born in Berkeley near the end of World War II and I still enjoy going back there from time to time. Even though my family moved away when I was a child, I've always felt a certain connection to the city, and especially its remarkable climate. Ever since the student rebellions of the sixties, I've followed events on the University of California campus. Needless to say, the news is almost never good. However, during my interviews for this book I arranged to meet with a young man, a senior staffer for *The California Patriot* alternative magazine, who offers a ray of hope that not everybody on that campus has gone berserk.

Amaury Gallais and his family emigrated from France to Canada when he was very young. Later they moved to Marin County, a toney area of Northern California, site of the famed Muir Woods and some of Northern California's wealthiest families. After graduating from high school, he enrolled at Berkeley where he immediately got involved in campus politics.

He became an officer in Berkeley's College Republicans, and was managing editor of the magazine and its Web site on campus.

After tracking each other down at Sproul Plaza, the central meeting place on the campus, we walked to a nearby coffee shop where we could talk freely. "Amaury," I said, "there's a lot I'd like to ask you: how you came here, how someone from France comes to be a conservative, particularly here in the belly of the beast, and what you think of all this stuff. But let me start with this: How did you become a conservative?"

"It was primarily from witnessing firsthand the effect of liberal policies in both France and Canada," he said. "It was pretty much at all levels, the economy, social programs, health care, and everything else of that nature. When I came to the United States I somehow discovered the Republican Party. In both of those countries, conservative politics are almost non-existent. Even the most conservative parties are liberal by American standards, which is unfortunate. I came to the United States during the 2000 elections, and at first I was rooting for Al Gore. The Republican Party had received so much bad press overseas—incredibly bad press because of the Monica Lewinsky scandal. All the French and Canadian media said it was a Republican strategy to take over the White House, so naturally I was for Gore.

"But when I started listening to the debates," he said, "I began to think that maybe there was more to it than I'd been told. Actually, it was the second debate that made a difference for me. I listened to George Bush, then I read up on the issues, and before long I realized I'd found someone who was saying what I thought. He recognized what was wrong with the liberal programs, just as I'd thought myself, and he had concrete solutions. So that's how I got involved."

"That's amazing," I said. "I think you're probably the first person I've talked to who has said anything close to that. You actually made up your mind based on ideas, and you thought about it and made a conscious decision to change your stand. I would say the majority of bright young conservatives I've met, all across the country, would say they were moderate liberals, not very serious about anything until 9/11. And when they saw what happened in New York and Washington, they realized they do love their country. It's not awful, as they had always been told by their teachers. But the people they were supposed to trust, in the media and the universities, were all saying that 9/11 was our fault.

"As remarkable as that is," I said, "it's not a terribly deep level of thought. Anybody could have that reaction. But then they met a few other people who agreed with them, people who didn't hate George Bush and who wanted to take part in Support-the-Troops rallies and things like that, and that's what caused them to wake up. But you, on the other hand, actually came to it by thinking for yourself, which is incredible. Were you in college at the time?"

"No, I was a junior in high school," he said.

"In Marin County?" I asked.

"Yes, the little enclave where liberals breed!" he said with a laugh. "Most of the people I knew there were liberals, but they were mostly harmless. They didn't have any strong opinions, and most of the students I knew were apolitical. Their parents were Democrats so they were Democrats."

"There are three things missing on most campuses," I said. "The first and most important is critical thinking. Basically, it's been de-educated out of them. But the other things are digital cameras and tape recorders to make a record of the lunacy that takes place on campus in the name of diversity and political correctness. There ought to be a Web site where students can post their digital images and audio clips, from colleges all over America, of the outrageous things that are happening on campus. They could never get away with this stuff anywhere else, but I think people accept it on the university campus because they think, *Well, professors are nutty and that's just the way it is.*"

"That's one of the reasons why extremely liberal professors, and pro-Communist groups like Spartacus stay on the university campuses," Amaury said. "The political system outside of campus doesn't permit the kinds of radicalism we see here. Public policy has very little effect on UC Berkeley. But the socialists who are completely against capitalism stay in the university system because they couldn't function outside of it."

RED-FLAG WORDS

Speech codes, speech zones, racist, sexist or heterosexist, hate speech, hostile unsafe environment [where people express their opinions as free Americans], privilege [all white people have this], threatened, vulnerable, violent heterosexist comment [they disagree], mean-spirited, insensitive, "peace and justice" issues, progressive, diversity, empowered, repressive, oppressive, oppressed group, offensive, homophobe, social justice, judgmental [people with moral values], heteronormativity, "the false conception of a society that holds that only heterosexuality is normal sexual behavior."

A SECOND OPINION

I said, "Let me ask you about something one professor said to me during a meeting at Harvard. He told me that he's not depressed by the liberal activism because he's seeing more and more conservative students, and they're passionate. Conservatives are now the counterculture, and they're changing everything. So he thought that was a reason to be optimistic. How do you feel about that?"

"Well, I'd agree with that to a certain extent," he said. "What I see are a lot of people who are just trying to get through. The radicals on campus, the leaders of the Socialist Worker's Party and the Spartacist Movement, for example, once they finish their B.A. degrees they're going to end up getting master's degrees in education or English so they can keep teaching. Then they'll go on and get their Ph.D.s and just stay in this little world as if it were the center of the universe—which it's not."

"From first grade through their Ph.D.," I said, "most of these people have never had to live in the real live world or earn an honest living."

"Exactly," he said. "But I do see strong passion among young conservatives. I think you'd be surprised how many people come up to me when they see my *Cal Patriot* T-shirt and tell me they support what we're doing. I'm actually chairman for the Bay Area College Republicans so I get to see what's happening on campuses all over the area, and it's awesome the way it's growing. There are people all over the Bay Area, and these people are incredibly passionate, and they're sacrificing a lot to advance the cause."

"I know that's not easy," I said. "If you want to stick your head up in this place you'd better know the arguments very well, and you'd better have some answers. Most of the time it's easy to win a debate, if you know your stuff, because the other side operates on feelings. They feel your pain but they have very little knowledge. That's why their arguments are based mainly on name-calling and emotionalism, because they have no real knowledge and almost no facts on their side. History has never supported that agenda, as we found out in 1989; history is always on the other side of the debate.

"But tell me," I said. "What other things influence what happens on campus? Television, newspapers, magazines, radio?"

"I think talk radio is huge for the conservative movement," he said. "I started with Rush Limbaugh, then I discovered Sean Hannity and Michael Savage. And Melanie Morgan here on KSFO Radio is very big on campus. Melanie is the star of Hot Talk KSFO, 560 AM, the conservative radio station in San Francisco. She's actually the one who first suggested we recall Gray Davis, and she's often called 'the mother of the recall.' She's really popular here among conservatives, and talk radio has been huge in terms of giving the conservative movement a voice."

"I've seen that all over the country," I said. "Everywhere I've been, without exception, there's somebody on local radio who has all the kids talking, even in the Ivy League where there's not a lot of thinking going on!"

"There's also a lot of Web sites that are incredibly popular," he said. "The Drudge Report now gets something like eight million visitors a day, which is awesome! There's also an incredibly strong and well-coordinated network of writers with Web sites, like Andrew Sullivan, Townhall.com, Opinion

Journal from the *Wall Street Journal*, *National Review Online*, *FrontPage* magazine, WorldNetDaily, and lots more. I read the *Wall Street Journal* every day, and I keep up with the *Weekly Standard*, Fox News Channel, and all the great shows like *The Beltway Boys*, *Hannity & Colmes*, *The O'Reilly Factor*, and all that."

"That's a great antidote for the poison you must see around this campus," I said. "But what about the classroom? What's that like?"

"It depends on the class," he said. "The mainstream social science classes are incredibly biased. The professors are biased and the textbooks they choose are all biased. The former president of the UC System, Richard Atkinson who stepped down a couple of months ago, passed a bill right before he left called the Academic Freedom Bill, and what it does is allow professors to use the classroom as a political forum so they can disclose their political beliefs in the classroom."

"Is it freedom of speech or honesty in packaging?" I said.

"It sounds good at first," he said, "because it gets it out in the open. But the problem is that it makes it very hard when you're just one person in a class of seven hundred and the professor, who has a Ph.D. in that field, is openly attacking everything you believe in, and then he's disguising his views as mainstream opinion. What's even worse, especially at Berkeley, is that a lot of these professors are great lecturers. They speak eloquently and they know all the issues on their side of the debate, so they have a lot of credibility with students."

"If students don't have critical thinking skills," I said, "and if the only news they hear is from MTV or ABC or the other networks, I can see how they'd be easily swayed."

"Exactly, and that's where the danger is," he said. "What you often see is little things that are passed off as truth. For example, they'll say we shouldn't have gone into Vietnam, which is untrue. Or the Million Man March, which they applaud as an expression of the heart of America, and that's obviously false. Or claiming that it was Democrats that passed the Civil Rights Act of 1964, when Democrats fought against it all the way. It was Republicans who passed that bill into law. The Democrats, led by Al

Gore, Sr., actually filibustered the Civil Rights Act. And there are lots of things like that where professors mislead the students."

"I've been reading your magazine, the *Patriot*," I said, "and I know these are some of the things you deal with. That takes a lot of courage, and I applaud you."

"If you've seen our latest issue," he said, "you probably saw the article about what's called the American Cultures requirement. All the UC campuses require their students to take an AC class, and that's where we see the most liberal bias of all. I took History 7B, which is American History from the Civil War to the Present, with Professor Charles Postel who's a self-proclaimed Marxist. He cancelled class a few times to protest the war in Iraq. He said in class that George Bush is a murderer. One time he delayed the mid-term exam so that students could participate in an antiwar walk-out, and he said things like, 'If we hadn't dropped the bomb on Japan and had sent troops in instead, the casualties would have been between twenty thousand and fifty thousand.' That's a complete lie and a total misrepresentation of what actually happened."

THINKING AHEAD

"Most of the time," I said, "there's no one in the room to challenge statements like that. There are no peers to challenge him, and the students, even if they know the truth, aren't willing to risk their grade or their anonymity by speaking up."

"Actually," he said, "I raised my hand and stood up when he made that remark. I said, 'What about the fact that the Japanese were so dedicated to their emperor that they were willing to give their lives? The kamikazes were the original suicide bombers.' Well, he was surprised, but he just dodged the question. He said, 'These are my sources, and they're military scientists and historians.'"

"And the implication," I said, "is that he's asking you, 'What? Are you questioning my sources? Are you questioning my academic credentials?'"

Amaury said, "That's right. That's how we understood it. But actually someone stood up on the last day of class and said, 'If you hate this country so much, why don't you just leave?'"

"That's great!" I said, with a laugh. "I'll bet he doesn't hear that one very often! But let me ask you something else. If you were going to speak to the typical student who's planning on coming to a university like Berkeley, what should they know before they get here?"

"Well, they should know that there's a heavy bias in most classes," he said. "Basically all the social sciences classes are far to the left. The political science department hasn't hired a conservative in thirty years. That tells you how liberal political science, history, and all the social science departments are. New students should also know that there's an alternative point of view, and that's the conservative and neoconservative view of those in the Republican Party and in conservative organizations like the College Republicans and a few others."

"So conservatives are at least visible," I said.

"Yes," Amaury said, "but unfortunately they won't find it in the classroom. On campus, the vast majority of students tend to be apolitical—they simply haven't thought deeply about these issues yet, in most cases. There's a strong liberal presence, and very vocal, and there's a considerable conservative presence that has a lot of limits placed on it, especially by the student government which is overrun by liberal activists.

"In campus elections last year, for example, a group called Cal Serve, which is the liberal group on campus, won every seat in the student government. Our group, which publishes *The California Patriot*, gets five thousand dollars from the university, but because they control everything on campus, Cal Serve gets literally millions of dollars to run their organizations and events. We raise forty thousand dollars a year from private donations to publish our magazine, but the other side has almost no limit to what they can spend. And it's all taxpayer funds, for the most part."

"What about the quality of education you receive," I said. "You have a basis of comparison, since you studied in both France and Canada before you came here. Do you feel that you're receiving anything of substance or is the bias just so overwhelming that truth gets lost in translation?"

"First off," he said, "I think a lot of the stuff that's taught in college should be taught in high school. High school is the place for a general education. When I was a junior in high school, I took a class here at Berkeley, Political Science 3, which is a course in research methods. It's supposed to be a pretty hard class because it's a fundamental course for political science majors, but I was able to ace it as a high-school student. If the high schools were doing a better job, they would teach classes at that level. But I think college ought to give you a better focus on what your major should be and what you want to do."

"What about grade inflation? Is that a problem here?" I said.

"Actually, it's more a problem of grade deflation," he said. "There are so many students and it's so competitive, that a lot of classes are what we call 'weeding out' classes. Math 1B is the math every math or science major has to take; it's basically calculus. It's very competitive because there are about seven hundred students in each section; the professor goes incredibly fast and a lot of material is crammed into one semester."

"Unless you already know calculus you're not going to pass," I said.

"That's exactly right," he said, "and you have to study really hard. I think the worst example is the introductory business class, B10, which I'm taking right now, where they grade on the normal curve and give as many F's as A's. You can get 95 percent and still make a B."

"A lot of campuses," I said, "have only three grades: A, A-minus, and B-plus, but it sounds like your situation is just the opposite."

"It's not fair," he said, "and it really impedes the student in my opinion."

"I know you're on the run with all the things you're doing on campus. But before I go, tell me, how big is your group? How many people are committed to this undertaking?"

"We have about five hundred and eighty registered members of the California Republicans," he said, "which makes us the biggest political group on campus. On average about forty will show up for meetings. But we have to start from scratch every semester. That's part of the bylaws of the Berkeley College Republicans; but we're still the largest group of our kind on campus."

"A lot of schools sign up lots of students for conservative clubs or College Republicans," I said, "but not many are active. They say they're busy, or in class, or whatever, but I suspect most of them don't want to be identified as conservatives in this liberal environment."

"It used to be that way here," he said, "but not now. Four years ago it was three or four people sitting in a room talking about how horrible the administration is. But a few people decided they were going to turn things around: Robb McFadden, Kelso Barnett, and Seth Norman, and they're all incredibly bright and excellent leaders. Robb is at law school now and working for the Republican Central Committee in Monterrey County. Kelso is completing his political science degree and working at a Republican consulting firm in San Francisco, and Seth is executive director of the L.A. County GOP.

"There's definitely growth in the conservative movement here," he said. "Each issue of the *Patriot*, we print between four to five thousand copies, and last issue we distributed every one of them in the first two days. Every month we have more people coming up to us asking for copies. So that keeps me going." Amaury was wearing his T-shirt with his group's name on the front, and as we were walking back toward the fountain at Sproul Plaza, a male student came up to him and said, "Hey, man, I really like your shirt!" On the front was the name of the magazine. On the back it said, "Proud to be educating Berkeley liberals!"

WINNING BY INTIMIDATION

After my meeting with Amaury, I drove back across the bay to Palo Alto for two days of meetings at Stanford. The Hoover Institution, located at the center of the campus next to the Hoover Tower, is one of the most distinguished think tanks in the country. My conversation there with Dr. Arnold Beichman, a Hoover fellow, gave me a chance to get acquainted with an ardent anti-communist, a distinguished scholar and researcher, and a prolific writer who has witnessed the leftist conspiracy in America since the thirties when he was a fellow-traveler of the Left. We spoke for an hour during lunch, off the record, but his stories of "spineless professors and even more spineless administrators" in the Sixties Revolution were amazing.

QUEER STUDIES

Over five hundred professors attended a conference at the University of Chicago called "The Future of the Queer Past." More than fifty panels on a variety of subjects were given for "scholars" in the Queer Studies field, such as "Eat Meat: Queer Cannibalism in Antebellum America." Roderick Ferguson of UC San Diego presented a paper on "Perverting Genealogy: Queer Sociology and the Radicalized Social Construction of Sexuality." Another academic presentation was given by Karma Lochice of Indiana University reading her paper, "Sister Acts: Medieval Nuns and Their Perversions." First night entertainment was lesbian performance artist, Holly Hughes, in her show, "Preaching to the Perverted."

—*Campus Report*, October 2000

Beichman was teaching at Columbia in 1968 when students, led by members of the SDS and their organizer, Mark Rudd, took over Low Library on the Columbia campus and occupied the offices of the president. Faculty members, deans, and university administrators didn't know what hit them at first, he told me. Some went into hiding while others decided to walk away and let the students take over rather than risk a face-to-face confrontation. They were, said Beichman, the biggest bunch of weasels he'd ever seen; and that flash of insight helped propel him away from the Left and more to the Right, where he now works tirelessly to keep the flame of resistance alive. His Tuesday pizza lunches with Stanford conservatives and members of the *Stanford Review* staff are legendary.

Subsequently I met with Joe Fairbanks, president of the Stanford College

Republicans and managing editor of the *Stanford Review*, which is the alternative publication on campus. As Suzanne Fields reported in her syndicated column in 2003, conservative politics has blossomed on the Stanford campus since Joe arrived three years ago. He had trouble getting the club started that first year, he told me: the administration mysteriously lost his paperwork, twice. But from the moment he set up the first booth for the Republican club, membership has soared.

"We were expecting maybe a dozen people to join up," he told me. "In fact," he said, "we had over two hundred."

"Why?" I asked. "Why so many?"

"Because they were happy to finally have a conservative group on campus," Joe said. "This campus is so radical with everything the liberals are doing, a lot of students just wanted to be able to be different and say, 'No! We're not buying into that!'" Later I attended the monthly meeting of the Republican club in the Tresidder Student Union Building and spoke to them about some of the things I had been seeing on campuses around the country. The stories these students shared with me, about liberal bias, political activism on campus, the hyper-sexualized curricula, and indoctrination inside and outside of class, were no less disturbing than those I'd been hearing everywhere else. It was not hard to understand the resentment they felt.

When I arrived in Los Angeles the next day, I drove to Westwood to make contact with a student on the UCLA campus whose brother had interned with my organization in Washington, DC. This student whom I will call Joshua, a junior at the time, began his college career on another campus in the UC system; but after a series of disagreements and clashes with left-wing faculty, he decided to transfer to the UCLA campus in West L.A.

"When I started my freshman year," Joshua told me, "I heard a lot of ridiculous statements in the classroom that had nothing to do with the subject of the course or anything related to it. One professor in a political science class started his first lecture by saying, 'If the dumbest man in America can be elected president, anybody can make it to the White House.' That was his opening statement, and I thought: *Man, high school was political, but this guy's bias is on a whole new level.* It was really blatant and never got better than that."

"I imagine that most of the students in the room were political science majors," I said, "so his goal was to transfer his liberal bias as quickly as possible."

"Exactly," Joshua said, "from the first minute of class. The rest of that quarter he would take any opportunity to take a stab at the president. But he never called him the president, and he never talked about patriotism. In fact, one of the biggest things I've noticed is the total lack of patriotism on these campuses. And another thing I find is that most of the students here just accept whatever their professors tell them, because they don't know what's going on and they don't much care. When they're told that America is the source of global terrorism, or that Israel is trying to take over the Middle East and kill Palestinians, they just accept it because they don't know any better."

"Does anyone ever object?" I said.

"Sometimes," he said, "but it's risky. I have a professor now who came here from MIT—granted, he's an East-Coast liberal!—but it was a class on the philosophy of language, and I thought, *There's no way this guy can bring politics into this subject.* So he was talking about language and he mentioned 'Bush-isms,' and he paused to ask, 'Just out of curiosity, how many of you voted for Bush?' Well, I raised my hand, and he said, 'How could you be so stupid!?' I almost got angry and said something rude, but instead I answered, 'I decided Al Gore was an idiot.' Well, he looked at me differently the rest of the quarter, and even though I did all my work and did a good job, I made a B-minus in the course, and I think it was entirely because he knew where I stood politically."

"Did any of the other students take your side in the debates?" I asked.

"Not during class," he said. "They knew better. But most students don't think on their own. They're not critical thinkers, and I spend most of my time doing damage control. They tell me some things that are so outrageous, and I say, 'Where did you hear that?' And it almost always turns out to be something one of their liberal professors said in class."

REALITY CONTROL

"The de-education taking place in the public schools has virtually destroyed students' ability to question, to think for themselves, or to learn." I said, "They've been led to believe that education isn't all that important. At some universities, I discovered, you don't even have to show up for class, particularly if you're a minority student. You just get the class notes off the Internet. The only thing most kids are passionate about these days is MTV. And their professors are saying, 'Okay, we've got 'em now! They'll believe whatever we tell them!'"

"And because they're professors," Joshua said, "people do believe whatever they tell them. But let me tell you, in that class of sixty people, I was one of only two who raised their hand and said they voted for George Bush."

"Which," I said, "doesn't necessarily mean you were the only two conservatives. . . . ."

"No!" he said abruptly. "We were the only ones with the guts to raise our hands. I'm sure there were plenty more but they didn't want to take the heat. In fact, a lot of guys in fraternities here are pretty conservative. One of the things going for conservatism on the college campus is that liberals are known as pansies, and there's good reasons for that. They don't want to attack anybody. They think, *We can negotiate our way out of anything, and we feel everybody's pain.* But this doesn't appeal to most guys. Most women on campus are still moved by that, but that may be changing, too."

"The problem," I said, "is that the university always has the last word. Not only is there tacit pressure not to say certain things, but there are legal and disciplinary penalties for saying certain things. The faculty can lower your grades—I call it the tyranny of the gradebook—and they can pitch you out of the course or the university. Even tenured faculty members can pay a price for daring to speak the truth if what they say goes against the liberal consensus.

"But there are ways around some of those things," I added. "The Internet has become an important resource for students and the conservative groups on campus. There are weblogs, or blogs as they're called, and a growing number of alternative papers. And several students have told me they're big fans of talk radio. How big a factor is that here at UCLA?"

"More and more all the time," he said. "Listening to talk radio I've become enlightened to a whole new arena of views. Talk radio is more effective with kids who aren't in college, to be honest, because they have more time to listen to it. I have some friends back home who are in construction work now. They listen to talk radio all day long, and they tell me, 'Wow! Man, this is great. We've never heard anything like this before!' So, it's growing all the time. I listen to it all the time, too, and friends come by and listen with me, and they say, 'Wow, that's so cool!'"

"I think students are looking for something to believe in," I said. "Whoever finds the way to get young people to say, 'The stuff that's happening on campus is wrong; it's dishonest. It's bad history, and besides that, it's anti-American, and we're not going to take it any more!' that person will spark a revolution in America—one that's long overdue."

Joshua said, "I have a friend at a college in Northern California who started out a liberal, but he was done in by Michael Savage. He started listening to Savage and he turned completely around. He's a minority student, very smart, and he really gets outraged when professors act as if he's not able to do the work on his own. But it was talk radio that got him to see the light, and I think that's happening a lot."

"Before I go," I said, "what's your assessment of the way things are going? Do you think you're getting a decent education? Is there anything worth saving?"

"It's still possible to get an education," he said, "but it's hard work. Let me give you one example. I took a class in ethics. It started with abortion and the professor began by saying, 'There are two views on this subject, only one of which is logical.' In other words, you have to believe in killing babies if you want to be ethical. The professor asked those who are pro-life to raise their hands and when they did she went into this long, angry tirade, and made two students cry. It was clear that her whole purpose was to humiliate those kids in front of a class of four hundred. The next subject was cloning, then euthanasia, and this professor is one of the most outspoken people in the country on this issue, and she made out that euthanasia is mainstream, and if you're not for it you're an idiot. So, from the first day, students were scared into a corner and afraid to say what they really thought."

"Nobody outside the university knows this is going on," I said, "and those who know either don't care or don't want to make waves. But how did you make out in that course?"

He said, "Basically, I lost an A because of the paper I wrote. I really worked hard on it. It was a serious paper and one of my primary sources was the English philosopher Bertrand Russell, who was an atheist. Sixty or seventy years ago there were professors who were non-Christian, but they still recognized the role that Judeo-Christian values have played in this society. Even if they wanted nothing to do with it personally, they were at least intellectually honest about it.

"So in the paper," Joshua continued, "I quoted Russell who said that it was Christians who believed that the world was orderly, uniform, and knowable, because it was made by God, and that made the Scientific Revolution possible. So I talked about people like Galileo, Bacon, Newton, and others who recognized the intelligent design of the universe and understood that they could probe the secrets of nature because it was ordered by God. I had incredible sources, but the professor went crazy. She rejected it outright and wouldn't even accept it. I had used secular sources, such as H.G. Wells. But, unfortunately, I didn't come to the conclusions she wanted."

"She was being intellectually dishonest," I said.

"Basically," he said, "she was rewriting history."

8

A Moral Freefall

A group called the "Queer Alliance" at the University of California at Berkeley receives nine thousand dollars in funds taken from student fees to carry out its sexual agenda on campus, which includes drilling "glory holes" in campus bathrooms. This practice, as reported by the *California Patriot*, is common at adult bookstores and certain public restrooms, and involves boring holes in the walls separating toilet stalls. Seth Norman and Ashley Rudmann, two former staffers of the conservative publication, reported that anonymous gay-sex seekers were using a university-sponsored Web site to locate partners and arrange times and places to meet for sex. The "glory holes" were then used not only to peer into adjoining stalls and solicit sex but also for completely anonymous encounters. As the article reported, there were as many as eighteen such vandalized stalls around the campus.

Part of the problem is that Berkeley's student code of conduct specifically prohibits "conduct which threatens or endangers the health or safety of any person," but campus police downplayed the problem and university administrators were not willing to condemn what was going on in campus bathrooms. The student magazine's publisher, Robb McFadden, said that, "to our knowledge, the University has taken no further action to stop this problem." When the *Patriot's* exposé appeared in print, staff members immediately became targets of homosexual hit-squads. And anyone who bothered to speak up was labeled a homophobe and a gay-basher.

Meanwhile, the campus health center at Cornell University, in upstate New York, has decided to sell "personal massage devices" to females on campus. According to a spokeswoman who responded to press inquiries on campus, women students were eager to buy the vibrators on campus rather than going to nearby sex shops or searching for them on the Internet. The health facility was more than happy to comply. In other news, it was reported that a local porn queen received college credit in her art class at the University of Southern California for an exhibit of hard-core "performance art." The class project that earned her rave reviews was undressing in front of the class and performing sex acts with two other women using vibrators.

COMING OUT

Sad to say, none of these are isolated incidents. Today's college campuses are hotbeds of extreme sexual activities of every kind, at all hours of the day and night. The habit of "hooking up" on campus these days—the trendy term for random and anonymous sex with strangers, male or female—is epidemic. Most such encounters are "unprotected" and a health risk both to the students involved, and potentially the general public. As Wendy Shalit, a recent graduate of Williams College, explains in her disturbing book, *A Return to Modesty*, "hook-up" is the term for having sex (or oral sex), or for what used to be known as "making out." She says:

> The hook-up connotes the most casual of connections. Any emotional attachment deserves scorn and merits what *Sex on Campus* calls a dangerously high "ball and chain rating." . . . in context, the typical exchange is, "I hooked up last night." "Yeah? Me too." Above all, it is *no big deal*. Indeed, hooking up is so casual, and the partners so interchangeable, that sometimes it's hard to discern a pattern in all the hooking and unhooking. It almost seems arbitrary.[1]

Far from discouraging this sort of behavior, many faculty members and administrators shrug their shoulders or merely look the other way. As Candace de Russy, a former professor who is now a trustee of the State University of New York, has pointed out, even the most bizarre sorts of deviant behavior have found a home in the universities. She says, "'Sex toys,' 'bondage sex,' and even 'pedophilia art' are now topics being taught in women's workshops on campus, English literature classes, art departments, and in new centers of 'lesbian, gay, bisexual, and transgender studies' at a growing number of respected colleges around the country."

As evidence, de Russy cites a conference on the campus of SUNY–New Paltz called "Queer Publics/Queer Privates," which featured panel discussions of topics such as "Sodomy, Miscegenation, and the Impossibility of Privacy," along with a performance by a Los Angeles drag queen known as Vaginal Creme Davis. A previous conference on the same campus, "Revolting Behavior: Challenges to Women's Sexual Freedom," promised to offer "cutting-edge scholarship in the field of lesbian sadomasochism" and "how-to" manuals for lesbian sex, and booklets on how to dispose of razors and other instruments used in "cutting rituals."[2]

At the same time, the annual conference of the Modern Language Association (once the most distinguished scholarly association in the humanities) featured a faculty presentation called "The Queer Child: The Pedagogue, the Pedophile, and the Masochist," and the *Chronicle of Higher Education* (still considered the primary news periodical of the academy) announced that "transgendered scholars" are now a standard feature on many campuses. Transgendered people are those who undergo sex-change operations or simply dress like the opposite sex. "Queer Studies" and the homoerotic analysis of literature have long since been recognized as accepted disciplines in departments of English, and few academic conferences today would consider offering a program without a gay and lesbian track.[3]

A course in session at Harvard College at the time of this writing virtually defines the crisis in the academy. The catalog description for Women's Studies 1160: "The Gendering of Music in Cross-Cultural Perspective," a conference course, says the following: "Drawing upon interdisciplinary theories of feminism, gender, post-colonial studies, and queer musicology, this course examines music, gender, power, and identity in diverse music traditions, including popular music, western art music, and world musics. We will also address special challenges of gender in Asian

American music traditions. Topics include: women's multiple roles in historical and contemporary music practices; women's images in music; sexual politics, gender ideology, and music, and gay and lesbian musicology." In fairness, Harvard offers fewer such courses than many of the major universities, but this candid declaration of purpose offers a striking portrait of what modern scholarship has become.

Only in such an environment could schools like the University of Michigan feel free to offer a course such as English 317: "How to Be Gay: Male Homosexuality and Initiation." The university's catalog says, "This course will examine the general topic of the role that initiation plays in the formation of gay male identity." In addition, students are told that the course will examine cultural artifacts such as "diva worship, drag, muscle culture, taste, style, and political activism." The professor told critics that the aim of the course was not to teach students to be homosexuals; but as pointed out by syndicated columnist Ben Shapiro—a recent graduate of UCLA and the author of a major new book on the collapse of ethical and moral standards on the university campus—the professor's own writings give him away.[4]

In a rare burst of candor, the homosexual teacher had written in 1996, "Let there be no mistake about it: Lesbian and gay studies, as it is currently practiced in the United States, expresses an uncompromising political militancy." And he went on to explain that professors in the field of "lesbian and gay studies" were the leaders of the militant gay movement, pushing universities and state legislatures to "recognize same-sex couples, to oppose the U.S. military's anti-gay policy, to suspend professional activities in states that criminalize gay sex or limit access to abortion, and to intervene on behalf of human rights for lesbians, bisexuals, and gay men at the local and national levels."[5]

THE GAYING OF AMERICA

While programs like these may surprise most people, the real surprise is that this is just the tip of the iceberg. On every campus, almost without exception, there are professors and associated gay-and-lesbian organizations working overtime to build a constituency for their "alternative lifestyles." At the University of Pennsylvania, for example, students can enroll in "Theories of Sexuality" which explores "the politics and meaning of non-normative sexuality." At the University of Maryland students can choose "Selected Topics in Lesbian, Gay, and Bisexual Literature." At UCLA, as Ben Shapiro points out, students are offered a class in "Lesbian and Gay Literature Before Stonewall."

And from the universities it's only a small step to the nation's high-school classrooms, particularly for those high schools affiliated with major universities. At the Amherst Regional High School, for example, which is the teaching school on the campus of Amherst University in Massachusetts, teacher Sara Just has created a course to help students deal with their "sexual identity." Her goal, she said, was to "make it clear that gay and lesbian people will be respected, celebrated, and recognized in our curriculum."[6]

Shortly after Ms. Just and her students began getting the "recognition" they wanted, it was announced that the school would sponsor a production of lesbian playwright Eve Ensler's controversial drama, *The Vagina Monologues,* as part of their "Violence Against Women Week" celebrations, which happened to fall on Valentine's Day—or, as it has now been dubbed by the sex lobby nationwide, "V-Day." The play took place over the strenuous objections of parents.

Ensler's play is a bitter, solipsistic, rambling monologue about one woman's miserable life and failings, which at one point celebrates a sex act between an adult lesbian and a thirteen-year-old girl. Further, the narrator tells the story of a six-year-old girl, interviewed by the author, in which the child is asked what her vagina smells like. It's apparent, at least from published descriptions of this revolting production, that the author's intent is not to speak "honestly" about sexuality but to desensitize and demean it, and to punish her audience for her misery. But is it something to be shown to children?

Dr. John R. Diggs, a Massachusetts physician concerned about the effects of sex-related issues on children, wrote an open letter to the Amherst school board to protest the performance, saying that the district's support of

The Vagina Monologues threatened damage to the culture of the school. "Even students who do not attend the performance are altered by the tone and content of conversations that follow," he said. Diggs further added, "How can we complain if a student makes a comment about a girl's genitals after the precedent was set by a school play, under the aegis of a superintendent, principal, and teachers?" And he warned, "The aftermath of this may become legally actionable."

HAPPY HOLIDAYS

From coast to coast, many colleges celebrate "Sex Week." Yale University announced faculty lectures, student talks on "the secrets of great sex," and promised that "all of campus is going to be involved." Princeton's Lesbian, Gay, Transgendered Student Services has an "Endless Possibilities Conference." Carnegie Mellon University has "Kama Sutra Bingo." Most U.S. campuses also sponsor a "Coming Out Week" for homosexuals. These activities are not only authorized by college officials, but are often paid for by your tax dollars.

The shame of it, as the doctor pointed out both in his letter and his public comments, is that, "The producers of this play are objectifying women in full view of our children. Further, the wholeness of woman is ignored, and the completeness of her humanity is caricatured into a single anatomical structure; one without a brain, emotion, or moral standing. This is much like the vocational viewpoint of a pornographer. Sexual violence against women is the result of them being discarded like objects."[7] According to Justice Department statistics, more than nineteen thousand sexual assaults occurred on school property all across the country in 1999 alone. The vast majority of the victims were women and girls.[8] But the rush toward more and raunchier sexual degeneracy is unrelenting, particularly in the nation's schools, as the advocates of "sexual liberation" push for ever more "openness" and "honesty" about the most questionable kinds of sexual intimacy.

In our conversation with Dana, a student at Middlebury College in Vermont, I was surprised to learn that the sorts of things that would be shocking to people in most neighborhoods are now common occurrences on the university campus. "The Open Queer Alliance on our campus," the student told me, "built a big closet in the middle of the quad for 'Coming Out Week.'" Gay festivals of this type, it turns out, are far more common on campus than Fourth of July celebrations or Christmas (now better known as "Winter Carnival").

"Obviously," she told me, "the closet was symbolic for students coming 'out of the closet' as gay or lesbian. That was bad enough," she said, "but they had also painted every vulgar sexual expression you can imagine all over the closet. I thought it was shocking to see that in the middle of our quad. And not just because I'm a straight person but as a human being it offended me. I don't enjoy walking across campus and seeing those explicit sexual words and curses painted all over something like that."

"Did anyone bother to complain to the administration?" I asked.

"When one of the other students asked the president about it," she said, "he just said it was a free-speech issue, and they had the right to say whatever they wanted."

I said, "Did anyone point out that obscenity is not protected by the Constitution or any other law?"

"No, I doubt it," Dana said. "But the closet had only been there a few days when somebody apparently got fed up and knocked it down. But think what that closet was saying to people. It was so offensive, and there were families bringing their kids on campus to take college tours. They were seeing all those words that I wouldn't even utter. But do you think the college was upset by those words or the image it gave the school? No, not at all! Instead, they were furious that someone had knocked down the closet, and suddenly it was like a campus-wide interrogation to find out who did it.

"They said it was homophobic, intolerant, and mean-spirited," she said, "and the faculty and the deans went out of their way to defend the homosexuals' right to spray graffiti and swear-words all over our quad. They even sent e-mails to all the students on campus saying they wanted the names of the persons who did that so they could be punished."

"We used to have 'standards of decency,'" I said. "Now the thought police have to protect the standards of *indecency*."

"That's right," she said. "They had absolutely no concern at all for my rights; I was offended, but if I had actually come out and said, 'I'm sorry, but that closet offends me!' I can't even imagine what the repercussions would have been."

"Homosexuality is sacred on campus," I said.

"It really is," Dana responded, "and the whole environment is repressive. But what I say is, if you want me to be sensitive to you, then you should learn to be sensitive to people like me who still have standards. We're a minority, too, and we need protection just as much as any other minority, when it comes down to it. But we're the only ones you can insult these days and get away with it."

Sponsoring Porn

Few people in the world of academia would ever think of speaking out against such things today. Sexual radicalism on campus is supported by public funding from organizations such as the Ford Foundation, the National Endowment for the Arts (NEA), and state and local government grants. The "Queer Faculty Group" at New York University has received funds for conferences and workshops not only from the NEA but from the New York State Council on the Arts. And university trustees, who have been "entrusted" with supervision of the academy and its educational objectives, have taken a hands-off approach. Their job, as one trustee explained to Candace de Russy, is fund-raising, not guarding the curriculum.[9]

The most troubling fact is not just that things happen on campuses in out-of-the-way places, but that the promotion and display of offensive and dangerous sexual behaviors—which amounts to the licensing of sexual exploitation on campus—is happening at even the most illustrious colleges and universities in the country. Connee and I heard stories like these in virtually every conversation we had with students. And even more disturbing was the fact that most of these students—and even their religious leaders on campus—were resigned to the hyper-sexualized climate. One part-time faculty member who also represents a well known Christian outreach told me, "I don't know about you, but that's how it was when I was in college! I mean, sex is everywhere on campus. What's the big deal?"

But even the non-religious students we interviewed were offended by the constant pressure to succumb to the sexual indoctrination on campus. A student at Yale told us, "When I first came here last year, I was struck by the sexual liberty that was everywhere in the dorms. One day my mom came to meet my freshman counselor and as we were talking one of the other girls came in and put a big bowl of condoms right in the middle of the table. I looked at my mom and her eyes were as big as saucers, but the student had to do that, it's part of the dorm rules. But I was sitting there and my mom and I were looking at each other, and she just took the bowl and said, 'Let's put this somewhere else.' And there was, like, sudden panic! They told her, 'No, you can't do that! It's required! It has to be there all the time or we get in trouble.' And we were thinking, 'Oh, my god!' I mean, stuff like that is totally ridiculous, but it's everywhere; you could make a satire out of the sexual politics around here. But that's just the way it is."

When Professor Harvey Mansfield was asked to speak to students at the Eliot House residence hall at Harvard last year, he decided to talk about something that has concerned him for a long time: the dangers of recreational sex on campus. According to an article published afterward in the student newspaper, the *Harvard Crimson*, Mansfield told the co-ed crowd that there have been advances in coeducational activities in recent years. Young men and women are able to interact now on an equal basis, but indiscriminate casual sex isn't a fair trade-off. Young women, he said, are just giving out "free samples" while the young men never have to make any kind of commitment. Most of the time the students who are "hooking-up" don't even know each other's name. Dr. Mansfield told them, "It's a man's game they're playing," and he said that the new trend of "hook-ups" is bound to have serious and long-term consequences for students.

So how did students react? Good advice? Practical wisdom from a distinguished faculty member with fifty years experience on the Harvard campus? Not even close. For many students who heard the talk, the shock wasn't the risks they face but that Professor Mansfield would have the audacity to criticize their sexual behavior. A female graduate student said it was a "very controversial" speech, and added, "I don't think anyone was expecting to hear anything so opinionated." Dr. Mansfield, much to the students' chagrin, had dared to challenge the new sexual orthodoxy, and the faculty member and house master who had invited him to speak was forced to confess, "I was trying to widen and deepen the boundaries of discussion at Harvard. I wanted to give an example of an unpolitically correct talk."[10]

A ONE-SIDED WAR

Another faculty friend at a prestigious Southern university, whom I'll refer to here as Kevin, told Connee and me recently that his biggest concern was the constant drumbeat "to make students at all levels accept homosexuality as a normal and natural way of life." As an example, he mentioned a film currently being shown on public school campuses around the country, called *It's Elementary*. "This film," Kevin said, "is very dangerous and exploitative, by design. But most students are so corrupted by all the talk of 'tolerance' and 'diversity' that they're basically incapable of seeing what's really there. In reality, it's overt brainwashing."

"I'm really sad to see that so many students today no longer seem to have any powers of discernment," Connee said to him. "They don't seem to realize the danger of all these risky behaviors."

"No, they don't," Kevin said. "But that's really the point: to desensitize them to what's happening. In making this film," he said, "the producers went into schools and filmed teachers using lessons that were designed to make people tolerant of homosexuality. At one school in Cambridge, Massachusetts, they were having an assembly and the soccer coach comes up and announces that he's homosexual. The students look like maybe they're second or third graders, and they're just totally accepting of all this stuff. Then, the most shocking thing is at the end of the student assembly when the kids are all singing, 'This little light of mine, I'm going to let it shine.' I mean, it's all you can do to keep your lunch down.

MLA DISCUSSES HOMOSEXUALITY, NOT LITERATURE

The once scholarly, staid, and oh-so-proper Modern Language Association, founded in 1883 to strengthen the study and teaching of language and literature, has ditched great books and taken up a radical homosexual crusade. Their December 2000 annual conference in Washington, DC—attended by ten thousand mostly university professors—discussed such topics as "Queering the Family," "Sugar Daddies and Chicken Hawks," and "Constructing the Transgender Subject."

—From *Campus Report*

"I couldn't help thinking," he added, "it's like something from Leni Riefenstahl, Hitler's filmmaker and propagandist. In all the films she made, like *The Triumph of the Will,* you see these young Nazis, innocent, blue-eyed, and beautiful, holding huge bouquets of flowers and singing German folk songs. But in this case, it's America's innocent little children being corrupted by deliberate brainwashing."

"That's a chilling image," I said, "but how do we deal with something like that?"

"I don't know," Kevin said, "but something has to happen. I actually showed this film to a group of my undergraduate students and I asked them to try to spot the semantic tricks that the filmmakers had used, and to observe how it was designed as an indoctrination piece. But they didn't see it, at all. They just watched and thought it was a fine, objective piece. No problem. I couldn't help but think, *It's already too late for them!*"

"The problem is that most Americans don't even know this is going on," I said. "They've turned their children over to the public school Gestapo, and their kids are being brainwashed."

"For your book," Kevin said, "why don't you use a title like, *We'll Get You through Your Children*? That's what the radical poet Allen Ginsberg said back in the sixties. He was gay, too, of course, and he really meant that."

"He's dead now," I said, "but apparently he was right. The children have already been captured by that agenda."

Connee said, "The Nazis were very successful at recruiting kids. They got them through brainwashing in the schools, just this way. But first they fired all the old teachers and hired new ones who would indoctrinate the children."

"You know, of course," Kevin said, "that one of the first meetings of the Nazi Party took place in a gay bar in Munich?"

"I didn't know that," I said, "but somehow it makes sense."

"It's a culture war and only one side realizes it," Connee said.

"Perhaps my biggest concern is seeing that a lot of young people today have an education but no formation, no values, no moral framework," Kevin said. "There's more freedom of speech in a barber shop or a taxi cab than there is in the average university. Faculty members sometimes come up to me on campus and they complain about the lack of academic freedom. But if it comes up out in the hallway, they don't want anyone to hear them admitting the obvious, so they say, 'Let's step into your office and close the door, so we can talk without being overheard.' At that point you know the propagandists have won, and they've done it by sheer intimidation."

The university's silent compliance with the propaganda and intimidation of the sex lobby on campus is not merely a matter of bad taste and inappropriate behavior by institutions of higher learning, but a legitimate health concern. Evidence of the physical and emotional problems young people are facing as a result of casual sex, "hooking up," and particularly the homosexual and lesbian activities, is everywhere. It's not as if the truth is not readily available either through the professional advice of a family physician, hundreds of books and pamphlets on sexually transmitted diseases, or from the thousands of sites on the Internet where such issues are discussed and examined. Yet, due to the intense pressure of the sex lobby and the silence of both educators and the mass media, lives are being shattered daily by a sexual epidemic.

Among college students who live away from home, according to one recent report, 56 percent have been sexually active while attending college. And of this large group of young men and women, fully 73 percent report engaging in unprotected sex, according to a survey by the Society for Adolescent Medicine (SAD). Underscoring the students' ignorance about the risks of sexually transmitted diseases (STDs), their online survey of 516 university students found that 68 percent of those who admitted having unprotected sex didn't feel they faced any risk of contracting an STD.[11]

Half of them, however, said they'd never been tested for infection, even though one in five college students (20 percent of those surveyed) said they did know someone who contracted a sexually transmitted disease in college. Dr. Helen Johnson, co-author of the book, *Don't Tell Me What to Do, Just Send Money: The Essential Parenting Guide to the College Years*, told the online journal, *HealthDay Reporter*, "I think part of it is people at this age really do feel immortal; they don't understand that their behavior has real consequences." And she added, "I'm actually troubled by the findings, particularly the one about unprotected sex."[12]

A MULTIPLE EPIDEMIC

College students who use alcohol are the ones most likely to contract sexually transmitted diseases. Because most colleges, as well as a growing number of dorms and residence halls these days, are fully co-ed, and because alcohol consumption is common on and off campus, the risk of contracting STDs is extremely high. College students spend $5.5 billion dollars on alcohol each year, according to a 2001 report, and they drink an estimated four billion bottles of beer. The total amount of alcohol consumed by college students each year exceeds four hundred and thirty million gallons, enough for every college and university in the United States to fill an Olympic-sized pool.

Seventy percent of college students admit to engaging in sexual activity, primarily as a result of being under the influence of alcohol. In many cases, students say, they engaged in activities they would not have done if they had been sober. A pamphlet from the national Centers for Disease Control (CDC) entitled "Drinking: A Student's Guide," concludes that the predictable result of mixing this much alcohol with young men and women who are away from their parents for the first time is "STD heaven." And a report from the Center on Addiction and Substance Abuse at Columbia University showed that 60 percent of college women infected with STDs such as genital herpes and AIDS say they were under the influence of alcohol at the time they had sex with the infected person. The report said, further, that 1 in 1,500 students on American college and university campuses is already HIV positive, and that the fastest-growing population of people infected with HIV are teenagers and young adults in college.[13]

Dr. Charlotte Gaydos, an associate professor of medicine at Johns Hopkins University School of Medicine cited in the article, said that the findings of the SAD survey were not really surprising. "Kids are having high-risk sexual behaviors, and they are not getting screened. One of the reasons is most of the sexually transmitted diseases are asymptomatic." In other words, students who have contracted a venereal disease don't necessarily feel discomfort, so they don't worry about it. Yet, untreated infections of this sort generally escalate rapidly over time, not only through the risk of passing along the infection to others but in the disabling and life-threatening impact it can have on the individual student.

The SAD survey found little awareness among most students about the risks of Hepatitis B, a potentially life-threatening viral liver disease, which is spread not just by sexual contact but by body-piercing, tattooing, contact sports, or simply sharing a razor or a toothbrush with someone else.

Researchers indicated that 40 percent of college students today already have a tattoo or body-piercing of some type, or they're likely to get one before graduation. And the survey also found that a third of all students admitted to sharing either a razor or a toothbrush with a roommate, partner, or friend.[14]

By definition, an epidemic is a disease that attacks a sizable group of people at about the same time. In an epidemic, a disease spreads from one person to another, and the disease often attacks areas where it would otherwise not be found—such as friends, spouses, and children. The STD epidemic among young people today, according to author Meg Meeker, is a ticking time-bomb because it involves more than one disease. Because of the implications of this new hyper-epidemic, the CDC have categorized the sex crisis among young adults and teens as a "multiple epidemic" which could involve as many as twenty-five separate STDs—actually, fifty STDs, scientists report, if all the variant strains of the same disease are included.

To make the point, Meeker offers a shocking illustration. "Imagine a high school football stadium filled with teenagers," she says. "Then start counting. One in five of the cheering kids has herpes. Herpes has no cure. Every third girl has the human papilloma virus (HPV). HPV causes 99.7 percent of cervical cancer cases that kills over five thousand women each year. One out of ten has chlamydia. Even if we pulled out the healthy kids, the stadium would remain nearly full."

Further, the author says, consider the statistics provided by on-site testing in the schools:

- Almost half of all students in grades nine through twelve have had sex.

- Half of all girls are likely to be infected with an STD during their first sexual experience.

- Nearly one in four sexually active teens has an STD.

- Teens will contract nearly one in four of the fifteen million new cases of STDs this year.

- Teens make up 10 percent of the population but contract up to 25 percent of all STDs.

- Genital herpes has gone up 500 percent among white teenagers in the last twenty years.

- One in five children above age twelve tests positive for genital herpes.

- One in ten teenage girls has chlamydia; half of all new chlamydia cases each year are diagnosed in girls fifteen to nineteen years old.

As shocking as such figures are, the problem is still worse, says Meeker. A February 2002 editorial in the *Journal of the American Medical Association* reported that the number of people with asymptomatic STDs (diseases with no outward symptoms) is probably greater than the number with diagnosed diseases, which means that the "multiple epidemic" may actually be twice as large as physicians suspect.

EVERYTHING TO LIVE FOR

Millions of teens are infected, writes Meeker, and millions more are threatened if the situation does not change. "Diseases are tearing into the bodies of our children in ways that will cause irreparable harm or possibly death." The reality is that the crisis exists, the author says with uncommon candor, because society has jettisoned the *moral standards* that direct sexual behavior. The shift began with the sexual revolution of the sixties when the effects of unbridled promiscuity were still largely unknown. But as society in general, and the universities in particular, began to adopt the values of the Sixties Revolution, the moral culture changed. Once unrestricted sexual gratification became the rule of the day, sexual disease took off like wildfire.

So who's to blame for the contagion spreading throughout the land? Dr. Meeker blames big media for targeting teens with the deliberate and irresponsible message that sex has no risks. Hollywood and the television industry have promoted promiscuity without mentioning the enormous harm that can come from sexual experimentation. Because of greed and moral recklessness, she says, an entire generation of young Americans—not to mention millions around the world who have been saturated by the values of Hollywood and the American idiom—will pay the price through illness, sterility, life-long struggles with medical complications and medications, and premature death.[15]

Dr. Helen Johnson says parents also have to take a large part of the blame when their college-age kids engage in risky behaviors. "I think too many parents today want to be their kids' friends and—sort of by default, not intentionally—they abrogate that important parental responsibility, which is making it really clear to your kids what your values are. Even though they will act like they're tuning you out, they hear you," she said, "and what I found working with college students is that they really care what their parents think about these things, and they generally don't know." But if the university is truly acting *in loco parentis*, as parents and other cultural institutions have always maintained, then university administrators will have to accept an enormous amount of blame for the situations they have condoned and encouraged—and the conditions that are now killing America's teens and young adults in record numbers.

The fallout from all of this is widespread and it takes many forms, not the least of which is the flood of suicides among teens and young adults— a flood that is high and rising. Suicide is now the second leading cause of death among college students, after accidents, claiming the lives of more than eleven hundred teens and young adults each year. And, as reported by the American Foundation for Suicide Prevention (AFSP), 90 percent of college students who take their own lives do so as a result of depression or related emotional problems.

"Too many lives have been lost to suicide and we need to educate people about this serious public health problem and ways it can be prevented," says Dr. David Satcher, who is a member of the AFSP board and former U.S. surgeon general. To help counteract this growing problem, the AFSP is providing copies of a documentary film to community colleges featuring students who have experienced suicidal depression or who have lost a friend to suicide.[16] But the problem is complex and dramatically on the rise.

Adolescence is a period of experimentation and adjustment, says Dr. Alan Lipschitz, a medical researcher and author, but since the fifties in this country, a growing number of teens and young adults have found the stress of coping unbearable. The despair they feel, he says, is reflected in a 300 percent rise in suicides among teenagers and young adults between 1956 and 1984. Psychosis and depression are among the principal risk factors for college students, but college students who commit suicide have different personality traits from non-students.

Most young adults who commit suicide have impulsive, high risk-taking personalities, and the abuse of sex, drugs, and alcohol is a frequent factor cited in this group. College suicides, by contrast, are often loners. They've withdrawn and become isolated from family and peers. Psychiatrists say that such students feel worthless and rejected by their families, and some of them struggle to gain acceptance through academic achievement or athletics. The depression they feel is complicated by a mélange of contradictory feelings, self-loathing, and hatred. Those who move from depression to suicide exhibit an attraction for death, which they see as a way of finding comfort and escape. Nearly half of all students who commit suicide have visited a physician for some type of medical treatment in the months before committing the act.[17]

The most widely publicized suicides took place in the fall of 2003 at New York University, where three separate incidents made headlines. In September 2003, a twenty-year-old from Evanston, Illinois, made a swan dive from a tenth-floor balcony, inside the university library, to his death. Less than a month later, on October 10, an eighteen-year-old freshman from Ohio climbed over the same library railing and jumped to his death. Then, on October 18, a nineteen-year-old sophomore from Brooklyn, New York, leaped from a sixth-story balcony to her death. Again, a near perfect swan dive. The provocation for the tragedies was never made clear, but drug use and the pressures of "fitting in" were named as contributing factors.

In the wake of their son's suicide during his sophomore year at the University of Arizona, grieving parents Donna and Phillip Satow decided to take steps to reach out to students who have contemplated taking their own lives. The organization they founded in honor of their son, the Jed Foundation, is currently working with a hundred and twenty colleges and universities around the country, providing resources and an Internet Web site, called ULifeline, to link students to mental health centers and confidential assistance. "A Web site doesn't solve the problem," Donna Satow told an Associated Press reporter, "but it might help one or two kids."

Recently the Jed Foundation joined with Harvard, Yale, MIT, and Columbia to begin developing suicide prevention programs for the college campus. The director of ULifeline says that many colleges have already developed programs urging kids not to binge drink and to protect themselves from STDs. They have rigorous policies for enforcing condom use, but suicide gets much less attention. And part of the problem is that psychologists tend to blame the problem of suicide on issues such as "perfectionism" and a desire to please their parents rather than on the risky behaviors—and the difficult emotional changes that often come with a new life away from home—that can devastate a young person's self-respect.

Ross Szabo, a twenty-five-year-old who speaks on behalf of the National Mental Health Awareness Campaign, says that communication is the key to prevention. In his speeches to high-school and college students, Szabo admits that his own failed suicide attempt when he was in high school was due to a long-term battle with bipolar disorder mixed with depression and anger. "One of the things I see," he said, "is that young people feel alone and don't know that they can talk about it. A lot of times they don't have the words to start talking about it. And their form of expression is to wind up taking their own lives."[18]

LOSING THE CONSENSUS

In his study of the breakdown of moral authority in American culture over the past forty years, Dr. Harold O. J. Brown has said that our society has lost its confidence and fallen into despair, in large measure, because we have willingly and wantonly cut ourselves loose from the spiritual moorings that provided meaning and purpose for previous generations. In this nation's tortured journey from self-determination to self-destruction we have already passed through the three stages identified by the late Pitrim Sorokin as evidence of a degenerate, sensate culture. We have gone from the ideational, in which spiritual truth is valued, to the idealistic in which reason and empiricism prevail, and finally to the sensate, in which materialism, sensuality, and self-indulgence reign supreme.

BRINGING SOMETHING HOME FROM COLLEGE

Two-thirds of college students today have sexually-transmitted diseases (STDs), such as AIDS, chlamydia, hepatitis B, gonorrhea, herpes, syphilis, and venereal warts (HPV) that can cause complications ranging from pain, infertility, and cancer, to death. Many are incurable. Due to mutation and drug resistance, the number of STDs has increased from two to fifty in the past thirty years. And, yes, "oral sex" is sex. Any or all of these diseases can be contracted through oral, anal, and vaginal sex. Condoms are not all-protective.

We don't need to revisit the issues in this or the preceding chapters to recognize that the world of the modern university is, by any definition, a *sensate* culture consumed by sensuality, self-indulgence, and materialism. But what we do need to do is to recognize that the collapse of standards on our campuses is the direct result, as Brown persuasively argues, of the willing surrender of moral authority by those whose duty was to preserve order. He says:

> One reason why authority in education has declined is that individual and institutional authority is based on the acknowledgment that such individuals and institutions exhibit virtue and serve the common good,

and contemporary culture has lost its consensus as to what constitutes the common good. This did not originate in disillusionment or rebellion among the common people but as a loss of orientation, abdication, and betrayal precisely where authority, dignity, and virtue should have been best safeguarded—in the institutions of higher and highest learning.[19]

It is without question that what has taken place, both on the campus and within the culture, is not merely a *loss* of moral authority but a voluntary *abdication* of responsibility. The wicked notion that somehow pluralism vitiates the obligation of leaders and other protectors of the commonweal to maintain moral standards has led to the loss of principle and a crippling rise in immorality throughout the culture. Those with the intellectual and academic resources and the responsibility to guide the nation toward reliable solutions to our common concerns have chosen, instead, to indulge in the behaviors of adolescents.

The opiate of the Sixties Revolution—which inspired a generation of young idealists to insist that libidinous self-indulgence was an entitlement of the young—eventually seduced the campus elite as well. Consequently, the deans, presidents, and other officers who had the duty to "Just say no!" said instead, "It's really not my concern." As Arnold Beichman made clear to me in our interchange at the Hoover Institution, the administrators who stood watch over America's universities in the summer of 1968 betrayed not just their own students and alumni but the entire nation when they capitulated to the drug-crazed and witless dissidents who took over the places of power. Insolence had won over honor; virtue succumbed to vice.

The attitude of compromise, complacency, and sloth that has incapacitated our great universities ever since that time has transformed many of our most ancient and distinguished centers of higher learning into playgrounds for corruption. As Brown puts it:

The prestigious institutions of North America (such as Harvard, Yale, Princeton, Stanford, the University of Chicago) and all their rivals and imitators entered the second half of the twentieth century with their authority, dignity, and virtue still apparently intact. The majority of college students, being less than twenty-one years old, were still legally minors, and the colleges saw themselves as *in loco parentis* (in the place of a parent) and consequently felt both obliged and authorized to teach moral principles and to uphold standards of behavior, civility, and morality, including sexual morality.[20]

But the seductions of the Sixties Revolution changed all that. Liberal administrators responded willingly to the siren-song of openness, tolerance, and intellectual equivocation that allowed the balance, self-restraint, and moral probity of that earlier time to be discarded, and, as Brown says further, "free speech came to mean the coarsest vulgarities and obscenities, and virtually all men's and women's colleges were made coeducational overnight (with far more emphasis on the *co* than on education)."

Eventually, he says, the barriers to sexuality were beaten down, and everything was permitted. "Indeed," writes Brown, "dormitories, floors, and sometimes even rooms were made open to both sexes, with absolutely predictable results: generalized sexual activity. Sexual behavior was removed from moral concern, and inasmuch as sex had always constituted a major concern of personal ethics, ethics became increasingly relativized and irrelevant."[21] When restraints upon heterosexual activity gave way, it was inevitable that homosexuality, bisexuality, and every imaginable perversion of human conduct would not only be allowed but positively encouraged on the campus, and even at times preferred to monogamous heterosexual relations within the sacred bonds of matrimony. The foundations had utterly given way, and short of a divine miracle or some unimaginable tragedy, there would be no stopping the moral descent.

BEGGING FOR ANSWERS

In this new permissive environment, much as the Founders of the Republic had warned, liberty has turned to license, while freedom transmogrified by the progressive notion of "liberation" has made a mockery of moral order. For there to be order in society, there must be strict limits on the behaviors that destroy lives, both individually and collectively, and there must be generally understood and accepted standards of restraint that set boundaries for the kinds of behavior that a just society can tolerate. But it is precisely these standards that have been abandoned, largely through the premeditated rejection of the principles of democracy and the Judeo-Christian beliefs the Founders believed were essential for national survival.

It was our second president, John Adams, who best expressed this view with his assessment that:

> Statesmen . . . may plan and speculate for liberty, but it is religion and morality alone, which can establish the principles upon which freedom can securely stand. The only foundation of a free Constitution, is pure virtue, and if this cannot be inspired into our people, in a greater measure, than we have it now, they may change their rulers, and the forms of government, but they will not obtain a lasting liberty.

Still more sobering are Adams' words that, "We have no government armed with power capable of contending with human passions unbridled by morality and religion. . . . Our constitution," he said, "was made only for a moral and religious people. It is wholly inadequate to the government of any other."[22]

As we have already seen, sociologist Christopher Lasch was startled by the pernicious deregulation of American society and the degree to which liberal permissiveness and disregard for law and personal responsibility had decimated the American character. In his analysis of the factors that led to this breakdown, he says:

> A lust for immediate gratification pervades American society from top to bottom. There is a universal concern with the self—with "self-fulfillment" and more recently with "self-esteem," slogans of a society incapable of generating a sense of civic obligation. For native as well as foreign observers, the disinclination to subordinate self-interest to the

general will comes uncomfortably close to capturing the essence of Americanism. . . .[23]

Lasch says further that, "Every culture has to narrow the range of choices in some way, however arbitrary such limitations may seem. To be sure, it also has to see to it that its controls do not reach too far into people's private lives. But if it allows impulse a public expression—if it boldly declares that 'it is forbidden to forbid,' in the revolutionary slogans of 1968—then it not only invites anarchy but abolishes the 'sacred distances' on which the category of truth finally depends. When every expression is equally permissible, nothing is true."[24]

This sage assessment turns the discussion naturally to the consequence of the current situation. As Dostoevsky and Solzhenitsyn famously remarked, "If God is dead, everything is permitted," by which they meant to say that only the moral order woven into the fabric of our civilization can truly preserve "domestic peace and tranquility." Yet, as if by design, we find ourselves in the throes of chaos. We are, as a decadent and permissive society, ripping away at the very few remaining threads of Western culture.

Ultimately, the future well-being of the American university and of the nation itself hinges upon our willingness to restore the framework of moral order. But we must ask ourselves these questions: Will we decide at long last to acknowledge the need for modesty and decency in our national conversation? Are we then prepared to give due credit to the foundational principles that men like Adams, Madison, Jefferson, Washington, and others prescribed? If there is to be any hope of arresting the moral freefall and restoring "the Blessings of Liberty to ourselves and our Posterity," as the Constitution proposes, this nation and the institutions that preserve our heritage of liberty must regain their nerve and evict the spineless men and their minions who have brought this crisis upon us.

The realization that Connee and I came to as we came to the end of research was that, indeed, a few students at these elite universities are getting a first-class education. They're being exposed to ideas and perspectives that will allow them to accomplish great things during their careers. There are honors programs in some places with very high standards, and students who are bright and willing to work hard and not settle for minimum standards can still learn a lot. Unfortunately, most of the students at Harvard, Stanford, Princeton, Vanderbilt, and practically any of the large state universities, are getting only a mediocre education. They are not being challenged, they are not being encouraged to stretch their minds, they are not being given meaningful instruction regarding the responsibilities of citizens, and they are certainly not being taught the benefits of moral restraint. Furthermore, they are being encouraged by an army of provocateurs to experiment with risky behaviors and to espouse utopian ideologies that will disappoint if not destroy them in the end.

While some of these students, by virtue of their character or upbringing, are able to survive the seductions of the college experience, others are not. Among the latter group are those who appear in the statistics cited above. Virtually without exception students on the university campus today are tortured by the vices and superficial values of a morally bankrupt society. To the degree that the compromises brought about by the Sixties Revolution still survive on campus today, the future of our culture is very much at risk. Is there still hope for stopping the descent and restoring sanity among the young? As Harvey Mansfield told us pointedly, "I think some of them know it: they know they're being cheated." That is, at least, a small step back from the brink.

A number of studies over the past ten years help to corroborate this belief. As just one example, a Zogby poll of American college students published in 2000 reported that young people are longing for more discussion of morality in the classroom. The survey, by the Foundation for Academic Standards and Tradition (FAST), found that an overwhelming majority of students want more discussion of morality and traditional values. They are exposed to sexually explicit materials of every description and many young people find this unsettling and frightening. They know instinctively that something is wrong. Nearly 56 percent of students in the FAST poll said that the pressure on campus to drink and use drugs is hampering their schoolwork; more than 73 percent said they believe cheating is always wrong; 98.8 percent believe in the concept of right and wrong; 83.7 percent reject the idea that "nothing can be true because everything is relative"; and 68 percent said there's not enough talk about morality and moral values in America's colleges.[25]

The response to such findings ought to be obvious: The ball is now in our court.

Part III
FINDINGS

9

Politics & Religion

At 8:46 A.M. eastern daylight time on September 11, 2001, a grim reality appeared suddenly on the American horizon. The world watched in shock and disbelief as three thousand men and women died in the deadliest assault to hit these shores in nearly four hundred years of history. It was the face of multiculturalism gone awry, a sobering moment for every American as we considered the carnage, the prospect that this unprovoked attack was but a prelude to something worse, and the even more disquieting feeling that something awful was about to happen and we were powerless to stop it. It was the fear that, in one terrible moment of unspeakable horror, the world had changed forever.

In many ways the attack by Middle Eastern terrorists and the devastating collapse of the World Trade Center towers on that radiant fall morning are emblematic of the world we live in. The clash of world religions that Samuel Huntington had predicted in his 1996 bestseller was no longer theory but a visible reality: catastrophe had come when we least expected it. It would take weeks, even months, to sort it all out, but for one hushed moment the din of controversy had subsided, and the flurry of accusations had not yet begun. America wept.

In his remarks to the nation that same evening, President Bush said:

A great people has been moved to defend a great nation. Terrorist attacks can shake the foundations of our biggest buildings, but they cannot touch the foundation of America. These acts shattered steel, but they cannot dent the steel of American resolve. . . . Today, our nation saw evil, the very worst of human nature. And we responded with the best of America—with the daring of our rescue workers, with the caring for strangers and neighbors who came to give blood and help in any way they could. . . . America and our friends and allies join with all those who want peace and security in the world, and we stand together to win the war against terrorism. Tonight, I ask for your prayers for all those who grieve, for the children whose worlds have been shattered, for all whose sense of safety and security has been threatened. And I pray they will be comforted by a power greater than any of us, spoken through the ages in Psalm 23: "Even though I walk through the valley of the shadow of death, I fear no evil, for You are with me."

The president concluded his remarks by reminding us all that, "America has stood down enemies before, and we will do so this time. None of us will ever forget this day. Yet, we go forward to defend freedom and all that is good and just in our world."

Soon afterwards, a joint statement was issued from the leaders of both Republicans and Democrats in the United States Senate, saying, "What happened on Tuesday, September 11, was not simply an attack against America. It was a crime against democracy and decency. It was a crime against humanity." Polls would show nearly unanimous support for the president, and 92 percent of the general public favored military action to root out "the enemies of freedom" and their enablers.

On the university campus, however, it was a very different story. One professor at MIT told an audience, "The best way to begin a war on terrorism might be to look in the mirror." The dean of the Woodrow Wilson School of Government at Princeton said, "There is a terrible and understandable desire to find and punish whoever was responsible for this. But as we think about it, it's very important for Americans to think about our own history, what we did in World War II to Japanese citizens by interning them." And a professor of anthropology at Brown University said that "the war can end only to the extent that we relinquish our role as world leader, overhaul our lifestyle, and achieve political neutrality."[1]

A War of Words

Such comments were mild compared to those of a history professor at the University of New Mexico who told students, "Anyone who can blow up the Pentagon gets my vote," or the physics professor at the University of Massachusetts at Amherst who said the American flag is "a symbol of terrorism and death and fear and destruction and oppression." A professor at the University of Hawaii—a state whose suffering had provoked America's entry into World War II—blasted the president and the nation, saying, "Why should we support the United States, whose hands in history are soaked with blood?" And most repugnant of all were the words of Nicholas de Genova, an assistant professor at Columbia College in New York City, who said, "the only true heroes are those who find ways to help defeat the U.S. military," and then added that he'd like to see "a million Mogadishus"— the military tragedy, featured in the film *Black Hawk Down*, in which eighteen brave Americans died.

Even as the nation braced for what was still to come by improving security precautions at airports, posting civilian and military guards in sensitive areas, and upgrading screening procedures in the nation's schools, universities erupted with antiwar demonstrations and protests on more than a hundred and forty campuses in thirty-six states. Professors at some universities sponsored "teach-ins" that, in the words of the American Council of Trustees and Alumni (ACTA), ranged from "moral equivocation to explicit condemnation of America." But who could have imagined that American intellectuals would have taken sides with our attackers?

An ACTA report published as the clean-up efforts were beginning in New York and Washington, said, "While America's elected officials from both parties and media commentators from across the spectrum condemned the attacks and followed the president in calling evil by its rightful name, many faculty demurred. Some refused to make judgments. Many invoked tolerance and diversity as antidotes to evil. Some even pointed accusatory fingers, not at the terrorists, but at America itself."[2]

As the partisan posturing began, politicians, special-interest groups, and the media began finding fault with the Bush administration and its plans to ferret out terrorist organizations who claimed credit for the September 11 attacks. The *New York Times* reported that anti-American sentiment was rising at home and abroad. When Pentagon chief Donald Rumsfeld announced that U.S. forces and their allies had begun a campaign in Afghanistan to eliminate the Taliban—rooting out Osama bin Laden and other Muslim zealots—most Americans applauded; but from the university campus there were cries of outrage and alarm. Liberal faculty members and Marxist student groups charged that President Bush was using the crisis to further his personal ambitions. Bitterness toward the president soon turned to invective against America, the military, and the American flag.

Many in the front ranks of the Left on campus, says New York University professor Herbert London, are "red diaper babies." They are the children of Marxist parents from the twenties and thirties, often affiliated with communist and socialist labor movements, and dedicated to the overthrow of the United States government. They imbibed the "blame America first" animus of the sixties and now spread this venom wherever they can find willing adherents. Among them are followers of the late Italian Marxist, Antonio Gramsci. "To a remarkable degree," writes Herbert London, "Gramscians marched through American institutions spreading a philosophy of group rights that resulted in the acceptance of affirmative action and other categorical ethnic and racial privilege." For such people, he says, America is a land of deep-seated racial antipathy, despite the nation's massive, long-term efforts to make up for past wrongs. But, because of their deep animosity, nothing will ever change their minds.[3]

The campus radicals are also, as I have written elsewhere, followers of Herbert Marcuse, the German-born professor and radical pamphleteer who taught the children of Haight-Ashbury and Woodstock the language of revolution. Marcuse was one of a large group of German intellectuals who made up what became known as the Frankfurt School of Social Criticism. Many of those individuals fled from Germany to America in the early-thirties and managed to find positions on the faculties of elite universities such as Columbia, MIT, Princeton, Brandeis, UCLA, and particularly the

University of California at Berkeley. They were the vanguard of the culture wars in America, and ideological pioneers of the Sixties Revolution. Many of the Baby Boomers who studied at their feet went on to become foot soldiers of the counterculture that continues, virtually unabated, to this day.

The aims of the Sixties Revolution—echoed in the phrase "sex, drugs, and rock 'n' roll"—were firmly rooted in Marcusian dogma. The culture war as they envisioned it was not merely a war of words or ideas but the radical transformation of commonplace institutions and everyday habits. Marcuse taught them to say, "Make love not war!" In one widely read tract he had said, "If the New Left emphasizes the struggle for the restoration of nature, if it demands a new sexual morality, the liberation of women, then it fights against material conditions imposed by the capitalist system and reproducing this system."[4] Marcuse tutored the political Left, and his influence was even felt in the Clinton White House, as both Clintons said on one occasion that Marcuse had been their main academic influence.[5]

Equally heated denunciations of U.S. policy came from former government officials who had been schooled in this environment. Among them, Ramsey Clark, who had served as attorney general under President Lyndon Johnson. Clark launched a fusillade of virulent rhetorical attacks on President Bush. Today Clark's organization still accepts funds from foreign governments to orchestrate demonstrations against the White House and the War on Terror. But even before the first bombs fell on Iraq, hundreds of demonstrators were marching in New York's Union Square Park, and on the Washington Mall. Marxist groups such as ANSWER—"Act Now to Stop War and End Racism"—responded to Clark's challenge to protest American military action and to demand changes in the government. And cover for all this acting out came from the universities.

SEEING THROUGH SMOKE

Yet despite the radicals' best efforts, patriotism in America remained high. Admiration for police, firemen, and military personnel reached the highest level since World War II; and the Pentagon reported that there is an ongoing surge in military recruitment, despite news of combat casualties in the Middle East. On every campus I have visited over the past year, and in dozens of e-mails and phone calls, I have heard from students who said their view of America changed on that day. For many, 9/11 was an emotional watershed.

For years, in some cases, they had believed what they'd been taught by teachers and textbooks since kindergarten, that America is an imperialistic and blood-thirsty nation. The land of their birth, they were told, was a nation not conceived in liberty but in blood and greed; it was a nation of exploiters, slavers, rapists, and "robber barons" who had slaughtered the Indians, desecrated the environment, and left a bloody trail of exploitation and capitalistic treachery around the globe.

But 9/11 made many of these young men and women pause to reconsider: Could this be true? "That's what happened to me," said Tom, a sophomore at Tufts University in Boston. "I was a sort of moderate liberal before September 11, but seeing that on television changed my mind about a lot of things. After that I stopped thinking about the world in idealistic terms and the way things ought to be, and I started thinking more about the way it actually is. I realized that the way to improve the world isn't always the way people might wish it to be. It's not as simple as that."

"There are people on this campus," I said, "including both students and faculty, who would say you've lost your mind. Bitterness toward America is deep in the academy, and going to war in Afghanistan and Iraq just made it worse. Now, some of them are rioting in the streets. How do you deal with that?"

"It's fine to say we can change the world by example," Tom told me, "but there's no proof of that in history. As far as I can see, and I read a lot of history, it's never been the case. Sometimes the only way to stop a corrupt government like the Taliban or Saddam Hussein is to do it by force. So that's what made me realize that President Bush was saying the right things and that if America didn't take steps to defend itself against future attacks, nobody else was going to do it for us."

"Have you said any of that in class?" I said.

"Oh, sure," he said. "I was still in prep school when 9/11 happened. Most of my teachers were liberals, but they were careful to qualify their own views and they allowed me to speak openly about my opinions on the war. I haven't found that in college, though."

"How is it different?" I asked.

"Most of my classes so far have been lectures, where the professor presents his own thinking and the students don't have much input. But, in general, there's an atmosphere in the classroom that you don't feel you can speak freely. It's mostly a bunch of liberal kids and liberal professors; they're having a dialogue, and there's no way to interject."

"So, basically," I said, "you don't feel you can say anything."

"For the first two weeks of class this term I didn't say a word," he said. "I just sat there and listened, but then one day I couldn't take it any longer and I said something, and there was this instant reaction! The liberals jumped all over me. But then, what really surprised me, was this whole group of kids spoke up and said, 'Yes, I agree with you!' Nobody wanted to be the first to say something, but once I spoke up they got on board with it."

"Have you run into many others who are changing their minds?" I asked.

"A lot of kids come here and they haven't looked into any of these issues," Tom said, "and they don't really know what they're getting into. So they come to college, and a lot of it is really subtle. The professors aren't going to bash you in the face with it, but they're going to exclude a certain viewpoint, or they're going to just weave an attitude or an opinion into what's being discussed, and it's hard to see that unless you know what to look for."

"Do you feel that you know what to look for?" I asked.

"Yes, I've read a lot of stuff," he said, "especially during the build-up to the war in Iraq. I saw the stories about all the different university protests and all the academic bias on campus. I read about people like that Professor de Genova at Columbia who said the Trade Center bombers were the real heroes and he'd like to see a million Mogadishus, and all that sort of thing. I've done a lot of research on it, so I knew what to expect. That's made it easier for me. But if I hadn't done that and spent a lot of time on the Internet,

I doubt that I would have seen through all the smoke and realized what was really happening."

TAKING ADVANTAGE

No sooner had the fires been extinguished in lower Manhattan than a whole new conflagration of accusations and partisan rancor began to erupt within the academy. At Central Michigan University, as reported by the Foundation for Individual Rights in Education, students were ordered by administrators to remove patriotic posters and the American flag from their dormitories. Thy were told that these items were *offensive* symbols and that they would not be *tolerated*.

Administrators at Duke University, in North Carolina, shut down Professor Gary Hull's faculty Web site because he had posted an article calling for a military response to the terrorist attacks on America. At Pennsylvania State University, a faculty member was reprimanded by the vice provost for saying that military action was the only logical response. The professor was told that his comments were "insensitive and perhaps even intimidating." And at Holy Cross, a Catholic college in Massachusetts, the chairman of the sociology department forced a secretary to remove an American flag she had put up near her desk in memory of her friend Todd Beamer, the young man on the doomed United Airlines flight 93 who spoke the words, "Let's Roll!"[6]

At Johns Hopkins University, in Baltimore, Professor Charles Fairbanks spoke at a public forum on how America ought to respond to the attacks. After saying that a military campaign against states that harbor terrorists was an appropriate step, he was attacked by fellow faculty members and administrators and accused of encouraging hate crimes. He was then summarily removed from his post as director of the Central Asia Institute on the Hopkins campus. And at the University of Massachusetts, antiwar protesters were given a permit to rally against President Bush and the War on Terror, but when students who supported those policies asked for a permit to hold a rally of their own, the request was denied.

At San Diego State, an Ethiopian student who overheard three Arab students in the university library celebrating the World Trade Center bombing was reprimanded publicly for telling the students, in Arabic, that they should be ashamed of themselves. At Florida Gulf Coast University the dean of library services ordered the library's employees to remove stickers that said "Proud to be an American" from their cubicles because they were offensive to foreign students. And the director of the University of Missouri's on-campus TV station told employees they weren't allowed to wear ribbons in memory of those killed in the September 11 attacks.

This is a mere fraction of the hostility that surfaced on American campuses. But how do normal people respond to this sort of anti-American bigotry? More and more Americans, as some observers have suggested, are beginning to believe that there is a fifth column ensconced in the Ivory Tower, working to undermine America's democratic traditions—they are men and women with academic tenure who wish harm to this nation no less damaging than the attacks of 9/11. As columnist Paul Craig Roberts writes, maybe it's time to pull the plug.[7]

Where do the left-wing groups get their funds? Many leftist faculty members receive substantial fees for political speeches, as well as grants and financial aid, from leftist groups, foundations, and Web sites. Funding for radical student groups, as has been reported by Eagle Forum and others, comes from student activity fees. Student fees are mandatory, and students' grades may be withheld if they're not paid in full. But students have no say in how their money is used, or which campus groups may be funded. On most campuses, the money is directed primarily to left-wing, feminist, gay, Marxist, and other radical clubs, and are often used to pay for anti-American tirades and graduation speakers pushing activist, socialist, or racially-divisive causes. The amount of money available to these groups is often quite substantial—as much as a million dollars each year at some of the larger private and state schools.

As one student informed me recently, there are 172 ethnic and cultural student groups that receive university funds at UC Berkeley, the majority of which are strongly to the left of center. Not only do these students and their faculty advisors agitate on behalf of homosexuality, women's rights, African-Americans, Latinos, Asians, and other "disenfranchised" minorities, but they fund conferences, speakers, protest rallies, "Get Out the Vote" drives, and other disruptive activities. Not least, they are behind the move for "theme program" housing on campus, isolating each of the preferred minority groups into communal quarters where they are subjected to "group think" indoctrination twenty-four hours a day.

ACADEMIC IMBALANCE

A widely publicized research project by professors from Berkeley, Stanford, and the University of Maryland provides a perfect picture of the kinds of ideological bias being pushed by activists in the universities. The point of the study, "Political Conservatism as Motivated Social Cognition," was to gain "a better understanding of what makes political conservatives tick." To accomplish this task, four scholars reviewed the words and policies of Ronald Reagan, Rush Limbaugh, Adolf Hitler, and Benito Mussolini—certainly no bias in their selection of subjects. According to their research report in the bulletin of the American Psychological Association, they based their analysis on eighty-eight statements by and about the subjects from books, conference papers, speeches, interviews, judicial opinions, and survey reports.

What they discovered, the APA article said, was that conservatives share a common resistance to change, an acceptance of inequality in society, nostalgia for an idealized past, and a desire to see and state things "in black and white ways that would make liberals squirm." They found that conservatives, as illustrated by President Bush, are less "integratively complex," which, they said, doesn't mean they're necessarily "simple-minded." But conservatives don't feel the need to jump through intellectual hoops in order to justify their positions. Particularly troubling, they added, was the attitude of most conservative leaders that, "I know what I believe, and I believe what I believe is right."[8]

No lofty reasoning is needed to recognize what these professors really had in mind. Of course the liberal media were quick to trumpet the results of the Berkeley study to the world. Anticipating that alert readers would notice that some of the findings could just as easily describe communist tyrants such as Josef Stalin or Fidel Castro, the professors added that the policies of those dictators actually classify them, not as socialists but as conservatives, since they had tried to maintain their power and policies, and to avoid change. But what, if anything, such "research" really shows is the deep rift between the Left and the Right, and by extension, the deep divisions between the majority of Americans and the academic elite.

In their defense of unfair recruitment practices that gave minority students a twenty-point advantage over whites, faculty members at the University of Michigan in their recent Supreme Court case had argued that a "critical mass" of black and Hispanic students was needed to ensure fairness and equality on campus. In their own recruitment of faculty, however, departments were more than happy to deny faculty positions to conservatives, making sure that the only "critical mass" for professors was a strong liberal bias. In an op-ed in the *Wall Street Journal*, John O. McGinnis, who teaches at Northwestern, and Matthew Schwartz, a law student at Columbia, reported on their study of political contributions of two hundred dollars or more by professors at the nation's top twenty-two law schools between 1994 and 2000. While the American public is split about evenly between Republicans and Democrats, they found that 74 percent of the professors on those campuses contributed primarily to Democrats, with just 16 percent contributing to Republicans.[9]

But even these sharply contrasting figures understate the imbalance on campus. At Yale University, where half the faculty actively donates to political parties, 95 percent of donations go to Democrats. At Michigan, the figure was eight to one, and at Georgetown, in Washington, DC, professors donated approximately $180,000 to Democrats and just $2,000 to Republicans. The far left Green Party, with donations of $1,500, was almost as close.

When researchers for the American Enterprise Institute and the Center for the Study of Popular Culture joined up to examine election records in communities surrounding America's top universities, they found that the majority of faculty members were registered Democrats, with a sizable number in liberal splinter parties, such as the Greens. Researchers said, "Colleges like to characterize themselves as wide-open places where every thought can be thought. . . . The demonstrable reality, however, is that you will find a much wider and freer cross-section of human reasoning and conviction in the aisles of a grocery store or city bus."

LOSING YOUR RELIGION

Don't think your student will be sheltered in religious schools, especially divinity schools. Boston College placed a "functional atheist" in charge of divinity students at the Jesuit-founded school. Many colleges and organizations are Christian or Jewish in name only. Check to be sure your school or group is not a "wolf in sheep's clothing." Many are wholly amoral and atheistic.

What they found was that liberal faculty members outnumber conservatives 166 to 6 at Cornell; 151 to 17 at Sanford; 116 to 5 at the University of Colorado; and a ratio of 6 to 1 at Penn, and 18 to 1 at Brown. The lowest disparity was at the University of Houston where the ratio was 3 to 1. At UCLA there were just 9 conservatives for every 141 registered liberals; at UC-Santa Barbara there was just 1 conservative faculty member among the 73 surveyed. Among political science professors in the entire UC System, there were just 5 conservatives and 90 liberals. Among all 32 schools included in the survey, the report says, there were 1,397 registered Democrats and just 134 Republicans. Another 1,891 faculty members were surveyed but listed as unaffiliated.[10]

Berkeley professor James Gregor, one of few campus conservatives willing to speak to reporters, told an editor of *Campus Report* that his university has gone out of its way to recruit liberal faculty members. "All these things,

I think, are in-house problems in any academic institution," he said. But the real problem, the professor added, reaches beyond the academy. "You know how Americans are," he said, "they mostly dismiss academics. . . . Ten miles from Berkeley, people say, 'Oh, Berkeley, what do you expect from that place?' . . . We have naked students walking on campus to test the limits of their civil rights. It's an outdoor lunatic asylum. And I think most people outside of academe treat it that way."[11]

ANTI-RELIGIOUS BIGOTRY

The problem with recruiting only professors of one philosophical bent is not merely that more Democrats will be chosen than Republicans, but that with this imbalance comes general disregard for the issues that are of concern to the majority of the public, who ultimately pay the salaries of these people.

Writing in the *Harvard Political Review*, Jordan Hylden and John Jernigan report that political bias isn't the only overt form of discrimination on the university campus. "Compared with the rest of the population, very few professors hold strong religious beliefs," they say. "While there is nothing wrong with this fact in and of itself, the danger is that anti- or non-religious viewpoints will seep into the classroom and curriculum, particularly in the sciences." As evidence, the article reviews the cases of Dr. Michael Behe, a Catholic scholar at Lehigh University, and Dr. William Dembski, who headed a biological research institute at Baylor University dedicated to the study of Intelligent Design—a field of research that accords with biblical teachings about creation—until anti-religious forces on that Baptist-funded campus managed to get him sacked and the institute shut down.

Commenting on Dembski's ouster, Baylor provost David Jeffrey told the Harvard reporters that "apparent anti-religious bias has certainly increased over the last three or four decades in the academy. Respectable institutions do not permit religion to be an item of discussion on the table, except in the abstract and clinical sense where we study it much like we study shards of ancient pottery."

At a time when "tolerance and diversity" are the most celebrated isms on the university campus, liberal faculty members take great pains to exclude not just conservative ideas but also religion. "The substance of all the concern," Jeffrey said, "is that you cannot articulate a point of view that might be considered by another party as exclusivist." In other words, the liberal view insists that we have no grounds for determining what is true; therefore, any claim to truth must be discounted and disavowed. This means, of course, that religious beliefs which rely upon revelation and absolute standards of truth, have no home in the academy.[12]

In a telephone conversation with Richard Halvorson, a 2003 Harvard graduate who was active with a large Protestant group on the campus, I asked if he'd experienced bias of any sort during his time at the university. "There's definitely a consensus in one direction," he told me, "in terms of politics, religion, and general worldview. It's not always explicit, or one that each professor at Harvard could explain coherently. It's more implicit and much more subtle, but it's there." When I asked if he had felt excluded because of his religious beliefs, he said, "I would say there's a lot of pressure. It's not people trying to pressure you into their ideology so much, but if you disagree with their view it's like, 'You don't care! Maybe you're a racist or a capitalist pig!'"

In an article for the *Harvard Crimson*, Halvorson expressed concern for the bias against conservative religious beliefs on campus, and particularly the bias against any view that does not support the reigning Darwinian orthodoxy. In his critique of this perspective, Halvorson said, "Intellectual honesty requires rationally examining our fundamental premises—yet expressing hesitation about Darwin is considered irretrievable intellectual suicide, the unthinkable doubt, the unpardonable sin of academia."

He went on to say that, "Although the postmodern era questions everything else—the possibility of knowledge, basic morality, and reality itself—critical discussion of Darwin is taboo. While evolutionary biologists test Darwin's hypothesis in every experiment they conduct, the basic premise of evolution remains a scientific Holy of Holies, despite our absurd skepticism in other areas." It's ironic that the university, which has made a fetish of skewering sacred cows, should be in the position of giving an unproven theory of origins by an uncertain nineteenth-century student of natural history the status of Holy Writ. Yet, that's precisely what has happened. The modern university has no religion but Darwinism, to which Halvorson replies, "We must reject intellectual excommunication as a valid form of dealing with criticism: the most important question for any society to ask is the one that is forbidden."[13]

THE ESTABLISHMENT VIEW

On my last day in Boston, I had a chance to sit down with four recent graduates of Eastern universities at the Massachusetts State House. They serve on the staff of the Minority Whip in the Massachusetts House of Representatives and share a common interest in campus politics. Chanel Prunier is a graduate of Assumption College in Worcester, Massachusetts. When I asked about her campus experience, she said, "I had some conservative professors, and I had a lot of liberal ones. Someone who comes to mind immediately was a professor in the political science department who tried to cast himself as a moderate; he said, 'Oh, I'm not on the left!' But when September 11 happened, his tone changed dramatically.

"He had always touched on his thoughts on war," she said. "He had a brother who died in Vietnam, so whenever the subject of America going to war came up, he was very closed-minded about anything students said in class or wrote in their papers. And while it didn't totally silence debate, I think it did make some students intellectually lazy. They said, 'We know how strongly this professor feels about war, so if we just go out drinking tonight and write a shoddy paper, as long as he agrees with it he's going to give me a good grade.' And they also knew that if they wrote a paper that disagreed with what he was saying in class, it would have to be a much better researched and written paper to get a good grade."

Another young man, Mark Buschenfeldt, is a graduate of Colby College in Waterville, Maine, where he had been active in College Republicans. "Considering what I've read about liberal bias in higher education," he said, "and considering some of the experiences that I know other College

Republicans have had, I think my experience wasn't quite as severe at Colby. Certainly, like most campuses in the country, there were far more professors who were partisan Democrats than Republicans—in fact there were only two reliable conservatives in the entire government department. But I felt that my ideas were respected, and as the token conservative I was often asked to speak out more than other students simply because they needed someone to take the other side in debates."

"So you didn't see a lot of bias?" I asked.

"The bias I've seen is fairly subtle," he said. "You have to have a certain character and self-confidence to be the token conservative. A lot of students have moderate to conservative views, even as young, idealistic college students, but they're afraid to share them, either because they don't want to rock the boat or they don't know how their fellow students will react. Also, they don't feel they know enough about the issues and don't want to look ignorant when they're challenged by their professors. The government department was fair, but if you talk about the sociology department or the American studies department, or certainly women's studies, African-American studies, and things like that, that's a different animal altogether.

"Where the real bias comes in," he said, "is that the same professors who are teaching the classes are leading the rallies outside of class."

"How does that work?" I said. "Did you attend any of those rallies?"

"On one occasion the College Republicans brought conservative author Dinesh D'Souza to campus. While we were eating dinner with him before his talk, there were students outside yelling that he was a racist and a bigot. One student burned a flag, and they were passing out American flags with 'Go Home, Nazi!' scrawled across them, which I thought was ironic since Dinesh is from India. Then when we got to the lecture hall, we had reserved a block of seats up front for members of the College Republicans who sponsored the event, but of course the protesters had taken those seats, and they interrupted him constantly. Before and after the lecture, liberal sociology professors staged a 'teach-in' where they were attempting to tell the students why D'Souza was wrong. There was one professor who paid lip service to the "devil's advocate" position, it was clear that as a whole the teach-in was little more than a forum to preach to the choir, and worse, to convince anyone who was still undecided about D'Souza's views that they were illegitimate.

"Another example," he said, "was a sociology professor who's basically considered a rock star for his ability to really get students involved in protest movements. He was doing teach-ins all over the place in the sociology department. It was pure left-wing ideology, to such an extent that even some of my liberal friends had trouble with it. The fact that he used his position as a faculty member, passionately espousing his beliefs, was unfair influence because it had the potential for radicalizing students in a way that's contrary to open discourse. If professors are intellectually honest, they'll be willing to let the other side express their views. But when they spend their time outside the classroom leading rallies, they make it clear to the student body that this is what 'right thinking people' should be doing. They believe so strongly that their worldview is the right one that it's impossible for them to remain dispassionate about the conclusions their students may come to on their own."

"What percentage of students on your campus bought into that?" I said.

"Because most of them didn't have very well-formed political ideas when they got to college," he said, "I think most of them were fairly liberal by default, and the media plays into that. The educational system before college has a lot to do with that, as well. The educational establishment, all the way through, is bombarding students whose ideas aren't well formed with a strong liberal perspective. I mean, look at the courses they offer to Colby students majoring in education: 'Teaching for Social Justice,' 'Revolutionary Multiculturalism,' and 'The Political Project: Education, Environment, and Social Justice.' This is the kind of education they give to future teachers; and we wonder why liberalism pervades our educational system? When all students hear is the liberal point of view, and especially if conservatives won't speak up for what they believe in, it's inevitable that a lot of students are going to think like liberals.

"A lot of what the students believed," he concluded, "was based on feelings, rather than reason or facts. When I went to the teach-ins, they always talked about human-rights abuses and massacres of women and children, and all that sort of thing—it was just so much hyperbole, but most students didn't see that. It was intellectually dishonest but they didn't know the difference."

TIPS FOR RELIGIOUS CONSERVATIVES:

Church for students: Get away from campus for more traditional religious beliefs. Those on or near campus are almost always very liberal. Conservative groups on campus, even religious ones, are not always *morally* conservative.

TOEING THE LIBERAL LINE

The next young man, Andrew Goodrich, graduated from Georgetown University. As a student journalist and a College Republican, he told me, he was often in the thick of controversy on that campus. "Georgetown, which is located in Washington, DC," he said, "is certainly a politically charged environment, and most of the students are very aware of what's happening in the political scene. But there are two different realms on campus: the academic realm and the student-affairs realm.

"At Georgetown," he said, "the academic realm was fairly balanced. It was interesting: I would go to a class on something like The Politics of Abortion, and the professor would be a director of NOW, and she would tell the class that she was coming at these issues from a liberal point of view. Then the next class would be with someone like Ambassador Jeane Kirkpatrick, who is a staunch conservative and former Reagan administration official, so we'd get a very different perspective on the issues. I think that was good, and I was pleasantly surprised that there was that kind of balance in the classroom.

"But in the student-affairs realm," Andrew told me, "it was totally different. One of my friends was writing in the campus newspaper, *The Hoya*, criticizing the sponsors of *The Vagina Monologues* for bringing that play to campus. After he wrote the piece, the editors decided to fire him for his conservative views. So he left and joined the staff of an off-campus paper called the *Georgetown Academy*, which has always taken a strong conservative stand against the liberal policies of the administration. The university was always giving money to abortion groups, pro-homosexual groups, and others like that, or trying to remove the religious symbols and crucifixes from the classrooms of a Catholic university. Of course, when the Jewish group on campus came out and said, 'No, they're not offensive!' the administration had to rethink their position.

"I also worked on the *Georgetown Academy* for awhile," he said, "and one time campus radicals didn't like something we'd written so they stole all the publications. And what was the university's response? Absolutely nothing. There were several other alternative papers, and we talked to them and asked for their support, but they wouldn't say anything. Well, a couple of years later copies of the most liberal paper, *The Voice*, were taken and what do you think happened? There was a full-scale investigation. The administration said, 'We've got to get to the bottom of this!' And all the other papers rallied around them to give their support. So that's basically how it is. The biggest problem," he added, "is free speech on campus."

The fourth person in the group was Justin Ryan, a graduate of Boston University who shared many of the same experiences I'd heard about earlier from David Carl, interviewed in Chapter Three. "Boston University was described in the sixties as the Berkeley of the East Coast," Justin said. "But shortly thereafter, John Silber became the president and he had a big impact and a moderating influence, not just on the faculty but on the political culture. A lot of the campus activism that came out of the sixties really dissipated under his administration, and he ruled with an iron fist. Despite running for governor thirteen years ago as a Democrat, he was really pretty conservative."

"I've heard much the same thing from other students," I said. "But tell me about your campus experience. What was it like?"

"My freshman year I had one professor who was a triple-Berkeley—he got his B.A., M.A., and Ph.D. degrees all from UC Berkeley—and he taught the introductory class for political science majors. He wasn't horribly left-wing, but what was abundantly clear was how much he hated teaching that class. You could tell he was much more interested in research than teaching. He would do the lectures and he had TAs administer discussion groups and give the exams, but it was really obvious that he just hated being there.

"Later I had a professor who told his students every semester, 'I don't vote, as a matter of objectivity.' He said he tried to remain non-partisan, but it was pretty clear he was on the left. The first day of his class on American political parties, he said that party disunity can be a disaster, as it was in 1968. He also mentioned Pat Buchanan's 'This Is God's Country' speech at the 1992 Republican Convention, and he just threw out that Pat Buchanan had managed to take time to shave off his square mustache. Well, that told us where he was coming from, not just politically but religiously as well. He said later when someone asked him about it that he had apologized for that remark, but I sure don't remember it. At the end of the course I wrote on the student evaluation form that he was guilty of the same intolerance he claimed to oppose.

"The Green Party chapter at BU is the largest on the East Coast," Justin said. "In 2000, Ralph Nader came to speak on campus, the night before the elections. I went to it and ended up as a stand-in for the Republican side in a debate with the Green Party. But by and large, I'd have to say that there's a lot of political apathy at that university, which I think has a lot to do with the fact that they're right smack in the middle of an urban area. The default position is liberal Democrat, but that's just because people never hear about any other options."

"But BU is right across the Charles from the liberal hotbed in Cambridge!" I said.

"That's right," he said with a laugh. "And that's one of the advantages of being here in Boston—going across the river. I saw former Special Prosecutor Ken Starr when he came to speak at Harvard. I also saw Pat Buchanan and a number of other people. David Horowitz came my junior year, and that was just weeks after he had pies thrown in his face at Berkeley."

I mentioned that the cover of Horowitz's book, *Uncivil Wars*, features a picture of him speaking at Boston University with bodyguards on either side. "Sure, I remember that," Justin said. "We reserved a 370-seat auditorium for that event and we were worried that we weren't going to fill it. But, as it turned out, that wasn't the problem. One of the local radio guys here in Boston, Jay Severin, was running advertising for us on the radio. He really built it up and we had to turn away at least as many people as we could squeeze into the hall.

"Outside, of course," he said, "there was a guy with a bullhorn saying that hate speech isn't protected by the Constitution, and so on. But it was great, and a marvelous event for our club. Cable news came and interviewed the chair of our College Republican club, and it was a real coup for all of us. As a Catholic and someone who was involved with the Catholic Club at BU, I'm concerned about hypocrisy, and it was evident to me from the way the other side responded to what was happening that they were very hypocritical. We had a distinguished African-American professor at BU, Dr. Glenn Loury, who has expressed reservations about affirmative action in its present form. He took so much heat from those on the Left, and they showed no respect for him when he asked people to consider other options. There was only one point of view that they would tolerate, and that was the typical liberal line."

A DIVIDED CULTURE

According to some recent assessments, the cultural divide in America really began with the 1972 campaign of Democrat contender George McGovern. A third of the white delegates to the Democratic Convention were secular and non-religious, compared to just 5 percent of the general public. By 1992, the year the "culture war" became a mainstream issue, fully 60 percent of first-time white delegates to the Democratic Convention were secular, non-religious liberals.

WE'RE NOTHING SPECIAL

A survey conducted by Americans for Victory Over Terrorism, chaired by former education secretary William Bennett, revealed that college students are remarkably ignorant about world figures and profoundly ambivalent about what America is fighting for in the War on Terror. According to the report:

- Students were more likely to identify Yasser Arafat correctly than any other major player (including our own cabinet) in the War on Terror.

- Students intensely and overwhelmingly disagreed with the statement that Western culture is superior to Arab culture. Only 16 percent believe Western culture is superior to Arab culture, and 79 percent do not.

- When asked whether they believe the values of the United States are superior to the values of other nations, a full 71 percent disagreed, and 34 percent disagreed strongly.

- While more than 70 percent gave President Bush very high marks for his handling of the presidency, a majority of college students believe the policies of the United States area at least somewhat responsible for the September 11 terrorist attacks.

- And while 79 percent believe the U.S. has the right overthrow Saddam Hussein, 58 percent said they would evade the draft if called on to fight.

Since that time most Americans recognize the Republican Party as the party of traditional values and religious faith. The Democrat Party, on the other hand, is now seen as a secular party dedicated to "progressive" politics and skepticism regarding religion and tradition. In the 2000 elections in New York, for example, exit polls showed that two-thirds of secular voters favored Hillary Clinton while two-thirds of religious people voted instead for her opponent, Rick Lazio. A Pew study subsequently showed that the most religious states in the country vote Republican, and the least religious states vote Democrat.[14]

Such findings impact the university campus not just in terms of politics and religion but in determining the standards that will be upheld and respected by the faculty and administration. Former University of Chicago professor Allan Bloom said in *The Closing of the American Mind* that it is the eternal questions—"the permanent concerns of man as man"—that have always been the guiding light and primary goal of universities. But, as we have seen in these pages, that is no longer true. Bradford Wilson, executive director of the National Association of Scholars, says, "The curricular disarray pervading undergraduate education for the past thirty years is a consequence of the university's having lost sight of that transcendent goal." For generations, the university curriculum believed that higher education should emphasize the nature and origins of civilization through the study of enduring monuments of philosophy, science, sacred texts, and literature. But, says Wilson, that curriculum is now all but dead.[15]

Nothing of comparable merit has been offered, but in the void left by the collapse of general education the academic theorists have brought forth a never-ending array of utopian schemes based not on science but feelings. This has been an issue of grave concern for scholar and columnist Thomas Sowell, who addressed this issue in his acceptance speech for the 1998 Sidney Hook Award of the NAS. The university's abdication of its responsibility for the intellectual and moral formation of undergraduates, he said, has led to a clash of ideologies on many fronts. "In one sense," he said, "it is a collection of fights over a wide range of issues—admissions policies, the curriculum, speech codes, faculty hiring—but, more fundamentally, the fight is over power because that is what our opponents have made their objective.

The opposite of power," he said, "is not power for opposite purposes, it is freedom."

The American War of Independence was not fought to set up a new king in America but to free Americans from British tyranny. Likewise, the battle for freedom-loving Americans today is not merely to take power from the Left, Sowell says, but to instill a new sense of freedom and moral responsibility within the culture at large. He says further that one of the most illegitimate uses of power is the idea that professors "have some sort of expertise in matters outside their own specialties—knowledge of why we should or should not have ROTC on campus, why we should or should not allow the Judge Advocate General's office to recruit in the law schools, why the institution's endowment should be invested according to ideological rather than financial considerations." While academic tenure may qualify them to teach, it certainly does not confer wisdom to pronounce on any matter of public concern. Unfortunately, Sowell says, "academic freedom has become a license to turn courses into indoctrination and recruitment centers for all sorts of fashionable ideological crusades."[16]

FALLING STANDARDS

In a comprehensive review of the changing moral standards of the universities, Harvard education professor Julie Reuben writes that "universities no longer have a basis from which to judge moral claims." At one time traditional moral foundations and shared values provided a sense of unity within the academy, but that is no longer the case. Ruben says:

> The Protestant synthesis that provided moral guidance up until the late nineteenth century did not survive the adoption of modern standards of scholarship or increased cultural diversity. Despite the hopes of its early advocates, scientific inquiry never produced authoritative intellectual standards for determining what it means to live "properly" or how to identify what constitutes social "betterment." Without a means of adjudicating

moral claims, contemporary debates about what college students should learn seem to be reduced to "politics."[17]

Ironically, she adds, the separation of "knowledge" and "morality" in the universities began as an attempt to define "more reliable ways of knowing." In the nineteenth century, some educators decided that learning ought to begin from a neutral point upon which they could naturally agree—outside the realm of religion, of course—and perhaps lead to a consensus of views that were empirically grounded. Based on science, they thought, colleges could adopt a form of "free inquiry." But this approach at first ignored and then discarded any notion of a moral framework for education, thus doing away with a view of higher learning that had existed for centuries. "Although the ideals of freedom and agreement seemed compatible in technical and specialized scholarship," says Reuben, "free inquiry when applied to moral issues produced conflict." Out of this conflict, then, it was inevitable that educators would decide that moral concerns had no standing in the university.

From that point, the history of the disciplines has been a record of the eradication of moral and religious principle from the curriculum. This is doubtless the origin of the current emphasis on "moral relativism," which claims that all truths are equal and no view of truth is superior to another; it is also the root of "postmodernism" which holds that nothing can truly be known since we have no reliable standards for judging right and wrong, good and bad, or even superior and inferior performance. In an environment that shuns judgment and denies absolutes of every kind, the university's mission devolves from "the pursuit of truth" to an empirical examination of random occurrences and surmises about "preferred outcomes."

What we are seeing, as Russell Kirk argues in a 1992 lecture at the Heritage Foundation, is the *decay of the cult*—that is, the philosophical breakdown of *culture* which arises from shared beliefs and common values. Citing the words of Russian dissident and exile Aleksandr Solzhenitsyn, spoken during his acceptance speech for the Templeton Prize in 1983, Kirk says it was the religious beliefs of the Founders that gave birth to this nation. Shared values gave life in America a unity of purpose and a sense of the transcendent. That common heritage, however, is being eradicated today by the educators and intellectuals who have been entrusted with the task of preserving it. And in the place of morality and religious standards, the universities have substituted a doctrine of secular morality based on theories of victimization and social oppression.

In that address, Solzhenitsyn had warned that, "the ideology of secular humanism, the ideology of democratism, and the ideology of negritude that lies behind professed 'multiculturalism,' all are assaults upon a common way of life that has developed out of Christian insights—or, if you will, Judeo-Christian insights—into the human condition." He then cautioned that, "Ideology always is the enemy of religion, and endeavors to supplant its adversary among humankind. But ideology has been unable to produce a counterculture that endures long—witness the collapse of the Soviet Union after seven decades of power."

Responding to the writer's indictment, Kirk says nothing better explains the confusion and rancor in the Ivory Tower today than the deliberate dismantling of moral standards. At the beginning of his Templeton speech, Solzhenitsyn had said, "Over half a century ago, while I was still a child, I recall hearing a number of older people offer the following explanation for the great disasters that had befallen Russia: Men have forgotten God; that's why all this has happened." And Kirk answers: "They were right, and so are their counterparts in the United States today."[18]

To be sure, the university is not a seminary nor should it be, and the purpose of higher education is not to instruct students in religion. One of the most troubling breakdowns in higher education is the corruption of religious institutions founded by Catholics, Jews, and Protestant denominations as colleges dedicated to preserving the religious framework of learning. Most of these schools have long since renounced their core values and turned, instead, to shocking abuses of their founders' beliefs. But without, at the very least, a moral consensus in the universities that allows standards of "right and wrong" or "good and bad," and that equips students to distinguish between "worth and worthlessness," the faculty may as well spend their time counting the number of angels that can dance on the head of a pin.

Plato argued that the purpose of higher education is to teach men to recognize the ideal, and to enable them to distinguish between the common and the sublime. But that sort of wisdom demands moral judgment and standards of excellence that universities no longer allow. The logic on campus that says, "Everything is political, and nothing is religious," short-circuits informed judgment and compromises the very purpose of the academy. A first-class education cannot be attained in a moral vacuum. Authentic learning demands authentic standards, and it is precisely the battle over standards—framed in the academic's taunt, "Whose morals do you want to impose?"—that is now the fulcrum of controversy on the university campus.

10

The Grand Delusion

The history of all hitherto existing society is the history of class
struggle." With these words, Karl Marx and Friedrich Engels began
their short dissertation on the rise of the working class and the fall of capitalism, known as the *Communist Manifesto*. The revolutionary ideas contained in that seminal work set out the principles of "scientific socialism,"
pitting the workers of the world, the proletariat, against the middle class
professionals, merchants, and aristocrats identified by Marx as the bour-
geoisie. "All previous movements," Marx said, "were movements of minorities, or in the interest of minorities. The proletarian movement is the
self-conscious, independent movement of the immense majority, in the interest of the immense majority."

In the summer of 1848, when that tract first appeared in London, all of
Europe was in a welter of economic stagnation brought about by years of
crop failures and civil unrest. Riots that broke out in Paris in early February
led eventually to the ouster of King Louis Philippe and the establishment of
a national assembly. A series of bloody clashes was finally put down in June
by the military, and a republican government was organized with Louis
Napoleon (the nephew of Napoleon Bonaparte) as the new French president. During that year, revolts also erupted in Austria, Prussia, Italy, and
Hungary, but in each case the rebels were crushed. Thus, the Revolutions of
1848 came to an end, but that was not to be the end of the matter.

"In bourgeois society," Marx had said, "the past dominates the present;
in Communist society, the present dominates the past." History, he argued,

244

was only a record of the exploitation of the workers for the benefit of their masters, and the revolution would put an end to the past. A foreshadowing of what was actually to come in 1917, when the Bolsheviks came to power in Russia, was to be seen in Marx's declaration that the communist enterprise would be an endless crusade to transform society, first by abolishing private property, then by redefining the family and transferring authority for the education of children from the home to the state. All this, along with appropriate industrial reforms, would lead to a worker's paradise within the new classless, borderless society that would arise from the ashes of the old order. "The Communist revolution," Marx confessed, "is the most radical rupture with traditional property relations; no wonder that its development involves the most radical rupture with traditional ideas."[1]

CONFLICT AND CHANGE

While Europe struggled with all these things for the next seventy years, it was not until the thirties, in the wake of the Great Depression when millions of American workers lost their jobs, that the threat of communism became a reality on this side of the Atlantic. By 1933, one American worker in four was out of work. The collapse of the New York financial markets combined with agonizing droughts across the Great Plains led to the dislocation of thousands of families and an atmosphere of widespread anger and resentment. A soft Marxism, like that of John Steinbeck's *The Grapes of Wrath*, threatened greater chaos during much of that decade.

The New Deal programs of the Roosevelt administration forestalled most of the violence by providing jobs and subsistence for millions, but it wasn't until the outbreak of the war in Europe in 1939 that the Marxists' hopes of revolution in America were dashed. The ideals of the *Communist Manifesto* didn't disappear, however; they simply went underground where they would appeal especially to artists, writers, and intellectuals. Some of these people joined the movement, convinced that the bubble of capitalism would soon burst, as in 1929. Others were attracted by the mystique of revolutionary culture—the lure of dark secrets, clandestine meetings, hidden meanings, and subterfuge. Thus, many in the elite classes began to see the utopian society that Marx had promised as a reality yet to come, and they began to work toward that end.

But the fall of the Berlin Wall in November 1989 brought a new reality. The entire world watched as the Soviet empire collapsed under its own weight, done in finally by capitalism and President Reagan's threat of an unrelenting military build-up. The communist dream of world domination, it seemed, had at last disappeared. The subsequent fall of governments in Eastern Europe shocked many, and one by one the communist leaders of Poland, Hungary, Romania, East Germany, Czechoslovakia, and a dozen more, were deposed and the former command economies were transformed into market economies. Meanwhile, Russia, under Mikhail Gorbachev and then Boris Yeltsin, underwent unprecedented "restructuring" and "openness to the West." Those terms, popularized in the media as *Perestroika* and *Glasnost*, soon became not just bargaining chips of global diplomacy but the realities of everyday life in the East.

To be fair, these events involved a process of change that Marx had predicted, saying that when the process of dissolution begins, the real struggle will be a battle of ideas waged among the ranks of the intelligentsia. In the *Manifesto* he says:

> Finally, in times when the class struggle nears the decisive hour, the process of dissolution going on within the ruling class, in fact within the whole range of old society, assumes such a violent, glaring character, that a small section of the ruling class cuts itself adrift, and joins the revolutionary class, the class that holds the future in its hands. Just as, therefore, at an earlier period, a section of the nobility went over to the bourgeoisie, so now a portion of the bourgeoisie goes over to the proletariat, and in particular, a portion of the bourgeois ideologists, who have raised themselves to the level of comprehending theoretically the historical movement as a whole.[2]

Alas, this is where we find the universities today, populated to a surprising degree by a generation of bourgeois ideologists schooled in the faddish

Marxism of the sixties. These men and women, who cut themselves adrift from the common culture and traditional beliefs, have taken the reins of power in the schools and are now laboring to transform the basic structures of society from the bottom up. In this, I'm reminded of the often-quoted boast of Norman Thomas, a Princeton-educated Presbyterian minister and a founding member of the ACLU who was defeated six times in his bid for the White House on the Socialist Party ticket.

MOST PC DEPARTMENTS

Be especially wary of social sciences, humanities (esp. English, which has thrown out "Dead White European Males" and instated "relevant" unknowns); all studies from race/gender/sexuality perspectives, such as Modern Ethnic Studies, Black Studies, Chicano or Hispanic Studies, Women's Studies, Queer Studies. Don't pay for a student to major in these; they're mostly propaganda and ranting about "feelings" and mistreatment. Few jobs await these graduates.

In 1952, no doubt, his words provoked only laughter, but today they offer a more somber warning. Thomas had once said in a candid interview that, "The American people will never knowingly adopt socialism, but under the name of liberalism they will adopt every fragment of the socialist program until one day America will be a socialist nation without ever knowing how it happened." By 1970, both Thomas and Gus Hall, the perennial candidate of the Communist Party USA, gave up their quest for the presidency because, as they said, the two major parties had already adopted their platforms. But their legacy is with us still.

The socialism of the academy today bears the tell-tale markings of the type of society prescribed by Marx: it is a controlled economy, fueled by large outside interests, and devoted to a radical transformation of culture. For all

248 | FREEFALL OF THE AMERICAN UNIVERSITY

that, the university is a place of intrigue and innuendo. There are so many rumors, factions, and internecine power struggles on the typical campus that it makes the court of Napoleon III look like a tea party. In this environment, where the quest for truth has long since been superseded by the clash of competing theories, the practical concerns of students and the demands of learning are often lost in the shuffle.

Among the most eye-opening statements in Professor Harvey Mansfield's *Wall Street Journal* article about grade inflation is the observation that, "Our liberals own our universities. To be a conservative professor in America—and especially at the most prestigious universities—is a lonely life spent fighting down your indignation, perfecting your sarcasm, and whistling in the wind. Liberals are so much in charge that they hardly know it."[3] Liberal orthodoxy has subdued all contenders; political correctness, despite the intramural rivalries and general discord among departments and faculties, is the common currency on every American campus.

This is a fact that should be troubling for parents and alumni, but according to a recent national survey conducted by the Higher Education Research Institute at UCLA, the number of leftist faculty members on campus is still rising. Among the 55,521 faculty and administrators at 416 colleges and universities nationwide, researchers found that the number identifying themselves as either "liberal" or "far left" has grown from 42 to 48 percent in the past three years, while the number calling themselves "conservative" or "far right" remains a modest 18 percent. In the middle, unwilling to admit to either label, are the 34 percent who identified themselves as "middle-of-the-road" politically. In any case, the trend is clearly to the left, as it has been for decades, particularly among women faculty, where the number of "liberal" or "far left" professors has increased from 45 percent to 54 percent.[4]

The End of Truth

This steady drift to the left puts a majority of the faculty, especially in elite colleges and universities, solidly in the Marxist camp. But the real danger of the new "progressive" orthodoxy on campus is that leftist thought today holds no regard for truth. I hasten to say that this is neither a calumny nor a rhetorical flourish on my part but a simple statement of fact. Postmodernist theory which dominates the academy is founded on the idea that truth is relative and ultimately unknowable; and relativism in all its forms holds that, since all truths are equal and none is superior, "truth" is merely a political or preferential claim rather than a valid category of judgment. Further, the modern university's devotion to policies such as diversity, tolerance, and multiculturalism has transformed the whole basis of judgment into a near sacred rite. As Bradford Wilson has said:

> There is a deeper and far greater threat to freedom of speech, and even of thought, on the campuses. . . . It is an orthodoxy that, in the name of diversity and multiculturalism, has elevated sensitivity over the love of truth, political consensus over disinterested inquiry, and intolerance of disagreement and contempt for "Western civilization" over political and intellectual pluralism. To accuse someone of not favoring diversity, Allan Bloom once said, is "enough to send him scampering with his tail between his legs." To think aloud, in a critical spirit, about diversity is impiety. To do so privately is to commit a sin.[5]

When you examine the public record on organizations such as the Department of Education, American Association of University Professors, American Association of University Women, Modern Language Association, American Historical Association, American Psychological Association, and many others, along with the National Education Association and the unions and activist groups dealing primarily with primary and secondary education, you can't miss the uniformly liberal perspective that informs and animates everything they do. For these progressives the past means next to nothing: as Marx expressed it, the present dominates the past. The central idea for university elites is the idea of change—for the sake of change. And as Senator Hubert Humphrey once said, nothing better defines the liberal view today.

The most singular responsibility of government is "to preserve, protect and defend the Constitution of the United States of America," and to mobilize the assets and resources of the nation to safeguard the interests of the people. The most important role of any government is to defend its citizens against enemies "foreign and domestic." Yet, when it comes to protection from dangerous ideologies and the anti-American brainwashing that infects our institutions of higher learning, the government of the United States has failed. It is true that some individuals and agencies have spoken out—most notably the National Commission on Excellence in Education which in 1983, under the guidance of New York University's Dr. Paul Vitz, dared to point out the failures of public education. But, in general, our government agencies have joined sides with the academics and the professional associations to advance a liberal agenda. Not only have they failed to intervene in the debates that have allowed liberals to dominate the academy, but they are also complicit in the fraud that passes for education at all levels.

As serious as the corruptions described in these pages may be, it's important to recognize that none of this could have happened without the complicity and silence of the individuals, agencies, and special-interest groups that surround and influence the universities. There are many willing collaborators. Administrators, faculty members, and academic institutes are abetted in their work by government bureaucrats and their agencies, teachers' unions and guilds of various sorts, the mass media above all, and even by parents who either aren't paying attention or don't want to get involved in the battles raging in the schools. Without their silence and moral equivocation, the freefall of the American university could not have happened.

This is a point that emerged most clearly in my conversation with Dr. Dallas Willard, a professor of philosophy at the University of Southern California, and a distinguished author and lecturer in philosophy and ethics. "A few weeks ago," I said to him, "I met with a young man at Bowdoin College who told me that a couple of days after President Bush's speech to the nation following 9/11, the faculty called a forum to review the speech and talk about the issues it raised. What surprised him, he told me, was the fact that the faculty members were horrified by what Bush had said while the students generally agreed that it was a great patriotic speech."

"It's an example of what I call 'the politics of contempt,'" said Dr. Willard. "This is now the main form of political thinking by those on the left. I have to admit that conservatives are not entirely without blame on this point, but the liberals have refined it to an art form. It's accusation by innuendo, name-calling, and suggestion. If you look closely, you quickly discover that they don't have any arguments, and that's the center of the issue. What we have now on the faculties of most universities is people who are basically governed by the professional associations. Their most important contacts are not with students or even fellow faculty members, and certainly not with the administration, but with their professional associations."

"They've got to be published in the right journals if they expect to get tenure and be promoted," I said. "But does this mean that they care more about the colleagues they see maybe once or twice a year than they care about the ones they see everyday?"

"Absolutely," he said. "This is because the conditions of their success are tied to that. You see, the university no longer evaluates its faculty; it asks other people to evaluate them, and these other people are people who are considered to be the luminaries in their professions. Professionalism had not really taken hold in the American university system until the seventies. It hadn't taken hold in the sixties, partly because the number of people involved in higher education in the forties and fifties was still so small. It wasn't like it is now, but the GI Bill changed a lot of that. Things like avoiding the draft changed it, as well. One of the interesting things that happened in the sixties is that whole segments of the population that never would have thought about going to college before were suddenly coming in.

"When I started teaching at USC," he said, "the annual dinner for the American Psychological Association was about ten to fifteen people. They were the ones who were active. Now it's thousands of people, and they don't have the dinners anymore. When you go to the APA Convention in New York or Boston, you see these massive crowds. Faithfulness to things like truth and research and students and love for teaching is nowhere to be seen:

it's all about reputation and standing and how you're evaluated by your peers."

THE END OF TEACHING

I said, "It's shocking to realize that even senior professors no longer consider teaching to be their primary objective."

"Yes, I agree," he said. "But it's very interesting. The reward for faculty members who do good work is more research and less teaching. I once asked a group of senior administrators, 'If the reward for good research is more research, then why isn't the reward for good teaching more teaching?' They didn't really have an answer for that. It's not what most professors are interested in."

"Several of the students I've seen recently," I said, "told me that part of the problem is that they rarely if ever see an actual faculty member. They see them sometimes for the first lecture, but then it's teaching assistants and discussion-group leaders for most of the actual class sessions."

"Yes, and they're not the quality of TAs we used to have," he said, "precisely because they're not interested in the fundamental things: truth, honest research, and pouring their knowledge of the subject into their students."

"Professors have always chosen TAs because they see something in them," I said. "It used to be that professors would say, 'I see something in that person that can be developed, and I want to guide them along and help them to become serious scholars.' But that's changed. And I suspect that many on the left are saying, 'Aha! Here's someone who will buy everything I say!' So they set out to shape and mold that person into a perfect little clone."

"Yes, and that goes to the heart of the matter," said Dr. Willard. "No longer do you evaluate a person in terms of their arguments; rather, you evaluate their arguments in terms of their position. And if the position is wrong, if they're not in some role that automatically confers distinction, then you don't need to bother with them. So *ad hominem* attacks on people are now standard fare. They say, 'You hold certain views, therefore you're disqualified from serious consideration.'"

LEAST PC DEPARTMENTS

Government (in some cases), hard sciences (not environmentalism), Math, and Computer Sciences are more objective majors for undergrads. Classes to seek out: Any course by a truly excellent teacher. Liberal professors who allow a "balanced" view to be presented are fine. Look for tips on student Web sites or in books that rate professors. Follow them to any subject or department; you *will* learn.

"And that also means disqualifying outstanding people like Justices Scalia and Thomas, or even Chief Justice Rehnquist, because they hold generally conservative views. It's outrageous, but that's what's happening."

"Sociologically," he said, "this goes hand-in-hand with something that started in the 1880s but didn't really take hold until the 1940s, and that is divorcing the universities from their religious foundations. In 1848, as George Marsden reports, two-thirds of the presidents of the state colleges were clergymen. The nineteenth century still valued the importance of religious instruction, and that's why they chose people who were religiously trained to administer public education. But things began to change about that time and the primary battles were fought around people who were willing to put their minds away to protect their denominational distinctives.

"At the center of this," Dr. Willard said, "was what they called 'The Thirty-Nine Distinctives' of the Anglican church, and there were some horrendous battles during those years as more and more professors began to resist loyalty oaths of one sort or another. You had to swear fealty to those thirty-nine articles or you weren't allowed to teach. Sometimes it was subtle and sometimes it was brutal, but it was a bad policy, and something had to happen."

"So was this going on in Britain and the U.S. at the same time?" I asked.

"It was a different denominational setting at Harvard and Yale than they had in Great Britain," he said. "It was important for the universities to divorce themselves from the church, but it was *not* necessary for them to throw the teachings of the church away in the process. Some of the reformers wanted to find ways to maintain a theological position, but they never managed to do that, so there was a wave of defections followed by a wave of institutions arising to combat that. Some of the most aggressive ones were not founded so much as institutions of higher learning as they were institutions for people who wanted to remain Baptists or Methodists or Catholics, or whatever."

"Sounds like they wanted to create their own alternative world," I said.

"Yes, it was an alternative world," he said, "but now that wave of colleges is on their way out."

"Which is not a bad thing," I said, "so long as they have the capacity to maintain both intellectual rigor and spiritual discipline."

"They have to do that," he said, "but the question is, How to do it?, and that hasn't been solved yet in the university setting. James Davison Hunter's book, *Evangelicals in the Coming Generation*, really tells that story. But if a college president who is a Christian reads that book, what's he going to do? What's he going to do about the situation that Hunter describes, where you have a faculty that is mostly Christian while many of the students simply don't believe the things the school says they need to believe?"

"They don't adhere to the school's charter anymore?" I said.

"No, they don't," he said. "So you have those two things sociologically: the divorce of the universities from the church and the loss of spiritual discipline, or any religious principles."

NO PLACE FOR TRUTH

"America's founding documents held that religion and moral instruction were essential for the maintenance of good government," I said, "and this, they believed, was why schools were to be established in every community—

for the education and moral instruction of the children. But that idea is considered intellectual heresy these days."

He said, "It's also why the first spelling books and copy books, like the McGuffey's Readers, taught children how to read and write using Scripture verses for instruction and writing practice. They would say things like, 'Love your neighbor as yourself,' and students would practice their penmanship by writing that phrase over and over in the copy books."

"Now we find ourselves in the position of having the words, 'You shall know the truth, and the truth shall make you free,' carved over the gates of our great universities. At Harvard," I said, "they're on the walls of the Widener Library, but nobody knows where they come from."

"Those words of Jesus," said Dr. Willard, "tell us what the university is supposed to be about. It's the one statement, in fact, most often carved into the walls of universities around the world. But, as you say, few make the connection to the one who spoke those words.

"Sociologically, it was the divorce of the universities from the church," he said, "that led to the divorce of the intellectual enterprise from the church. I believe that was not necessary, but after the Civil War the country began to realize that the development of knowledge was an economic and political necessity. That's when the German model of the research university first appeared in this country. The British model, which was designed to teach truth and train character, was put aside. So today every college wants to be a university and every university wants to be a research institution. None of them wants to be a knowledge university any longer. The idea of teaching students specific information has become a laughable proposition."

"No one wants to train the next generation in the values of the current generation," I said, "which means that the fundamentals of Western civilization are scorned and virtually forbidden on most campuses. I spoke to Donald Kagan at length about the controversy at Yale over the proposal from Lee and Perry Bass to expand the history curriculum. The faculty simply wouldn't consider it, and the administration drug their heels so long the money went away. It was a total dismissal of the idea of Western civilization. The professors at Yale said, in effect, 'How outrageous of you to ask us to put twenty million dollars into a program that teaches the history of our culture!'"

"It didn't make sense to them," he said, "and that's the tragedy. That's because the only moral model left is the model of the 'rebel,' and the rebel's job is to attack hypocrisy."

"We tend to think so much has changed since the sixties," I said, "but in reality not much has really changed, because the only thing the Left had to offer when they took over at Berkeley and Columbia was invective, accusations, name-calling, and anger. They had nothing to go on but untested theories and empty rhetoric, and that's what we see from leftist faculty members in university lecture halls to this day."

"The Marxist idea was that rhetoric is everything, and everything is political," he said. "And, of course, people like Jacques Derrida and Richard Rorty are still saying that. Rorty famously defined truth as 'whatever your colleagues will let you get away with.' What they will let you get away with today depends on your rhetoric, and your rhetoric depends upon being an outsider or a rebel, and having that model. In the classrooms, people can morally pontificate *ad nauseum*, so long as it's against traditional values, because that means they're a rebel, they're authentic, and there's even the possibility they're persecuted for their 'courage.' So that's the standard, and then you get all the sub-rhetoric that comes out of the specializations. And that means you're really okay because someone else in your area of specialization says you're okay."

"If you pass muster at the APA," I said, "then, 'You're okay by me!'"

"Precisely," he said, "I think that's the sociology on the issue of change."

"How about students?" I said. "How have they changed since the sixties?"

"One of the wonderful things about our students," he said, "is that they're new, and they're still young. But they're tremendously gun-shy."

"The faculty member is like a super-parent," I said, "and if he or she doesn't like. . . ."

"Oh, no!" he said abruptly. "They don't admit that. It's the old *in loco parentis* principle. The model now is to deny *in loco parentis* while you practice it in the classroom. One of the things you have to understand about the present situation is that professors influence students' thinking by their body language, intonation, by the things they assign and the things they don't assign. They negotiate a position of objective distance but with authority over the moral context of the classroom. The university may have no use for religion anymore, but it teaches a morality that's more rigorous than any Puritanism you've ever seen! All you have to do is get cross-wise with it and you'll find out suddenly that you're a bad person!"

LOSING THE LOGIC

After a moment of reflection, I said, "I was very disturbed by my conversation with a student at UCLA who told me his professor asked for a show of hands to see which students had voted Republican in 2000. When this young man raised his hand, the professor basically called him an idiot, and said, 'How could you be so stupid?!' I asked the young man if he was the only person in the room who had voted Republican, and he said, 'No! I'm sure at least half of them did, but I was the only one with the guts to raise my hand.'"

"That's exactly what happens," said Dr. Willard, "and that's what I mean by their being gun-shy. If any student attempts to take a position that is not anointed by the faculty, they're shot down immediately, and in such a way that they're much less inclined to try it again next time. I was talking with a young woman a couple of days ago who said a professor asked if anyone in the class believed in Satan. As a Christian, she of course did, so she put her hand up, and she was the only one who did. Now, I know this person and she's one of the brightest students at USC and the professor knew that, too. And he just about blew a fuse, and he started taking her apart bit by bit, and he wouldn't let up. After class a large number of students came up to her and said, 'We're so ashamed that we didn't stand up with you, but we knew what he was going to say and we just didn't want to be attacked.'

"You see," he added, "the students discover very quickly that the system isn't fair, and I think this is where students have to start suing professors. Your young man should sue that professor for abuse."

"I'm generally against grievance litigation," I said, "but I think you may be right about that. If no one stands up and says, 'You can't do that to your students!' then it will never stop. And what makes me angry is that the students are paying the salaries of the people who are doing that, which means they're paying to be abused!"

"The ironic thing," he said, "is that alumni and the public generally cannot believe that this is happening. They would never believe what's actually being done in the classrooms at these large universities. But it's not just that students are called idiots. It's worse than that. Students are made to *feel* like idiots. Professors tell them that certain kinds of people are idiots, and if they just happen to be that kind of person, then they know where they fit in. So they learn to keep a low profile."

"The sad thing," I said, "is that those who are not critical thinkers are made to believe that the leftist notions being peddled by their professors are actually mainstream, so therefore if they want to fit in then they'd better believe that, too."

"There are courses on all these campuses called 'critical thinking,' run by the government," he said. "They aren't critical thinking in any sort of logical or philosophical sense; it means criticizing all these people with whom you happen to disagree. You're not learning to think, you're learning 'group-think,' and it's a fraud. It's so ironic, because most of these people don't know the first thing about critical thinking and wouldn't recognize it if it ran over them in the middle of the street. The teaching of simple logic has disappeared."

"A professor at another university," I said, "told me he'd once asked the chairman of the art department why they no longer offered a basic survey in Art Appreciation. And the response, which shocked me, was 'Who would teach it?' More than likely it would have to be a junior professor, and he wouldn't be qualified. Furthermore, professors today are so specialized in these tiny, esoteric subjects that they don't have any sort of comprehensive knowledge of their own discipline. I think it would be shocking to most parents to learn that nobody on campus is qualified to teach the history of their discipline. That's shocking!"

"Unfortunately, that's true in every field," Willard said. "The one thing you do not learn in your field is the history of it. And one reason is because it would be embarrassing, because regardless what your field may be, what you would inevitably find is the deeply Christian roots of that discipline."

"Particularly the sciences," I said.

"And also the social sciences," he added, "which were basically founded in France by Christians—Claude Saint-Simon and others; Auguste Comte eventually took it over and made it atheistic, because he was looking for the "religion of humanity"—but no one knows this because the history of the disciplines has largely disappeared. I would have to say this is less true in philosophy than most other majors, due to the historical and empirical nature of the subject matter, but it's still true.

"The other thing is that logic has disappeared, as well," he said. "There are reasons for this, of course. But think about the implications of that. Once history and logic are jettisoned, what guidelines do you follow? What goes into the curriculum? Political interest groups and career advancement are practically the only guides we have left for deciding what goes into the university catalog."

A WAKE-UP CALL

"If you pause to think about how the curriculum has been altered to favor certain politically correct perspectives and ideologies," I said, "you see why this would have to happen. Logic is like a fact of nature: logic gives you rules by which you can judge the truth or falsehood of any statement. If the faculty are afraid that what they want to teach can't pass the test of truth, then the last thing they want is students who are trained in logic and have the ability to challenge them."

"That's exactly right," he said. "I'm sure there are sessions at the Modern Language Association, the American Psychological Association, and the Comparative Literature Association, or whatever it's called, where logic is attacked as a Eurocentric male conspiracy, and people like Derrida and the deconstructionists are behind it. Logic, they say, is oppressive, and prevents them from extrapolating beyond the range of the known. You don't want to be restrained by something like logic, for God's sake!"

"Destroy truth and you can do whatever you like," I said. "If God is dead, as Dostoevsky, Sartre, and others expressed it, everything is permitted. And basically that seems to be the point. If they can get rid of the natural laws, and especially the theology that restrains them, then they can do whatever they like with impunity."

"That was extended by Nietzsche and others to truth," Dr. Willard said, "because they came to see that it wasn't enough just to get rid of God; they had to get rid of truth, too. And you have to think of reasoning only as rationalization. A lot of this stuff comes to a head in the nineteenth century. Nietzsche, especially in the literature department, is often regarded as 'The' great man on campus; I don't think he wrote a thing that could pass as a Ph.D. dissertation in any philosophy department, but he is lionized by the academic elite.

"It's pathetic, the kind of so-called reasoning that goes on in many departments," he added. "It's basically in the form of telling stories, or meta-narratives as they're called. Nietzsche tells little stories about how the slave morality of the Jews and Jesus triumphs over the noble morality of the people—there's not a shred of historical reality to it, but it appeals to a certain kind of audience. He tells a story he's invented out of whole cloth and people who want to believe that Christian morality is nothing they need to deal with will accept that story, and so much of the fascination with 'deep interpretation' and postmodernist theorizing turns out to be story-telling."

"What frightens me," I said, "is not so much the story, because ultimately lies will be shown up as lies. Unless, of course, you have de-educated the receiver of those lies to the point that they can't question what they're told. It seems like that's where the public schools have been complicit in this whole ordeal. It almost had to start there so it could eventually work its way up through the universities. The point was to build a cadre of ignorant people who then end up teaching illiterates who have no knowledge of the facts. I believe that's the only way they could sell some of these ideas; and what does frighten me is that they have done this over the past thirty years, so that today, from kindergarten through graduate school, the sources of truth have been turned upside down. Entire generations of young people don't know the essential facts of our history or culture."

"And they think they're educated because they've gone to school," he said.

"The only thing worse," I said, "is that a great many of them don't even care. What troubled me most when I was teaching was not so much that students didn't know much about the subjects they were studying but that they didn't much care, and didn't really want to know. We've always had people like that, but they never made it into the universities. Now suddenly we have students with no real interest in learning—let alone of doing responsible research of their own—ending up with teaching diplomas, masters degrees, and even Ph.D.s, who don't have the basic educational attainment or study skills, and they end up being hired to teach our children."

"We had one guy a few years back who couldn't read and he received his bachelor's degree," Dr. Willard said. "He even started teaching. He had never been in a course where he had to read; all he had to do was listen and take multiple-choice exams, and fill in the blanks. He was smart enough to find ways to do that. He eventually wrote a book about his experience and how he pulled it off. He said he found ways to get other people to do things for him that he couldn't do. And he learned how to listen.

"When I saw that," he added, "it made me think of the famous experiments with 'Hans the Intelligent Horse,' who was supposed to be able to count. They would say, 'How many apples are on the table?' and Hans would paw the dirt three times, and it was astonishing, but they discovered that when Hans couldn't see his trainer, he couldn't count. He was getting his clues from the trainer's body language, and I suspect a lot of that goes on at the highest levels, reading body language. Students are experts at it. When they come into the classroom, they watch for clues to find out what sort of person this teacher is going to be, whether he's smart or mean or a push-over or whatever, and they're looking for clues on how they can get the grades they want with the least amount of effort."

"It makes you wonder if they want an education or just a diploma," I said.

Dr. Willard smiled and said, "I often ask my students when I take up their tests, 'Did you believe what you wrote?' They always laugh because they know you don't have to believe it: you just have to know the answers. So they have developed a form of life that totally insulates them from this system that they're stuck in."

"In a column earlier this year," I said, "George Will offered the sad truism that the main preoccupations of university administrators today are parking for faculty, football for alumni, and sex for students. That's outrageous but, sadly, I suspect it's probably true."

"It's an exaggeration, of course, but like most humor it contains a grain of truth," he said.

"In a couple of my interviews with students," I said, "I heard of parents who grew up in the sixties and they were really upset when their kids became conservatives. They said, 'College is for experimentation, for sex and parties, and trying stuff you've never done before!' The freefall of morality is of no concern to them, even though it can have devastating consequences, both physically and emotionally. But kids in that situation are getting it from both sides; not only are they getting it from the faculty who are pushing them to try it all, but parents are pushing them as well. My long-term hope is that I can wake up some of these people to what they're doing to their children."

THE FAILURE OF ATHEISM

"Obviously, a lot of parents don't have any idea what's really happening on campus," he said. "But now that you've been all around the country doing these interviews, do you get the feeling that the academy is in denial about what's happening?"

"As a matter of fact," I said, "Arnold Beichman at the Hoover Institution suggested I read the new book by Haynes and Klehr called *In Denial: Historians, Communism & Espionage*, so I've been taking it with me to read on the plane. Essentially it says that professional historians in this country have defended the whole sordid history of socialism and communism, and they're in denial about the tragic consequences of that belief system through-out its entire history. Because they refuse to admit the dark secrets of the death camps, of mind-control, and the other horrors of socialist indoctrina-tion, the Left in this country has been pushing socialism down our throats so successfully that it's now the dominant view—not just in the history departments but in the university as a whole. Liberals on the campuses refuse to see that the values of Western capitalist societies are just the oppo-site of that. Wherever you look, you find that benevolent free-market economies have lifted people out of darkness and put them in charge of their own lives. But the academy refuses to see any of that. Instead, they just look the other way, and continue defending the evils of Marxism and socialism."

SO MUCH FOR TOLERANCE
"We cannot tolerate the intolerable!"
—College administrator, when a student was
"offended" by a Christian magazine found
in a DePauw University classroom

"I believe there's an element of truth to that," Dr. Willard responded, "but I think you need to be sure and do justice to the good will of many of these people. I think where many of the books on the problems with the modern university go wrong is that they come across as attacking the intentions of these people. What one has to do, I believe, is to recognize that there's a problem; an ego investment often leads people to falsify facts in order to make things come out at the right place. It's the same way with the media, when you look at the liberal bias of the media. For the most part, they're very liberal, but frankly, they're also uncomprehending of what people are talking about when they accuse them of liberal bias. They don't intend to be biased, so they protest their innocence. But if you don't want to be biased, you have to take an active stand against it. I wish I could teach logic more often, but when I do teach it, I tell the students that being logical is a moral commitment. You have to take this as something you do to be a good person, and if you don't do that, you'll be overrun."

"That's another reason why logic is foundational to any course of study," I said.

"Another thing is that a lot of people within the professoriate don't really understand the positions that are dominating the academy," he said. "That's less true in the sciences, but it's overwhelmingly true in the humanities. They're dominated by glittering personalities and phraseology and they go to professional meetings and warm themselves in that glow for a while, but they don't understand the issues or the arguments. There are exceptions, of course, but if you take the ordinary person on a faculty in a good university and ask them to explain a position that is behind some popular position, they will generally not be able to do it."

"Especially in political science," I said. "If you look back into the history of the profession, you eventually come to people like John Locke and John Stuart Mill, and the ideologues on the faculty can't deal with that because they've long since turned all that stuff into invective. They have a certain number of catch phrases to say about Locke or Mill or Hume or de Tocqueville, but their knowledge level is not much deeper than that."

"To make a serious debate," he said, "they would need to spend a year studying Locke, but they haven't done that. They get their Ph.D.s now by learning to play ping-pong in the academic journals. You can earn a Ph.D. if you start doing something that might function in that field, but you don't have to know the history of your subject."

"That sort of mentality has happened to a lot of intellectual endeavors," I said, "not just political science, but the humanities, history, and much more."

"That's right," he said. "Too often these days research just means coming up with weird stuff."

"So someone like Peter Singer gets a richly endowed chair at Princeton for coming up with the idea that mothers can murder their babies up to the age of three," I said.

"That's exactly right," he said. "The underlying premise of the modern academic enterprise is that something has been found out. Someone somewhere has found out that there is no God, that the Bible is a made up bunch of fiction, that no one really knows anything about truth, and this just infects the whole system. It turns the intellectual world into a rumor mill and the center of that is the university, which is now the dominant authority in our culture."

"And if it's not checked somehow," I said, "it can destroy the entire culture."

"It will do it," he said, "if nothing else, just by negligence of teaching what is fundamental for human life."

"So was Nietzsche right?" I asked. "Has the university succeeded in killing God?"

"Yes, Nietzsche was right," he said. "He was right in saying that this world cannot remain the same if you accept the idea that God is dead. There isn't a single field of knowledge, including divinity—or 'religious studies' as it's sometimes called—where belief in the reality of God is a part of the essential knowledge. No one proved that, of course; it was decided through a process. It was not true, but there is this idea that someone somewhere found out that all that Christian stuff was wrong. So now the university has become a rumor mill.

"There's a fascinating book," he continued, "by A.N. Wilson called *God's Funeral* which shows you all the absurd arguments that convinced people that God was irrelevant. On the other side is a book by Owen Flanagan called *The Problem of the Soul*, which is merely the most recent stroke in the battle. Basically it's an attempt to establish decency on the basis of pure secularism, and the problem is what to do once the notion of the soul is gone. But the idea is pervasive that someone found out that all our ideas about God and the Bible are wrong. No one did, but it was decided so that the university could get on with its research without having to worry about God. Once that was decided, then the university—and the popular media who live a symbiotic life with the university—can function as a rumor mill to spread this new secular gospel."

"I cut my teeth as a young reader," I said, "on the great Russian novels, like *Fathers and Sons* by Turgenev and of course Dostoevsky's *Crime and Punishment*, in which the pre-Marxist brew of the late 1800s was already visible—you could see that a revolution was coming. The Bazarovs and Raskolnikovs of the world, who were a foreshadowing of Lenin and Engels and so many others, were all beating their chests saying, 'I'm a free man! I can do whatever I wish!' But you know, at the end of all those novels the rebels were always proved wrong. And they always had terrible lives and horrible deaths."

"The reason," said Dr. Willard, "is because all of those novels had a moral vision of human goodness, and they recognized when it was betrayed. Dostoevsky, Turgenev, Tolstoy, and others like that, including Aleksandr Solzhenitsyn in our own time, understood that if you betray that basic moral reality then you'll have hell to pay. Even if they didn't see it work out in their own society, they knew it to be true, and that's why those novels have such a ring of truth to them today, and why our students need to be reading them over and over again."

"Then, and I suspect even now," I said, "those who say 'There is no God!' really believe that there probably is a God. It's undeniable that there's something going on in our midst that's bigger than we are."

"Absolutely," he said. "Atheism is highly overrated!"

RENEGADE LIBERALISM

One of the greatest ironies of the transformation of the American university from a center of higher learning to a center for leftist indoctrination is that it has been done under the banner of "liberalism." The common view of liberalism—its lexical definition, at least—is a view of society based on faith in the innate goodness of man and the right of individual autonomy. Classical liberalism is in favor of civil and political liberty, and a system of laws that protects each individual from the imposition of arbitrary authority. At the same time, the classical liberal favored limited government and greater freedom of expression for the individual, whereas today liberalism looks to government for its power and its funding, and to regulatory power for the right to punish any form of expression that cannot be controlled by social restraint.

As Robert Conquest has said, liberals say they believe in social justice and freedom of thought; yet, the intellectuals who prosper within our universities rely upon dogmatism, social oppression, and Marxist-style thought-control to maintain their power base. This is a puzzle.[6]

It was this paradox, in fact, that attracted the interest of George Orwell, who struggled to understand the strange schizophrenia that allowed intellectuals who passionately defend freedom and equality to suddenly turn a blind eye to the brutal repression and dishonesty of Stalinism in the thirties—and, we might add, to the charlatanism of Ivory Tower Marxism today. Reacting to much the same paradox, Thomas Sowell has said that, "the grand delusion of contemporary liberals is that they have both the right and the ability to move their fellow creatures around like blocks of wood—and that the end results will be no different than if people had voluntarily chosen the same actions."[7]

The climate on the campus has been so utterly compromised by socialist thought and duplicity that university faculties and administrators willingly allow conservative opinion to be silenced. This is clearly how student publications critical of liberal bias on campus can be confiscated by outraged minorities and burned without repercussions; how faculty committees are allowed to recruit and hire only other liberals who share the dominant ideological view; how Shakespeare and Twain and Keats have been stripped from the canon and little-known (and much less-talented) radicals suddenly infused. The liberal academic has bought into the rage of the Marxist and now turns that rage against the culture that enables his right of dissent.

In testimony before a Senate committee on Health, Education, Labor, and Pensions in October 2003, looking into the lack of intellectual diversity on the university campus, Anne Neal, who is president of the American Council of Trustees and Alumni, addressed the atmosphere of intellectual intolerance on campus. In particular she spoke about the problems of dis-inviting controversial speakers, the punishment of faculty members who fail to conform to the dominant ideology, and the predominance of one-sided courses and opinions among the faculty. Students on the typical university campus live in daily fear of reprisal or caricature if they speak their minds, and they are routinely victimized by draconian speech codes and ideological litmus tests that place unfair restraints on their constitutional guarantee of free speech.

Neal's recommendations to the committee focused primarily on the responsibility of trustees and alumni to influence change, and then on the role of government to provide suitable oversight. Trustees, she said, need to adopt resolutions that faculty members are expected to present a balanced view of topics where the issues are debated, allowing viewpoints other than their own to be explored. They should stress, further, that the focus of higher education is intellectual development and the acquisition of actual knowledge and professional skills, and not merely the manipulation of attitudes or the promotion of social and political activism.

Trustees, who are charged with overseeing the mission of these institutions, ought to insist that departments offer survey courses designed to expose students to the best that has been done and said in the field. They also need to ensure that students have a sense of the history of their discipline and not merely exposure to the latest fads. In addition, trustees and administrators should insist that speakers invited by the university or by recognized student groups represent a wide range of views. Ideological and political discrimination should not be allowed, either in the classroom or in the hiring, firing, and promotion of faculty.

Congress, said Dr. Neal, should endeavor to raise public awareness of these problems, and encourage faculty, administrators, and boards of trustees to conduct reviews from time to time to ensure that academic freedom is respected on campus and to make sure that students, parents, and the taxpayers are actually getting what they're paying for. Congress can also target grants to promote the study and teaching of American history, politics, and law, and thus ensure that our great heritage is not forgotten or submerged under the rhetoric of the trendy specializations that now dominate the academy.

While serving as president of Yale University, Benno Schmidt warned that, "The most serious problems of freedom of expression in our society today exist on our campuses. . . . The assumption," he said, "seems to be that the purpose of education is to induce correct opinion rather than to search for wisdom and to liberate the mind."[8] Sadly, little has changed since he spoke those words in 1991. Renegade liberals are in charge, and students' prospects for receiving a liberal education have never been worse. Unless we decide at long last to heed these words of warning, we will have lost the battle for freedom in America and Karl Marx will have won.

11

A Mandate for Change

What is truth? Who's to say what's right and wrong? Whose morality are we going to follow, professor? For thousands of academics and a growing number of students at the nation's most hallowed institutions, there is now no truth and no reliable standard of authority. Who's to say what's true or good anymore? Everyone's entitled to his own view: that's what they say. John Stuart Mill argued in his 1859 essay, *On Liberty*, that the most moral act is that which offers the greatest good for the greatest number; but for today's educators, even that formulation is unacceptable. Who's to judge, after all? Who gets to decide the values we live by?

A familiar story is told of Dr. Frank Rhodes, then president of Cornell University, who participated in a 1987 conference on the future of the university. At one point, Rhodes stood and urged his fellow conferees to begin paying more attention to the moral well-being of their students. But before he could even finish his remarks, a member of the audience leaped to his feet, shouting, "Whose morality are we going to follow, professor?"

Clearly there was a perfectly good answer that Rhodes could have given: the Judeo-Christian standard built into America's founding documents has allowed this nation to steer a true course through civil war, national tragedy, and domestic emergencies of every kind for more than three centuries. Surely that would do very well, particularly since this also happens to be the moral standard upon which our laws were founded, and some 84 percent of the American people have said in Gallup polls for at least four decades that they choose to live by. But, alas, Dr. Rhodes could not answer the question.

Confused and affronted by his interrogator, the scholar returned to his seat in silence.

As disturbing as this sort of moral surrender may be for most of us, liberal academics hold precisely the opposite view. Most of these elites would be horrified to think that any sane person would dare to prescribe any set of moral and ethical values for a nation. When the inflammatory comments of Professor de Genova at Columbia and others who defended the actions of the 9/11 terrorists were made public by the American Council of Trustees and Alumni—along with anti-American tirades of 116 other faculty members—suddenly leftist weblogs and listserves on the Internet were ablaze with the venom of professors accusing ACTA of "patriotic correctness," "right-wing bigotry," and "stifling of academic thought." And this is precisely the problem: the entire moral worldview of the academic Left is upside down.

As a former operative of the National Organization for Women, and president of its Los Angeles chapter, author Tammy Bruce has seen through the "looking glass world" of Left activism and witnessed the culture of moral deregulation first-hand. Everything is backward in that world, she says. Left is right, up is down, and black is white. That's why speech codes, sensitivity sessions, group-think, and indoctrination are necessary: the beliefs that most liberals cling to are so illogical and corrupt they simply cannot compete in the marketplace of ideas.

As a child of the sixties, Tammy Bruce accepted those values wholeheartedly until, who knows how, she emerged one day to see the destruction that brand of liberalism had unleashed on America. Her conclusions, contained in the book *The Death of Right and Wrong: Exposing the Left's Assault on Our Culture and Values* are disturbing and painfully direct, but they leave nothing to guesswork. "The Left Elite," writes Bruce, "has worked for years to brainwash us into a sort of values lobotomy." By turning traditional morality on its head, the Left has succeeded in changing the entire context of the debate. She writes:

> One now-accomplished goal is the brainwashing of society into believing that because of the color of their skin, or their gender, or their sexual

preference, some in our "multicultural society" can never be understood by others, making judgment and punishment inappropriate. The corollaries are that traditional concepts of personal responsibility are outdated, and that expecting others to behave with dignity, and expecting society to recognize the concepts of right and wrong, is contrary to the ideal of liberty. Every idea, every act, has the same value—none is more worthy than another. Of course, this effort has to start with convincing you that the standards by which you were raised were wrong. Your ideas about religion, family, and sex are wrong, perhaps even harmful.[1]

The logic on today's campus is that only the socially and politically informed—the anointed *cognoscenti*—have the right to decide "the greatest good" in the realm of academia. It's a philosophy that's incompatible with any previous vision of American society. It favors group rights over individualism, and the authority of the enlightened over the will of the people. PC logic makes no place for historical standards of right and wrong. It's inimical to the rule of law, and stands in defiance of all our traditions of common decency. Despite growing resistance from all sides, the PC university continues to practice a type of Gnosticism in modern dress—divining secret wisdom by cryptic revelation. This is the worldview of the elites who've been chosen to teach our children. But now it's time we ask: what are the prospects for change?

CULTURAL ILLITERACY

In my conversation with Donald Kagan at Yale, I mentioned that a couple of the faculty members I'd spoken to on Ivy League campuses had told me that they were not bothered by the liberal climate, and they thought that things would have to change very soon because, basically, it can't get any worse. Dr. Kagan shook his head and smiled. "No, that's wrong," he said. "I can easily imagine how it could get worse. But the truth of the matter is, however much worse it gets will not be very significant, which tells us that we're pretty close to bottom now from the standpoint of any measure that we care about."

"Something that concerns me," I said, "is, *Who's going to teach the next generation?* I was an undergraduate in the sixties, and that was the last generation to be taught the great canon of Western literature and culture. The generation after us is less educated in matters dealing with the foundations of civilization and culture, and each subsequent generation knows even less. So who's going to teach the ones who come after us?"

"There's not going to be anyone left who remembers when it was anything else," he said.

"You've written about the fall of Rome," I said, "and how those who should have been the leaders of the empire didn't want to do it. For one thing, they didn't have the knowledge to do it, and they had become dissipated. But I wonder if we're not in the same situation today. Classical education—or 'cultural literacy' as E.D. Hirsch expressed it—helped make this a great society, but it's not the same anymore. The great tradition is not being taught."

"That's a real problem," he said. "But there's so much going for us. Intellectually, morally, ethically, we have been in decay for a long time. But our economic prosperity is so enormous, I don't see anything likely to interrupt that for the foreseeable future. There's never been such a gap between one nation and the other nations. It would take some years for the breakdown to do sufficient damage to the culture to utterly destroy it, but if nothing happens to reverse the trend, then, of course, we could go the way of Rome. Nothing is forever."

I asked him, "Do you think any of your students understand what's really happening? Do they have any idea where we stand as a culture?"

He said, "It's fascinating to be a dinosaur like me. My lecture classes normally have about a hundred and fifty kids, and I think the young people in those classes know there's something they're missing. Some of them come up to see me after class and they say they want to be like me. They know there's this package of something that they're not getting, and they want to know what it is. I think that's a good sign."

Later that afternoon, Connee and I stopped for a cup of coffee with a bright young woman who was part of the Directed Studies program at Yale.

She's one of the students Donald Kagan had told me about who realizes that there's something more to be discovered, and that the university isn't providing it. "I think I had a pretty good idea what to expect when I came here," Catherine told us, "so the liberal bias on campus wasn't really the issue for me. But what bothered me the most was the complacency and passivity of most of the students, and the timidity of conservative students to speak up."

"I suspect they know there are penalties for speaking up," I said.

"Yes, but if we can break through that barrier," she said, "so that students on campus understand that 'conservative' isn't a dirty word, and 'Republican' isn't a dirty word, then I think things will begin to change. Dr. David Gelernter is a well known computer-science professor here at Yale, and he has said pretty much the same thing. Actually, I would have expected the most depressing view to come from someone like him—he's been fighting the liberal bias for so long—but he said he's actually very optimistic, and he thinks it can still turn around if enough students will start standing up for what they believe in."

"There are always a few fair-minded liberals on any campus," I said, "but there's an important caveat: often these liberal professors only teach the side of the issues they want you to hear. Most students don't have a broad enough knowledge to ask for the other side and they tend to believe they're getting the whole story. In fact, they're only getting the information the professor and his liberal textbooks and discussion materials provide.

"It's the rare professor," I said, "who will say, 'Okay, there's a difference of opinion on this issue, and here's what the other side has to say.' Even if you believe that Yale has a pretty good record on this, there are a lot of smaller schools, state universities and two-year colleges, where there's an overt totalitarian mindset among the faculty, and that means that the vast majority of college students in this country are only getting one side of the issues—and it's a side that's most likely slanted to the left."

"I think it's possible to get a decent education," Catherine said, "if you take the time to study the catalog, talk to people who've taken the classes, and especially if you get to know your professors. What's neat about Yale is that we have a shopping period: we have at least two weeks to visit lots of different classes and check it out, to see what's being taught and what the atmosphere is like in the class. So I'd say, tell incoming students to shop everything! Go to the classes, even if you know you're not going to take them, and see what's there. You don't have to register for a class if the professor's on a soapbox. In fact, I shopped one class this year that looked good on paper, but it was taught by two women who were bitter and angry, and I felt suffocated by the atmosphere in the room, so I just got up and left. They didn't know me, I didn't know them, so I just went somewhere else and found a class I liked a lot better."

"Are you aware of many other students who feel the way you do?" I asked.

"Well, there are a lot more liberals," she said, "but I think 9/11 was really important, because it allowed conservative students to see what it's really all about. I think it made a lot of us more outspoken. As far as conservative faculty here at Yale, even though they're much fewer in number, they're giants in their field and they're highly respected by the students. People like Donald Kagan, of course, and Stephen Smith, Charles Hill, Norma Thompson, and several others. These are names people know, and they're the best things we've got going."

"Yes, and you could use a lot more of them," I said, "but in the current environment that's not likely to happen. But tell me what the other students think about all this. How do they keep from getting sucked in by the Left?"

"Talk radio has played a really big part in my becoming more active as a conservative," she said, "and a lot of students are listening to that, visiting conservative sites on the Internet, and subscribing to magazines like *National Review* and the *Weekly Standard*, reading *FrontPage* magazine online, and things like that where they get a more honest point of view. Jonah Goldberg is great! And all those things are making a difference."

"Somehow I hadn't pictured a bunch of Yalies sitting around listening to talk radio," I said with a laugh. "How does that work?"

"I mean, why not?" Catherine said with a laugh. "Here are all these talking heads who are hilarious, irreverent, and personable, and it's a source of substantive arguments about the things we hear about on campus every day.

You hear what these guys have to say, and then with the callers you get to hear both sides. Not only that, but now we have people like Michael Medved, who is really excellent, and I understand he was a leader of the SDS at Yale back in the sixties, and a big liberal activist. He's obviously changed a lot, but listening to him argue with liberals on the radio empowers me to do the same thing."

"That's right!" I said. "If you've got a brain, you can do that. If you don't, and all you have is feelings and emotions, then you can be a liberal!"

CLASS WARFARE

One of the most outrageous accounts I heard during my conversations with students was from Lenny Edwards, a graduate of the University of Akron with degrees in political science and international relations. When I asked him what was happening on that very liberal campus in the wake of 9/11, he told me about a clash of worldviews that made his life a misery for years.

"Professor Rula Abisaab is originally from Syria," Lenny told me, "and she teaches in the history department at the University of Akron. The first time I took a class from her was in 1998, supposedly a class on medieval Islam—at least that's what the catalog said. But almost immediately the class steered away from what was presented in the syllabus and became a long-winded attack on America and the West. It went on like that for weeks—an all-out attack on Western culture and civilization. I eventually got so sick of it I asked her, 'Excuse me, but what does this have to do with the course we signed up for? This is all your personal opinion, when it's supposed to be a history course where we focus on facts.'"

"Good for you!" I said. "But what was the reaction?"

"Well, she didn't like that a bit," he said. "She didn't appreciate the fact that I dared to say the obvious, so for the rest of the semester she was on my case, and she took it out on me in my grades. Now, I was a serious student with a 3.9 GPA, so I was accustomed to doing very good work. But in that class, which was at the tail end of my undergraduate program in classics, she gave me a D+ in the course."

NEW CONSERVATISM ON CAMPUS

A recent survey conducted by the Higher Education Research Institute at UCLA shows that even at the most liberal universities, a surprising number of students are becoming more conservative: a slight majority leaning Republican, in huge contrast to the "old days" and the predominant liberal views of their professors.

"That's what I call the tyranny of the gradebook," I said, "and that's what these people will do. If you dare to ask, 'Why don't you get back to the subject?' they use the gradebook to intimidate you, or to hurt you, as this woman did."

"That's exactly what happened," Lenny said. "After I graduated, I didn't see her again until about two weeks after September 11. It was my first semester of grad school in political science and there was a public forum on the attacks and the War on Terror. She was giving a presentation and, for at least an hour and a half, she just railed against Israel and America and everything Western you can think of. She said it's America's fault that 9/11 happened. She felt no sorrow for the people killed in the World Trade Center. It was utterly sickening to hear her giving her diatribe, so about halfway through the program I just got up and left. She had no sympathy, no remorse, no regrets about any of it."

"Was anybody buying it?" I asked.

"You could tell that some students were taken aback by what she was saying," he said, "but she was very slick about it and she shifted the conversation to the 'Palestinian struggle' and why they should be called 'freedom fighters' and not terrorists. It was the typical leftist drill."

"So what happened after that?" I said. "Did you ever run into her again?"

"The next time I saw her was at a forum on the war in Iraq, in which I was one of the speakers," he said. "A friend of mine and I spoke on behalf of the College Republicans, and on the other side were the College Democrats. There were some points of disagreement between the two sides, but basically we all agreed that Saddam Hussein had to be removed from power. But then, at one point, Mrs. Abisaab marched into the room with her husband, who is also Syrian, and they started passing out flyers about how many people America had killed in Third World countries, and things of that sort. Frankly, I was shocked: why would they pass out something like that at a public forum? We were having a sensible discussion where people could get together and voice their opinions."

"Obviously, she had an agenda," I said, "and she wasn't interested in a polite discussion."

"But that wasn't all," Lenny said. "At the end of our presentations, there was an open microphone and Rula Abisaab was the first in line, and she assaulted me like you wouldn't believe. It got to the point where it became a personal attack on me. She singled me out by name and lambasted me for my position. I had said that Saddam Hussein had twelve years to prove that he wasn't a tyrant, and to prove to the UN Security Council that he had disposed of his weapons of mass destruction. Failing that, he needed to be removed from power. Those were the terms of the UN resolution; so it wasn't about preemption.

"But she didn't like that," he said, "and for the next half hour she went on a vicious tirade. I didn't know it at the time, but she and her husband, along with some other faculty members who agreed with them, had planted people all over the audience, so when anyone spoke out on our side of the issue, the goons would shout them down. It was outrageous."

"Did any of this make it into the newspapers?" I asked.

Lenny laughed. "No," he said, "the problem is that the Akron *Beacon-Journal* is very liberal and the university newspaper is worse. The opinion columnist for the student newspaper, in fact, worked for the *Beacon-Journal*, so unless a story had a liberal payback it wasn't going to be reported by either paper. Earlier, when I wrote an article for the campus newspaper in support of President Bush and the war in Iraq, I was attacked in print for three solid weeks. After that, I went down and applied to become an opinion writer for the campus paper—now, understand that I had been on the staff of the newspaper for two years as an undergrad, as an editor, so it's not like I wasn't qualified. But the editors wouldn't return my calls. They threw away my application. I called and left messages, and they never responded. Yet, they continued to print articles that attacked me personally."

"What strikes me as odd," I said, "is that they would do something like that, attacking you personally because of your opinions, particularly when you're an African-American. You'd think they'd be concerned about getting the whole African-American community on top of them!"

"Yes, well that's part of the problem, isn't it?" he said. "Because if you're an African-American conservative, you don't get much support from either side. I can't begin to tell you how bad I've had it from both sides. And, unfortunately, that's really typical for that campus. The place isn't just liberal, it's leftist, and extreme leftist at that. They talk about diversity but there's absolutely no diversity of thought, and if you're a conservative you have no voice on that campus. I tried to fight for a year and a half, but since they controlled the newspapers and every other means of communication, it was almost impossible to get a word in edgewise."

PRACTICAL MORALITY

"The good news," I said to Lenny, "is that you've finished your master's in international relations, and now you're beginning to get more involved in other things. But tell me, how did you come by your views? Obviously, you came to these perspectives on your own. No one told you what to think. But how did that happen?"

"As an undergrad," he said, "I majored in history and classics. I studied Greek and Latin and things of that nature, and I've always been an avid reader. I have a fifteen-hundred-book library at home, and I've read on every subject—history, political science, sociology, and anthropology. In international relations my area of interest is the history of warfare. So I'm very interested in defense policy, and you don't really have to read very far in that field to see how important American ideas about freedom and self-defense have been in modern times. I realized that most of the stuff I was hearing about multiculturalism and America's failures from my teachers was dishonest and wrong. So I think that made me start looking a little deeper, and one day I woke up and realized I was a conservative."

"What does your family think of your political views?" I said.

"Oh, wow!" he said with a laugh. "All my family are Democrats, so I've gotten into some heated discussions about why I'm a Republican."

"Is your family religious?" I asked.

"Yes, they're Christians, and I am too," he said. "But they haven't made the connection between their faith and the state of the culture. I think I changed because I knew a little more about all that."

"The main theme that runs through this issue," I said, "and the thread that seems to tie everything together for people who've thought it through, is that those who care passionately about preserving our heritage and culture tend to have a strong moral sense that derives in large measure from faith—either their own faith or the religious principles designed into the Republic. If you look at it from that perspective, you realize that anyone who could work against the interests of their own country can't have a moral framework that informs how they think and act."

"I see that," he said. "Look at the kinds of policies the other side supports today, like abortion, gay rights, pushing for homosexual marriage, and things of that sort. To me that's unacceptable. This past year we've seen all these Hollywood actors coming out against the president—people with no credentials at all questioning the secretary of defense, the president, and the administration. Obviously, there's a knowledge gap, and it's a one-sided conversation. They don't go on facts; they go on emotions. That's no way to live."

"I couldn't agree more," I said.

As I reflected on my conversations with Lenny, Catherine, and others, I realized that the real danger of the demoralization taking place on the university campus is not what's happening on the micro scale of current events and the various cultural topics that make headlines but the changes taking place on the macro scale of the human spirit, and how the beliefs of students are being shaped by the "looking glass" values of liberal culture. In a 2002 poll of college seniors conducted by the Zogby organization, three-fourths of the students reported being taught that right and wrong depend on "differences in individual values and cultural diversity." Only a fourth reported their professors taught the traditional view that "there are clear and uniform standards of right and wrong by which everyone should be judged."

Three-fourths also said they'd been taught that pursuing progressive social policy was a higher priority than "providing clear and accurate business statements to stockholders and creditors," a standard once regarded as the bottom line of accountability. With such a view, it's not surprising that 56 percent said the only difference between the highly publicized crimes of Enron managers and normal business procedures is that the Enron executives "got caught." But most depressing, 97 percent of the college seniors surveyed believe their education has equipped them to perform ethically in their careers, and when they were asked which ethical statements were most often transmitted by their professors, 73 percent said "what is right and wrong depends on differences in individual values and cultural diversity." The idea that there are clear and uniform standards of right and wrong by which everyone should be judged is now the minority view.[2]

As troubling as these findings are, the evidence of decline keeps compounding as other surveys and polls offer a portrait of what's been done to the minds of the next generation. When the Independent Women's Forum conducted an Internet survey of the attitudes and political views of college students between the ages of eighteen and twenty-four, they learned that students are being told to check their personal beliefs at the door if they expect to make good grades. Sixteen percent of respondents to the winter 2003 poll told the IWF that they feared their grades would suffer if they openly disagreed with their professors' political opinions.

Insecurity about their ability to speak freely led, in turn, to lower class participation and less honesty in their written work. Nearly a fourth of those surveyed said they were afraid to contribute to the general conversation in class, and just under a third said they were required to take moral or philosophical positions they were uncomfortable with in their assignments. Bias of this sort in a university classroom isn't just dishonest, it's also bound to have a chilling effect on freedom of speech, and to change behavior in many ways.

One of the surprises of the poll was that a majority of students, 74 percent, indicated that they're registered to vote, and 57 percent said they expect to vote in upcoming national elections. In contrast to recent years when most college students neglected this privilege, this next generation is apparently more interested in political issues and is eager to take part in the elective process. Fully 52 percent of respondents to the IWF poll said they're either "extremely" or "highly" interested in the outcome of the presidential elections. It's clear, not only from these results but from the 2003 UCLA poll and others, that 9/11 has had a profound effect on many of them, causing them at long last to begin thinking for themselves.

BITTERSWEET FAREWELL

Dr. Richard Zeller, resigning as professor of sociology, wrote: "I bid Bowling Green State University a bittersweet farewell. After a quarter of a century on the once-proud faculty at BGSU, I am glad to leave. BGSU has sold its soul to the thought police of political correctness." Zeller mourns for students who self-censor their ideas so they can pass their classes. "They are the ones most damaged by the totalitarian thought control so regularly conducted in the social sciences and humanities at BGSU."

—*Campus Report,* October 2000

And that level of interest adds further drama to another discovery of the IWF poll, which was the disparity between the political views of professors and their students. Thirty-seven percent of students said their professors are either very liberal or somewhat liberal. Just over 13 percent characterized their professors as conservative. And while 70 percent of students indicated that professors often express political opinions during class, they said that ideological diversity doesn't exist.[3] Clearly, many faculty members are using the classroom for propaganda. But more and more students are resisting that sort of programming, and some recent polls even suggest that they're beginning to take conservative ideas more seriously. In some cases it's the passion of activist professors that's driving them back to reality.

A CHANGE OF HEART

Alex Compton graduated from the University of Texas in 2000 with a degree in molecular biology. Since that time he's been admitted to medical school at the UT Health Science Center in Dallas, and is now preparing for his residency in radiology. His journey, he told me, was fairly direct, but there were some surprises along the way. "When I first got to the University of Texas," he said, "I was basically an atheist. I had come from a stable, upper middle class family, but I was really open-minded and naïve, not really knowing what I believed. Most eighteen-year-olds don't have a very good sense of themselves or their direction in life, and that's how I was. The culture myth is that you go away to college and find yourself, and that's basically what I expected to do."

"Did you know at that point what you wanted to study?" I asked.

"My plan," he said, "was to get my bachelor of science degree in molecular biology and a bachelor of arts in English. But during my junior year I found out about the humanities program that allows you to design your own major, so I switched over to humanities."

"That's amazing," I said with a laugh. "It's certainly not a combination that anyone would normally expect to see!"

"I know," he said. "I didn't realize it then, but I think I was looking for a moral justification for life."

"An English major would give you the words to be working with ideas," I said, "and the science would help you to be looking in places where life began. That's very interesting, but it's not something the average high school teacher would be able to point you to. How did you come by that combination?"

"The first time I knew I wanted to study biology," he said, "was when I was in an advance-placement biology class and they went over how trees photosynthesize. Unbelievable! It was a symphony of work. It was magnificent! From that moment I knew I wanted to learn more about science. I decided to study English because I had a fantastic English teacher in high school, and I gravitated toward the humanities because I wanted to explore the world of ideas."

"So when you got to UT," I said, "did the reality match your expectations?"

Alex paused for a long moment. I could see that he needed a little more time to think about the question. But then he said, "When I got there I didn't know what to expect. Maybe I shouldn't have been so naïve, but I really thought that everyone was going to be objective, and they were going to look at the world as it really is and not try to impose their worldview on it. I would never have labeled myself as a conservative. I wasn't at all religious. But in a rhetoric class in my freshman year everything was suddenly extremely political, and very liberal, and I didn't realize that the instructor was extremely liberal as well. I didn't have any strong political opinions, but I constantly found myself defending basic common sense, and I realized I was probably the most conservative person in the class."

"Sounds like it was you against the world!" I said.

"It was," he said, "but it was really a kind of set-up, and the conclusions were already decided before we ever got started. The readings were supposed to explore two sides of a contentious issue, like abortion for example, but when we got to the class discussion it focused on how one worldview was better than the other, and almost invariably that was the liberal worldview. So that's how it started."

"That was intellectually unfair," I said, "and you knew it."

"Absolutely!" he said. "I mean, you're dealing with a population of eighteen-year-olds who don't know what they're doing. They don't even know what to think, and here are all these professors bending their minds to fit their own conception. This happened in discussions, in peer groups, and every-thing else; there was a paucity of people who had a conservative worldview."

"Or if there were people with a conservative worldview," I said, "they probably didn't feel they could speak freely."

"As I got older," he said, "I realized that the Left controls the language. They control what diversity means, what racism means, and they control what's basically right and wrong. Their rhetoric is set up such that they always have the moral high ground, and the whole system is rigged. I think some students kept quiet and didn't feel they could express themselves out of inhibition. And anyone with a religious perspective was totally constrained. There was a policy in the dorm that we had to discuss homosexuality, and we had to agree that it's acceptable. But we couldn't talk about anything reli-gious, especially Christianity."

"This wasn't Harvard," I said, "it was a major, state-funded public uni-versity in middle America—the Bible Belt. So how did you react to that?"

Once again, Alex paused to consider his words: "I had one professor," he said, "and I won't give his name, but I could see that he was different from the others. He was more logical, more practical, and he was very highly regarded academically. He had published articles in all sorts of journals and you could read anything he wrote in a fairly straightforward secular nature; but I began to wonder if there wasn't something else, too. And I realized that he was probably a closet Christian. This all happened at a time when I was really reading and searching and looking for meaning, and I eventually came to the conclusion that there has to be a God—nothing made sense without it. What I'd seen in high school when we were studying photosynthesis was part of that, I realize now, but of course I didn't see it at the time. The com-plexity, the sophistication, and the beauty with which it all fits together was just too much.

"On the idea side," he continued, "I realized there has to be a reason why molesting children is wrong. You can't tell me that there's some relative way that that's all right; you can't tell me that murdering a child is no big deal. And when I began to see that, it was the absolute necessity of a belief in 'right and wrong' that finally tipped the balance. I couldn't accept the fact that there is no right and wrong. And if there's right and wrong, then there has to be a Creator who made it that way."

DON'T BE IMPRESSED

Don't be too impressed by an impressive-sounding résumé: This person is a Harvard honors graduate. Harvard gave honors awards to 91 percent of its 2001 graduating class. "Law school admissions officers ignore *magna cum laude* and *cum laude* honors from Harvard as meaningless." To present oneself as a "Harvard honors student is misleading, since so few know that it is a grand anti-intellectual scam." A Harvard senior says, "In some departments A stands for average; since so many of us have A averages our grades are meaningless." At Cornell the percentage of A's doubled from 1965 to 1993; C's dropped from 40 percent to 12 percent. At Princeton fully 41.2 percent of all grades are A's. The average grade at Harvard today is A-minus to B-plus. Stanford, promising to reform, is bringing back the once-banned F.

—Martin Gross, *The End of Sanity*

What's most striking for me about Alex's story is that he was able to see through the hypocrisy and illogic of the academic world and walk away from it. And this is my main concern: saving the next generation from mistakes that can only lead to utter self-destruction. It may be too late to save the leftist faculty. They're all mostly dinosaurs who will continue their predatory behavior until they drop in their tracks and pass silently into the sediments of time. The most striking aspect of Tammy Bruce's story is that she came to her senses, at least to some degree. She awoke from a nightmare, and when she did, she was able to walk away from dogma. I can't imagine there will be many others, but the changes in her were remarkable. We still have much to learn, but one of my main concerns from the start has been to find out how major change might come to the universities. And that was the subject of my next conversation.

COMMUNITIES OF MIND

As I approached the end of my research, I arranged to spend an hour with Dr. J. Budziszewski, a well known professor of government and philosophy at the University of Texas. In addition to his academic publications and conference papers, he has written several important books. Two of these are *Written on the Heart: The Case for Natural Law* (1997) and *The Revenge of Conscience: Politics and the Fall of Man* (1999). Another, *What We Can't Not Know: A Guide* (2003), isn't just for scholars but has been enthusiastically reviewed and widely read. His two newest, *How To Stay Christian in College* and *Ask Me Anything*, deal with some of the logical fallacies of postmodernism and popular culture, helping students and their parents deal with the questions that inevitably arise in any learning situation. *How To Stay Christian* has sold in outrageous numbers, is easy to read, and helps Christian kids heading for college defend what they believe to be true.

Over the years, some of the critics of higher education have said that faculty tenure is the real problem, and doing away with this guarantee would help weed out the worst and force those with a tendency to use the classroom as a soapbox to change their evil ways. But Budziszewski strongly disagrees, and said that ending tenure may only put the best at the mercy of the worst who are already entrenched. In the long run, he said, issues such as tenure, curriculum, and the racial or sexual environment on campus are secondary issues. Of course it's important to deal with weakness and abuse in these areas, but genuine reform calls for a bigger strategy.

"There are three ways that you might imagine the reform of the university system taking place," he told me, "and I think they deserve greater attention. The first is a complete revolution of the intellectual culture. Revolutions like that certainly can occur, but they take centuries and can't be master-planned, so it's not the most practical approach!"

"That idea came up in a previous conversation," I said, "and we decided it was like moving a mountain."

"Yes, but not just moving a mountain," he said, "it's a mountain too big for us to see. We can't begin to anticipate the results that our efforts might have two centuries down the line. Consider the passing of the medieval university. It's not as though nobody was trying to change it, but the changes that actually took place during the Renaissance, the Enlightenment, and the Reformation weren't the ones they were planning. So I don't think any of us can manage a revolution from the top down.

"The second approach," he said, "might be called the seat-at-the-table method. In some ways the contemporary university resembles the Hindu social system in India, where the castes aren't just social strata but compartmentalized, coexisting subcultures. There are a lot of different subcultures in the university, too. Some people say the postmodernist movement contributes to a kind of compartmentalization because it doesn't believe in any sort of grand meta-narrative—or a 'big story' that's true for everyone. What it does claim is that all the different subcultures have a seat at the table, and they all co-exist. The problem is that the seat comes with a high price. You have to accept the rules of the table: you have to sit in your assigned seat, and it's difficult not to compromise your principles. Basically it's called being captured by the institution."

"There's an admission price to sit at the table," I said.

"That's right," said Dr. Budziszewski. "But if you can avoid being captured by the institution—and that's a big if—then the seat-at-the-table strategy can work. At some universities, traditionally-minded scholars are trying to establish alternative degree programs—something like small liberal-arts colleges within the structure of the university. At others they're making places where visiting scholars can work without ideological pressure. The success of Robert George's Madison Program at Princeton, for example, suggests that it may be easier to do that than most people think. By their nature, universities will try to capture those programs—that's just the way they are—but they don't necessarily oppose them, because the programs give them something to show their donors. When someone from the outside says, 'What are you radicals doing down there?' they can simply say, 'Let me show you this new institute or degree program,' and they've got cover."

"Now there's something they'll understand!" I said.

"Yes, and I think that approach is a good one if you go about it realistically," he said. "But my guess is, that sort of initiative can only remain independent for about one generation. Then it will be captured by the university, absorbed into the system, and you have to find *another* initiative.

"But there's a third approach," he said, "and this is to foster alternative institutions not *within* the universities but *alongside* them. You have to keep your eyes open, because you don't know what alternatives might be possible. Nobody anticipated that monasteries would save Western learning, for example. And, for that matter, nobody anticipated universities. At one time higher education didn't happen in universities. They were a historical surprise, based on an ideal of *universally integrated knowledge*, where all the parts were connected. That's why they're called uni-versities. Some people say we don't really have uni-versities anymore, we have multi-versities which reflects the view that knowledge is disconnected, that it doesn't always hang together, and that it's all a matter of perspective. But people are trying all sorts of new alternatives to the multi-versities, and I suspect we need to keep an open mind."

I said, "Would you include things like 'distance learning' and the 'electronic universities' on the Internet in that category?"

I'm not encouraged by distance learning," he said. "I've had some experience with it and I'm afraid it's just going to be another way to pull in educational consumers—a way to make money. You can provide certain kinds of purely technical education that way, but you can't provoke searching reflection of ideas. It's not a solution, but a symptom of the problem."

Relational Learning

"A better example of what I mean by alternative institutions," he said, "might be the Christian studies centers that are being established alongside many campuses—or something else along that line. This is a burgeoning movement, and the centers operate on a different sort of educational ideal. They have a different view of knowledge, how it works, and what it means to cultivate it. They aren't at war with the universities, but their perspective is all their own, and it contributes to a helpful intellectual tension, and a new kind of discussion."

"My own experience with these organizations," I said, "is that there's a lot of genuine enthusiasm about ideas among the students who get involved. In fact, it's a striking contrast to the kind of apathy I often see in the typical lecture hall."

"I agree," he said, "and I think that's another reason why this sort of thing is going to grow. Who would have anticipated that Christian studies centers would be popping up all over the place? And then we have to wonder, what other sorts of institutions are going to develop? We don't know, but we have to be ready, and wherever we see something that seems to be promising we ought to work with it and explore the possibilities. Who knows? Perhaps one hundred and fifty years from now we may see a whole new system of higher education! We can't *engineer* such a thing—I criticized that approach earlier—but if something good starts to happen we should just get out of the way!"

"That is long-range planning!" I said with a laugh. "But one of the things I've observed on virtually every campus I've visited the past year is just how prone students are to self-segregate into communities of one kind or another. The trend toward 'theme programmed' dorms is a version of that which is not very helpful, because it's often done with the express purpose of creating barriers between groups, to foment bitterness and disharmony instead of what the Left euphemistically refers to as 'unity' and 'tolerance.' Dividing up by race, gender, or class is, to my mind, a bad idea. But the idea of establishing relational communities within the university based on a common commitment to a philosophy, a set of principles, or perhaps certain professional disciplines sounds like a good one."

"If it were done in the spirit of 'My truth as contrasted with your truth,' it would be as bad as theme dorms," he said. "But if it's done in the spirit of the search for *universal truth*, it could make all the difference. Bear in mind that I'm using these institutes merely as examples. There may be many other possibilities on the horizon that we don't yet see. Think of institutions that aren't the university, but live in the same world as the university. They have an influence on education, they have intellectual transactions with their people, but their aims are different—and more sane, perhaps. Theme dorms and things like that, I'm afraid, weaken the search for universal knowledge because people aren't interacting with one another."

"Instead of ending racism," I said, "they actually breed it."

"Yes, racially themed dorms are an especially virulent idea," he said, "but on the other hand, suppose that you had an alternative degree program that's really a classical education. You really want those students to interact with each other intellectually, outside the classroom, and to encourage them without requiring them to live in a common dorm."

"To get them reading great books together and debating ideas," I said.

"Exactly," he said, "and trusting the ordinary dynamics of young adult intellectual energy to keep it all going. Now there's something worth thinking about."

"That's an exciting concept," I said. "The closest thing I've seen to it would be the Directed Studies program at Yale where students are encouraged to study together and spend free time together reading and arguing about great books and all the ideas they're dealing with in this fairly intense program of study."

"At the same time," he said, "I think it's very important for young people who are looking ahead, preparing to go away to college, to think not just about which courses they'll take, but what sort of influences they want to be exposed to. That means looking for mentors. The university isn't going to provide appropriate influences for them, but there's really no substitute for the teacher-student relationship. So this is something to keep in mind. As students begin to find their way around the university, discovering what their interests may be, they need to be looking for professors who may be suitable mentors. Not just people who can write letters of recommendation when they graduate," he said, "but people to whom they can entrust a part of their intellectual formation."

A NEW REALITY

When he spoke to students and faculty at Westminster College in Missouri, in March of 1946, Sir Winston Churchill said, "From Stettin in the Baltic to Trieste in the Adriatic, an iron curtain has descended across the continent." Those words are well known, but in the remainder of that famous "Iron Curtain" speech, the British prime minister also said the following:

> People of any country have the right, and should have the power by constitutional action, by free unfettered elections, with secret ballot, to choose or change the character or form of government under which they dwell; that freedom of speech and thought should reign; that courts of justice, independent of the executive, unbiased by any party, should administer laws which have received the broad assent of large majorities or are consecrated by time and custom.[4]

The values Churchill described were easily understood in those days because they were the values of all Americans. They were the beliefs of the Founders who had inscribed ideas much the same in the Declaration of Independence and the United States Constitution. They're among the beliefs that distinguish Western civilization from communist treachery and fascist totalitarianism.

But some sixty years later, and with so much of our history now unlearned and forgotten, we can no longer take those noble sentiments for granted. "Today," writes an Auburn University graduate, "a new iron curtain has descended, but this time not on Eastern Europe. Instead, it has come down on university campuses nationwide, as debate on key issues is nonexistent, and intellectually the faculty of many of the top colleges are overwhelmingly liberal and some, downright anti-American."[5]

In the wake of 9/11, University of New Mexico professor Richard Berthold said to his students, "Anyone who can blow up the Pentagon would get my vote." Sadly, those remarks were majority opinion on many American campuses at the time. But are they still? Can anything happen that might alter the attitudes of a radicalized faculty, or reverse the kinds of thinking that allows such words to be spoken in the first place? As I considered these questions in the light of Dr. Budziszewski's remarks above, I realized that what happened in the sixties was, in fact, the first model of change that he described—*a complete revolution of the intellectual culture*. And just as he said, no one was prepared for the transformation it unleashed upon the nation.

For there to be genuine reform of the universities, it will take more than cosmetic surgery. Long-range planning is surely needed—where there is no vision the people perish—but we also have issues of much more immediate concern. The generation of the sixties is almost past and another radical brood is coming along behind them. How to deal with this reality? How to prepare for changes that may be just ahead? These are questions we must wrestle with now. Our concern for the future of higher education and the well-being of the next generation means that we must turn our attention to a new reality—to the looming specter of a type of change that may transform the universities in ways we cannot yet imagine.

12

The Coming Revolution

What happens when an irresistible force meets an immovable object? Philosophers will tell you the argument of that ancient riddle is invalid because, in a world of immovable objects, no irresistible forces can exist. And in a world of irresistible forces, nothing is ever immovable, so the conditions of the paradox can't be met. But a question of greater concern, and a matter less of physics than of history, is how institutions long established and deeply entrenched become the victims of sudden and momentous change. For most of the eighteenth century, France was the most populous and powerful nation in Europe. Louis XIV and his successors ruled a colonial empire that spanned the globe, with the greatest military and most prosperous economy of any nation. By all appearances, the empire of the Sun King was invincible; but change was in the air.

It's said that on the morning that Louis XVI looked out his bedroom window, in July of 1789, and saw the legions of peasants marching on the Bastille, he turned to his adviser, Duke François de La Rochefoucauld, and exclaimed, "My God, it's a revolt!" Glancing over the king's shoulder through the open window, the nobleman realized what was about to happen and said, "No, Sir. It's a revolution." Three months later, Louis and his entire court were in seclusion, hiding from the leaders of the new French Republic. By mid-October of 1793, both Louis and his queen, Marie Antoinette, were dead—victims of the guillotine.

Revolutions, whether in the realm of politics or physics or genetic engineering, are unstable and volatile phenomena. They come, by and large, only after years of agitation, fed by the contradictory emotions of despair and hope. They are never one thing or one movement but a coalition of forces brought together by a common need and the expedience of a shared antipathy for the source of that need. Malcolm Gladwell offers a provocative anatomy of revolution in his 2002 bestseller, *The Tipping Point: How Little Things Can Make a Big Difference*. There are many factors that can set off a sudden change response—whether it's a flu virus, pop culture, or mob psychology—but there are, he says, three essential attributes of every revolution. *The law of the few* says that the initiative usually comes from a small group of "mavens, connectors, and salesmen" who spread the energy and vision of change. The *stickiness factor*, Gladwell says, has to do with packaging the new idea to make it persistent and irresistible; and *the power of context* provides an environment or a medium through which the energy is allowed to grow and thrive.[1]

A Time for Change

Gladwell's idea certainly applies to business, which thrives on fads and fashions that spread like wildfire. But there's a commonality to every movement in which these and other factors described in *The Tipping Point* can be seen. When the environment is right, things can change suddenly and dramatically. Whenever I've spoken on the crisis of culture in America, and related topics such as this one, I've often been asked by someone in the crowd: "Is there any hope? Can we turn it around?" My answer is always the same: "Yes, I believe we can." To say otherwise would be to condemn this and future generations to hopelessness and despair. It would be cowardly, and a surrender to the fear that we may not have the resources or the right to demand the kinds of changes that can stop the madness.

From a faith perspective, it would be heresy to say that the collapse of our culture can't somehow be avoided; it would be denying that we have other even greater resources that may empower us—by some type of divine intervention we can't even imagine—to cross over to dry land. But for all my bravado in responding to such questions, I am not always as convinced as I sometimes make out to be. We're forty years into the breakdown in higher education and the mechanism is massive and unwieldy. But one thing I know: we do have resources. If all those who care passionately about the crisis in the academy begin to react with appropriate alarm, demanding that corrective action be taken now, we can make an enormous difference.

It's not too late to restore the dignity and purpose of these great institutions. It's not too late to demand that universities actually teach students their own history and literature and the core disciplines in a manner that reflects the dignity and grandeur of our common heritage. For all the damage that has been done, millions of young people have somehow managed to make it through the minefields of academia and accomplish the impossible: they've gotten a reasonably good education and, at the same time, rejected the leftist dogma thrust at them daily by their professors.

Some of them have even emerged stronger and more resilient because of their personal commitment to hold passionately to truth, to what they believe in, and what they believe to be the real issues of concern. In this category I would include my own children who survived the university environment, not entirely unscathed, but with their integrity and self-respect intact. This same strength of character is clearly visible in each of the young men and women I've interviewed in these pages. Surely this should give us hope. But just because there are still some young people who have the moral fiber to resist the indoctrination and forge ahead, we must not assume that this will always be the case. A great many have already been lost. We can't afford to lose any more to the star chambers of political correctness and moral deregulation.

The real source of the problem, as David Horowitz has said many times, is a lack of accountability among university faculty and administrators to the people who pay their salaries. Furthermore, it's a sign of utter contempt for those who will ultimately employ the graduates of these institutions. University chancellors, trustees, presidents, deans, and faculty members have become accustomed to using their endowments and the funds provided by donors, foundations, tuition monies, and other industry and federal grants, to do as they damned well please. The belligerence of the faculty at Yale who could not bring themselves to use a twenty million dollar gift for courses in Western civilization is just one conspicuous example of this sort of arrogance. Losing twenty million, or ten times that amount, hardly phases the Ivory-Tower elite. As one faculty member said to me, "I mean, you can't take Harvard or Yale down that way. They'll go down slightly after the continent sinks into the ball of liquid ore at the center of the earth." And that's how they really feel.

Stanley Fish, who made his fame at Duke University and served most recently as dean of liberal arts at the University of Illinois at Chicago, has been traveling the country on what he calls his "farewell tour." He's retiring soon, he says, but speaking at Stanford in November 2003, Fish told a campus crowd that "Tolerance, mutual respect, and freedom of speech are always bad ideas. They are cheerleading, flag-waving, and slimy! Censorship and regulation comes first, free speech comes second. Free speech requires constraint, which is thought to be opposite." Without censorship, he told the audience, original and provocative speech is just so much noise. Tolerance and mutual respect must be directed toward specific ends. "Disrespect," Fish declaimed, "is a prerequisite for respect."

Admittedly, Fish, who has written several provocative books, including *There's No Such Things as Free Speech, and It's a Good Thing, Too*, is one of the many "rock-star" radicals who plays for the crowds. He takes delight in tweaking an audience and provoking both laughter and outrage. But this, in reality, is a form of desensitization to ideas that are repugnant. College students flock to his lectures, not because they comprehend or even care what Stanley Fish has to say, but because he's good for a laugh and, to his credit, brings out into the open ideas that are often left unsaid. But Stanley Fish believes most of what he says, and he points to the "repressive tolerance," as Herbert Marcuse phrased it, that is the dark undercurrent of faddish progressive thinking. No one on the Left, particularly Fish and his ilk, is the least concerned if conservatives and traditionalists are forbidden to speak. Censorship, after all, is a good thing, so long as it's the disenfranchised minority that's being censored.

Today's university is a censorship gulag, where freedom of conscience is little more than an amusing catchphrase. The universities know this to be true, but they prefer to ignore it. Robert Berdahl, chancellor of the University of California, said in 2002 that, "It is imperative that our classrooms be free of indoctrination—indoctrination is not education."[2] But either the chancellor doesn't believe what he said or he has no idea what's actually happening in practically every classroom in the UC system. Hugh Hewitt, a Harvard grad and former Reagan staffer, makes the point very well:

> Even casual observers of elite academia know of the thorough-going decay within its ranks, with its attachment to absurd theories and rejection of anything like a traditional core curriculum. For a quarter century, undergraduates have been fed a diet based on intellectual junk food that will eventually cripple the eater. The faculties of elite institutions have become less and less important in circles with any claim to influence. The hard sciences continue to be hard and continue to thrive, but the rot in the departments associated with cultural and political leadership is hard to disguise.[3]

ORGANIZED RESISTANCE

All Americans, not just those currently enrolled in colleges and universities, have been betrayed by this system. We've been cheated, lied to, taken advantage of, and ripped off. We've paid for our children to be properly educated, given suitable professional skills, and equipped as loyal citizens and taxpayers, and that has not happened. Worse, hyperpoliticized and oversexed pseudo-specialists have twisted the curriculum to suit their own alien vision of reality and, in the process, they've done real damage to some of our most promising young people.

But rest assured, there will be a high price to pay when the modern university comes tumbling down, as it surely will. The freefall of the American university is happening, not just as a result of lost jobs or lost respect, but because of what we have become in the eyes of history. A collapse is coming, one way or another, because the intellectual leadership of the nation has sold its soul to a treacherous orthodoxy and lost its *raison d'être*—that is, it's reason for being.

Future generations will judge us by what happens now, and that's a trust we must not betray. Ultimately, as Alan Charles Kors and Harvey Silverglate conclude in their masterful work, *The Shadow University*, the academy "will have to answer for its betrayal of the nation's and its own traditions."[4] But for that to happen, every person who genuinely cares about the future of this nation and the type of education we're providing to future generations—and at costs that are so much higher than ever before—must stand up and say no. We're well past the tipping point, and it's high time for a revolution to begin.

How to begin that process was the subject of my conversation with Professor Gerard Bradley at Notre Dame University. Bradley earned his bachelor's and law degrees at Cornell University and served as an assistant district attorney in New York before joining, first, the faculty at the University of Illinois, and then the law school at Notre Dame, where he's been since 1992. In addition to teaching, Dr. Bradley has served as president of the Fellowship of Catholic Scholars. In our conversation, I asked about the PC environment on the South Bend campus and whether, as I'd heard, the climate there was a little less oppressive than at most of the other big-name institutions.

"Things are different at Notre Dame," he said, "but probably less different than you've been led to believe. The law school is a notable exception. We've succeeded in maintaining most of our Catholic identity. The culture here is actually the reverse of the typical classroom culture, and students who are pro-life or anti-gay marriage are in the majority. But outside the law school, I'd have to say that Notre Dame is not very Catholic at all, and the university and most of the other departments are hiring faculty as if they were trying to be just like Princeton or Harvard, or any secular institution."

I said, "Is there any pressure on the administration, either from students or parents, to resist that trend?"

"The climate is generally liberal here," he said. "It may be getting better. At least to the extent that apathy has supplanted the sort of raw ideological passion that we saw in the nineties, it's getting better. It's less intense. And insofar as the students are apathetic, and the faculty becomes just a bunch of careerists and less ideological, I think things are marginally better. Also, I think things will get better on campus as some of the cultural issues are settled. As the level of controversy subsides, I think the Left may be more tolerant of those who hold different positions on these issues. They're not threatened by them because, for now at least, they're winning. So, on the whole, things are getting better, but for the wrong reasons."

"What will it take to change that balance?" I asked.

"One place to look for signs of hope," he said, "would be in the next generation of students. I sense that they're getting tired of all the BS, and they really want to know what's what. There's always reason to hope for improvement on these campuses with regard to openness, honesty, and genuine pursuit of the truth, but if the students ever get fed up, then I think things will begin to change. And I think there are reasons to believe that's happening now."

"What do you base that on?" I asked.

"I think that students are restless spiritually," he said, "and they feel oppressed by the careerism around them. They're already prone to see college as vocational training, which is not the way it's supposed to be, but that's what they expect. They may take some liberal arts courses, but in the end what they're really here for is to get a diploma so they can get a job—and so they can live the way they think they're supposed to live, which is suburban and comfortable."

"To make a great deal of money," I said, "as a recent UCLA poll reported. The number of students who say their main goal is to be 'very well off financially' has jumped from 42 percent in the mid-sixties to 74 percent today."

"That doesn't surprise me at all," he said. "But while students tend to buy into that, I think by nature most of them are inclined to sense that it's oppressive. Kids don't naturally think of college as a way of planning for the rest of their lives. They want this to be a 'now' experience, and if they have any good professors at all, then a desire to really know what's going on will be instilled in them. I think that's the place to look for change. The faculty's not going to change, and these big institutions aren't very likely to go through any sort of soul-searching and change their ways."

"The main concern for most administrators is building the endowment and raising more money," I said.

"Exactly," he said. "At Notre Dame the endowment is bigger than the budget of most countries, and that's how it is at most of these big schools. For the most part the amount of money they can raise through fund-raising is so enormous that the universities aren't going to change. The faculty all know they're protected and they don't have to do anything they don't want to do. But on the other hand, it's still a consumer market, and if the kids and their parents ever start demanding changes, then things will have to change."

"Do you really think it's possible to use the money as a bargaining chip?" I asked.

"It's a consumer-driven culture," he said. "Colleges are very concerned about meeting demand, at least of their paying students. Unfortunately, I think a lot of parents are complicit in what's going on. They want to believe that things are going well at their children's college, and they let themselves get sucked in very easily. It's like a Ponzi scheme. Somebody says to you, 'Give me five thousand dollars and I'll double it in two months,' and you say, 'Wow, sure!' So you lose all that money and then you call a lawyer. But, come on, really! Do you think any legitimate investment is going to double your money in two months? We know better, but I think some of these parents are basically Ponzi-scheme victims. They really ought to know better, and in their heart they know it's not really like they've been told. But they want to believe it."

"The sad part," I said, "is that a lot of parents are saying, 'You know, I don't care if Johnny or Suzie has to endure some indoctrination at college, just so long as they come home in four years with that sheepskin!' So they allow the faculty to browbeat and intimidate their children, filling their heads with dangerous ideas, so that the parents can have the pride of having a child with a degree from a major university!"

"I'm afraid you're right," he said.

"So what's the secret?" I asked. "How will it ever change?"

"Parents just have to demand clear and honest answers," he said. "Unfortunately, each individual parent is just a drop in the bucket, and the universities can find ways to ignore them. Those who complain are looked on as nuisances and passed along to some community relations person who will just say nice things and then do nothing about it. The college is getting ten thousand applications a year, which is more than they can possibly take in, so losing a few troublemakers here or there is no big deal. The individual trying to change things can only influence their own kid's trajectory, which is all to the good. But in terms of changing the institution? It would have to be through some kind of organization of radicalized people that, frankly, I can't imagine."

"There's no structure for that," I said.

"That's right," said Dr. Bradley. "The power is in the money. It's not in the faculty or the administration. Only occasionally do you see major change initiated by the administration. If you look around to see where the radicalizing forces are, they're outside the university in those sectors of the society that are potentially clients of the institution, and that would be primarily the next generation of students. But unless they're organized in some way that I can't imagine, I don't know how it will ever have any effect on the institution."

AN ORDERLY APPROACH

Recognizing that the principle of organization is very important, the Center for the Study of Popular Culture created a new initiative called the Campaign for Fairness and Inclusion in Higher Education. Co-opting the Left's own code words of "fairness" and "inclusion," this plan calls on university administrations to implement five basic demands:

1. Conduct an inquiry into political bias in the hiring process for faculty and administrators, and seek ways to promote fairness towards—and inclusion of—diverse and under-represented mainstream perspectives;

2. Conduct an inquiry into political bias in the selection of commencement speakers and seek ways to promote fairness towards—and inclusion of—diverse and under-represented mainstream perspectives;

3. Conduct an inquiry into political bias in the allocation of student program funds—including speakers' fees—and seek ways to promote fairness towards and inclusion of diverse and under-represented mainstream perspectives;

4. Institute a zero tolerance policy towards the obstruction of campus speakers and meetings and the destruction of informational literature distributed by campus groups;

5. Adopt a code of conduct for faculty that ensures that classrooms will welcome diverse viewpoints and not be used for political indoctrination, which is a violation of students' academic freedom.[5]

The plan is simple enough, and it draws attention to five distinct areas which have been ignored by the universities for years. Knowing how such demands have been met in the past, however, many will be skeptical that university officials may be willing to help resolve the problems they've created. So the CSPC campaign calls on state and local government to get involved, too, to begin making inquiries into the ways the institutions are being run.

The principle of diversity is not just a code word but a matter of federal law, says David Horowitz, and extending that concept beyond race and gender to matters of conscience, including political and religious affiliations, can help the universities regain their credibility. But will they willingly adopt such a policy? Frankly, without additional pressure from other sources, there's not a chance. And that's where you and I come in.

One of the main sources of influence upon university administrators, says columnist and author Stanley Kurtz, ought to be the federal government. If there's to be any hope of preserving America's cultural legacy, the government must enter the fray, extending not only its power of influence but its legislative authority to call the academy back to its original purposes. Congressional hearings can help bring national attention to these problems. And closer scrutiny of how government monies are being used by universities and research centers will get the attention of administrators and fund-raisers right away.

DO YOU TRUST YOUR DOCTOR?

Diversity means giving minority groups a chance, right? They wouldn't give credentials to an unqualified person, would they? "Professional schools are prime participants in affirmative action." ... In medical schools, for women and minorities, the Association of American Medical Colleges admitted its "bias for affirmative action, apparently even if those would-be doctors are less qualified than others for that life-and-death job. . . . Even if they have lower grades in college and lower scores on the Medical College Admission Test (MCAT)—too low to guarantee that they can properly practice medicine." Won't they flunk out? No. "[E]ntrance into medical school virtually assures an MD degree and a license to practice." And similar quota systems are in place for law schools as well.

—Martin Gross, *The End of Sanity*

By any standard, the prospects of such changes are grim unless the stranglehold of the Left is somehow broken, because the radical Left still has tenure and authority and plenty of money. And we can't expect the media to help: they're co-conspirators and fully compromised. As Kurtz points out, the tenured radicals were hired by old-fashioned liberals who believed in giving people with different perspectives a fair chance. But as soon as they moved up the ladder into the ranks of leadership, the radicals slammed the door on everyone else, thereby "reproducing themselves and squashing their opposition."[6]

The leftist domination on campus is not total, however, as we've seen in these pages. Some of the "best and brightest" are conservatives who find their way onto important faculties by various means, where they've joined ranks with older conservatives who earned their tenure long ago. And there are a few honest liberals who appreciate the importance of ideological balance. But these people are in the minority and the chances of greatly increasing the number of faculty members who are concerned about the academy in this way are slim—that is, unless state, local, and federal officials begin taking steps to clean up the mess.

Short of such dramatic changes, however, it falls to people like you and me—parents, students, and others who truly care—to take matters into our own hands, and to band with a growing coalition of like-minded groups who are ready to lend a hand. The most conspicuous victories for free speech and equal access in recent years have come from legal challenges, including litigation through the full range of judicial options, by groups such as the Center for Individual Rights (CIR), the Alliance Defense Fund (ADF), and the Foundation for Individual Rights in Education (FIRE). These nonprofit organizations, all privately funded and passionate about their mission, are having a profound impact on campus debates by providing an escape valve for students and faculty who find themselves caught up in the web of censorship and viewpoint discrimination.

Among the best known recent cases is CIR's Supreme Court victory in the case of *Gratz v. Bollinger*, challenging affirmative action policies at the University of Michigan. In this widely publicized case, as mentioned briefly in Chapter Five, the system of awarding admission points to applicants on the basis of race was found to be unconstitutional. While the use of race in admissions to the Michigan law school, in the companion case of *Grutter v. Bollinger*, was allowed by the court, the message of these challenges was clear: affirmative action is in big trouble, and under very close scrutiny by both the public and the courts.

More recently, CIR filed suit on behalf of a student at California Polytechnical University who was punished for simply trying to post a flyer on campus promoting a speech by the black conservative author, Mason Weaver. That case, *Hinkle v. Baker*, was filed in September 2003 in U.S. District Court and resulted in an out-of-court compromise by the university. In the case of *Columbia Union College v. Oliver*, CIR defended a small religious college in Maryland when state officials denied them the same financial aid benefits they had extended to other private colleges, entirely on the basis of the school's religious speech and beliefs. CIR won that suit, as they've done with dozens of others, simply by exercising due diligence and being willing to stand up against oppressive liberal policies.

The ADF has to its credit a large number of victories in state and local jurisdictions as well as before the United States Supreme Court. In one case the organization sued the University of Texas and eighteen top officials for censoring the speech of members of a registered campus group, Justice For All, during a pro-life rally. The ADF suit alleges that preferential treatment was given to pro-choice groups who were allowed to disrupt the pro-life rally, and that a professor with a bullhorn was allowed to shout down the pro-life group's invited speaker.

Rutgers University officials agreed to settle a case filed by ADF on behalf of the campus chapter of InterVarsity Multi-Ethnic Christian Fellowship. In that case, the university decided the fellowship could not require that its leaders subscribe to the organization's statement of faith. To enforce compliance with university policies, Rutgers had denied the organization equal access to campus buildings and a fair share of student activity fees. Under the settlement, however, the university gave assurances that the student-led organization was within its rights to have a credible profession of faith, and that funding would be fully restored.

Starting a Fire

Victories like these are happening more and more today as students and conservative faculty members are, as Professor Bradley says, getting "fed up" with the liberal BS. In some cases, a telephone call or a letter from an attorney may be enough to turn things around; but sometimes it takes civil action. Of all the groups that are shaking things up on campus, none has struck greater fear into the hearts of administrators than the Foundation for Individual Rights in Education. As faculty members themselves, Alan Charles Kors and Harvey A. Silverglate know how the system works, and they're not timid about rushing in where angels fear to tread.

Their first big case was the defense of a Christian group at Tufts University that refused to elect a lesbian with unorthodox views of scripture and sexual morality to a leadership position in the organization. When the woman complained to the administration, the Christian group was surreptitiously put on probation. But after a brief telephone interview, FIRE intervened, pointing out to the officers in charge of student activities that a gay student group would not have been put on probation for refusing to choose an evangelical Christian for a leadership role, so the idea of holding the Christian group to a different standard was not only illogical but illegal. Oddly enough, the university had a sudden change of heart.

Among FIRE's most celebrated cases was an action on behalf of a young man who had yelled from a dorm window to a group of African-American female students, asking them to stop making racket in the courtyard while he and others were trying to study. Because the women were horsing around in the water fountain, he called them "water buffaloes" and told them to go back to the "zoo." The next day a firestorm erupted and the male student was hauled before university officials who threatened him with expulsion. From there it only grew more intense. The student contacted Professor Kors who brought in outside legal help and soon the battle was under way. The case dragged on for nearly two years, and only ended when the University of Pennsylvania finally conceded and ended the contest. It was a bitter fight and nobody was entirely happy at the end, but the young man (who was an Israeli) was vindicated.

More recently, FIRE jumped in when conservative students at the College of William & Mary, in Virginia, were censored for holding an affirmative action bake sale. These bake sales have been held on campuses all across the country. By selling cookies to white males for one dollar and at half price to women and minorities, conservative students are trying to illustrate the basic unfairness of university admissions policies based on race, gender, or other preferences. Liberals on campus don't like the idea, but free speech is not a one-way street, as FIRE has been helping the colleges understand.

FIRE maintains a running list of cases under way on their Web site (www.thefire.org), so student groups and administrators can see how these battles are being won and, at the same time, so that students will be encouraged to resist attempts by campus liberals to take away their rights. Other recipients of FIRE's unwelcome attentions include the University of Connecticut, which attempted to outlaw "inconsiderate jokes," "stereotyping," and "inappropriately directed laughter," as interpreted by campus thought police; and Colby College, which tried to forbid speech that causes "a vague sense of danger" or a loss of "self-esteem."[7] Colby's speech code was being applied only to conservative speech, and not to the inflammatory antiwar and anti-Bush rallies taking place on the university quad.

Officials at Brown University, one of the most liberal schools in the country, have tried to ban "verbal behavior" that produces "feelings of impotence, anger, or disenfranchisement." Again, FIRE was only too happy to jump in and help them change their minds. In virtually every case, campus speech codes are enforced by kangaroo courts run by left-leaning student-affairs directors, liberal faculty members, and like-minded student government leaders. But defenders of student freedoms, at FIRE and elsewhere, are quick to point out that penalizing students for their beliefs is a clear violation of the First Amendment, which guarantees freedom of religion, speech, press, and assembly, and star-chamber tactics have no place on any university campus.

It's a shame that it takes court action or threats of action to force universities to back down from such acts of intolerance. But as the level of resentment continues building among students and others, court cases like these are just an early warning of other things yet to come. Furthermore, the real victories aren't just the ones happening in courtrooms and boardrooms, but those in the hearts and minds of the people once they begin to see and react to these outrages.

The biggest threat to the liberal orthodoxy is the atmosphere that's coming to college now as conservative students are becoming a bigger and more powerful force. A recent Harvard poll indicates that more than 60 percent of currently-enrolled college students support the policies of the president and the administration, at a time when just 53 percent of the general public support them. In the annual survey of college freshmen by the Higher Education Research Institute at UCLA, researchers found that 21 percent of college students now identify themselves as conservatives. This figure is growing, and just 24 percent say they're liberals, which is a sizable drop from the nearly 40 percent who identified themselves as liberal in the seventies.[8]

USING TECHNOLOGY

In a review of the newest edition of an excellent resource for parents and their pre-college children, called *Choosing the Right College: The Whole Truth about America's 100 Top Schools*, published by the conservative Intercollegiate Studies Institute, Boston College graduate student David Bobb writes, "The liberal arts provide a foundation for thinking, a way of ordering into coherence the questions of those things that matter most. In celebrating post-modern confusion and the lack of a foundation for knowledge, modern radicals rob their students of the noble task of the pursuit of knowledge and wisdom. Students guided thus fail to delve deeply enough into the most fundamental questions, mired as they are in the muck of the politicized academy."

One student from Amherst University quoted in the article expressed disappointment at the kinds of transformation taking place under the watchful gaze of university faculty. "Before I came to Amherst," he said, "I wasn't thinking about race or class or gender or sexual orientation. I was just thinking about people wanting to learn." But that's not what the university delivers. As Bobb says, "So diluted is the core now that at some schools the only true requirement is the 'diversity' class, frequently designed to expose the student to a 'non-hegemonic discourse' (the reality is often little more than anti-Western seed)." Sometimes, as the writer suggests, a decent set of core subjects can be cobbled together by those who truly want a first-class education, but it takes thought and planning, and good advice is needed for that, which makes a resource like the ISI Guide a valuable reference, well worth the price.[9]

Parents and prospective students will be well advised to use any tools they can find to resist the leftist monopoly they'll face in the universities, both before and after they arrive on campus. A group of conservative students at the University of Texas is using technology to give students a preview of what they'll find. Fed up with liberal bias in the classroom, Austin Kinghorn, who is chairman of the UT chapter of Young Conservatives of Texas, created a watch list of professors who use their classes for indoctrination. "There's a lot of professors out there who don't just teach the facts," said Kinghorn, "but also mold the curriculum in a way that attempts to produce a certain mindset in their students. These are the kinds of professors that the Professor Watch List was designed to identify, and the idea is that we can give a little bit of control back to students in how they're going to determine their own education."

One journalism professor on the UT watch list teaches a class called "Critical Issues in Journalism." In fact, the list reports, this class introduces unsuspecting students to a crash course in "socialism, white privilege, the truth about the Persian Gulf War and the role of America as the world's prominent sponsor of terrorism." Under the guise of objectivity, the professor, "half-heartedly attempts to tie his rants to 'critical issues' in journalism, insisting his lessons are valid under the guise of teaching potential journalists to 'think' about the world around them." But that's not how students see it. The same professor is renowned for using class time to get students to "come out" and to compare today's gay rights with the civil rights movement of the sixties and seventies.

Another professor on the list teaches African-American Studies. On one occasion, the watch list reports, a black student asked this professor what's wrong with being a black conservative, and the professor scolded that anyone who is black and conservative simply isn't black enough, and they're not working for the best interests of the black community. Such ideas are not only silly but dangerous, and Kinghorn and his associates want that fact to be made known. But in addition to the list of liberals to watch out for, they've also included an honor roll of professors whose classes are consistently fair and balanced. "We think there are a lot of students who'd be interested in knowing who those professors are," Kinghorn told a CNS News reporter. By checking the list on the group's Web site, students don't have to wonder what to expect from their professors anymore.

WHEN THIS NEWS GETS OUT!

At a dinner party discussing this book's premise, most guests were shocked to hear about the decline of the university, especially the Ivy League. Not so with one guest, president of one of America's top companies. "Yes," he said, "I've noticed the decline in the quality of graduates. I used to travel to the Ivy League every year to interview potential executives, but no more. The elite university graduates had a real lack of general knowledge—they were not helpful to my company. They were smart, all right, and thought they knew it all. They knew nothing. Now I never recruit from the Ivy League, only from second-tier colleges and state universities. These grads have been much more satisfactory; they're willing to learn."

Kinghorn said his list isn't entirely unique, and he recommended that students check out other Web sites such as NoIndoctrination.org, which provides ratings of professors at schools around the country. He updates the list continually during fall and spring registration periods, and said he's encouraged that professors are taking the list seriously enough to dedicate classroom time to discussing it. And well they should![10]

A PLAN OF ACTION

There are organizations with a national presence, such as the National Association of Scholars and the American Council of Trustees and Alumni, that are tackling the major issues of higher education reform at the institutional level. Some of the action plans they've prepared take the battle to local, state, and federal government officials, to help them understand the problem and the imbalances that exist. In a sense, this is the back-door approach, or the top-down approach. There are also activist groups and student organizations that are taking a front-door approach by organizing and educating students, and providing access to information and contacts of all sorts. But there's still a crying need for those in the middle, including parents, alumni, and funding organizations, to take the campaign to the next level by demanding accountability.

I've been amazed by the resilience and imagination of students on the frontlines. The solutions they come up with are often quite amazing. Alternative newspapers funded by the Intercollegiate Studies Institute and Accuracy in Academia are among the most compelling weapons in the students' arsenal because they give students a voice on campus and a chance to say things, in print, that might otherwise be forbidden or simply dismissed. The boom in alternative publications really took off in the eighties when the *Counterpoint* began giving conservative students at the University of Chicago a way to counteract liberal bias.

Before long, publications such as the *Dartmouth Review*, *Harvard Salient*, *California Patriot*, and the Tufts *Primary Source* began attracting lots of attention, and the Collegiate Network was on the map. The network of conservative publications that operates under the banner of ISI got its start in 1979 when a couple of Chicago students asked a national think-tank to help them start an alternative newspaper. Tod Lindberg and John Podhoretz, then freshmen, founded *Counterpoint*, which had an immediate impact on the campus culture. Later, both men went on to become distinguished authors, editors, and columnists involved in national politics. Lindberg served for a time as director of the editorial page at the *Washington Times* and is now editor of the Hoover Institution's *Policy Review*. Podhoretz is a columnist for the *New York Post* and a well known pundit and author.

SOMEONE WHO CARES

Studies show that parents can reduce students' risky behaviors just by talking to them. Young people who talk with their parents take fewer risks—particularly fewer sexual risks. It's not necessary to give them information or advice but to show that you care, that you take an interest in who they hang out with and what they're doing. What can you do? Stay connected, talk, write, e-mail, call, visit. Students, phone home!

—Julia Rosenbaum, Academy for Educational Development, cited by Joel Epstein

Today the Collegiate Network sponsors eighty student newspapers and magazines at colleges and universities around the country. Free of university oversight, these publications are able to speak for the students they serve. The network has been written up in the *Columbia Journalism Review*, *New York Times*, *Wall Street Journal*, *Boston Globe*, *Los Angeles Times*, and many other places as a leader in defending free speech rights on campus. Graduates of these publications have gone on to work for the *Wall Street Journal*, *Los Angeles Times*, *Detroit News*, *Washington Post*, *Investor's Business Daily*, *Weekly Standard*, CNN, Fox News, *Newsweek*, *National Review*, and many other news organizations. Some are now in government and politics; several have been awarded Rhodes, Marshall, and Fulbright scholarships; and all have used their skills to combat the bias in the academy.[11]

But what really makes these publications successful is the pent-up frustration of students with the leftist culture on campus. As many of the students and professors cited in this book have said, they know something's wrong. Students sense instinctively that the indoctrination and mind control are wrong, and they're open to any ideas that will allow them to regain the feeling of being in control of their own lives. Whether it's alternative newspapers, Web sites, or joining clubs such as College Republicans, Campus Conservatives, or a religious group of some kind, many young people are eager to step out and get involved, and there are more and more resources every day for them to do just that.

At Colorado University, students decided to make a statement by organizing conservative "Coming Out Day" on the Boulder campus, an event designed to give students who are fed up with the campus culture a chance to declare their values to the world. In addition to a kick-off ceremony on the campus mall and an affirmative action bake sale, the group declared February to be Conservative Coming-Out Month at CU, and encouraged students to "profess publicly and proudly" their conservatism. "As long as other minority groups are encouraged to publicly express their real identities," said the group's spokesman, "I don't see why it's a problem that this particular minority at CU—conservatives—follow suit."[12]

There's no limit to the kinds of things that can be done to shake things up on campus. But the best way to get started is to "stop, look, and listen." First, stop ignoring the problem and assuming that it will just go away. That's how campfires become forest fires, and how ridicule that goes unchallenged leads to full-scale persecution. Parents, of all people, need to look at what's happening and get involved; and students and like-minded faculty need to start thinking creatively about what they can do to make a difference. This usually begins by getting together with friends who share your concerns and brainstorming new ideas, from joining existing clubs to forming new ones, and then coming up with activities or programs that can help build ever larger coalitions. Of course, looking around and listening to what others are doing is a great way to start.

One of the best suggestions Connee and I heard during our travels around the country came from the student we met at Bowdoin College in Maine, interviewed in Chapter Six, who said that parents who want to find out what's really happening on their child's campus, or, equally important, to find out what it's like before their son or daughter enrolls, ought to "Get a subscription to the student newspaper." Because these papers are always lacking for real news, he told us, they cover all the crazy things that happen on campus, "and they don't even realize how outrageous this stuff looks to people outside the university." What could be more logical than that? Before investing upwards of a hundred grand to send your kids to a PC gulag, check out what's happening in the news. And if that doesn't get you on your feet, nothing will.

COMRADES IN ARMS

As so many of the young people in these interviews have said, talk radio is another medium that's having a huge influence with students these days. In addition to national celebrity talkers—such as Limbaugh, Hannity, Savage, O'Reilly, Michael Reagan, Laura Ingraham, and others—there are local conservative hosts with a substantial radio audience in practically every college market in America. The young woman we met at MIT told us she'd never put two-and-two together until she starting tuning in to what her mother was listening to in the car on the drive to school. Others told us that they automatically turn on the radio after class, because the political commentary is not only funny and outrageous but it gives them specific information and ideas for defending their beliefs in the classroom.

Another important way of finding out what's happening is to attend lectures and conferences where you'll have a chance to hear some of the outstanding speakers who appear regularly before college groups all over the country. Among them are people with frontline experience such as author Dinesh D'Souza, University of California regent and activist Ward Connerly, columnist Don Feder, columnist and author Pat Buchanan, talker and author Oliver North, advice guru Dr. Laura Schlessinger, lawyer and author Ann Coulter, former secretary of education William Bennett, and many more. Sometimes these speakers are sponsored by local student groups, and sometimes by service or political organizations. Occasionally they're invited by college or fraternal groups. Some organizations listed in

Appendix II provide schedules for these speakers on their Web sites. Young Americas Foundation is a great place to start.

In addition to these things, it's also important to listen to the concerns of students on the campuses. Prospective students, in particular, should begin keeping up with campus news before they even complete their applications for admission, and try to talk to students currently enrolled to find out what it's like and what kinds of restraint are placed on students' personal, political, and religious beliefs. Freedom of conscience is essential in a free society, so you'll want to know how far faculty members and others on campus may go in their attempts to invade your privacy. Dorms are a huge concern, and a visit to campus to inspect accommodations will tell you a lot. Be sure to ask students what they think about the housing situation, how roommates are determined, and what sort of sexual indoctrination may be required.

Along with these things, be sure to visit the Web sites of professional groups, think tanks, and public policy institutes who take a specialized interest in the welfare of university students. Among these I would recommend the Heritage Foundation, American Enterprise Institute, National Association of Scholars, Foundation for Individual Rights in Education, American Council of Trustees and Alumni, the Institute for Humane Studies at George Mason University, Intercollegiate Studies Institute, Leadership Institute, the College Republican National Committee, and student activist groups such as Students for Academic Freedom, Accuracy in Academia, and the Young Americas Foundation. Most of these sponsor conferences and events of their own to help students find the kinds of information they'll need to defend freedom of speech on campus, and to resist the attempts to change their beliefs and behavior.

It's also important to have access to more comprehensive information, and for this there are many important books and periodicals worth checking out. The bibliography in the back of this book offers a fuller list of resources, and I've mentioned quite a few in previous chapters. But to single out some exceptional volumes, I would first suggest that every student and concerned parent check out the Intercollegiate Studies Institute bookstore online. In addition to interpretive works by renowned scholars such as William F.

Buckley and Russell Kirk (whom I count as an important influence on my own thinking), you will find books, pamphlets, and monographs by some of the foremost conservative thinkers of our day.

For a more political approach to these issues, visit Townhall.com and Townhall Book Service on the Web. Sponsored by the Heritage Foundation, Townhall is one of the most popular meeting places anywhere for young conservatives and activists, and a forum for dozens of Townhall member groups who share a common interest in the issues described in these pages. Not only will you find the hottest new books on critical issues, but classics and reference sources, as well, often at exceptional discount prices. Townhall also maintains an archive of timely articles, reviews, surveys, fact-sheets, and white papers that provide excellent preparation for college writing and discussion-group assignments. All these things are useful and can help students and parents gain a new sense of control over their educational opportunities.

FINAL THOUGHTS

In its statement of principles on academic freedom and tenure, the bylaws of the American Association of University Professors state the following: "Institutions of higher education are conducted for the common good and not to further the interest of either the individual teacher or the institution as a whole. The common good depends upon the free search for truth and its free exposition." There was a time, which some of us can still remember, when those words actually had credibility on campus. But it's a different story today. Words like "truth" and "free exposition" don't even make the lexicon anymore.

I still remember the words of one of my major professors when I first started classes in 1962. He said, "This is not a vocational school. This university exists to form your mind and help you to become a fully literate and educated person. If you've come here for any other reason, then pick up your bags and leave now." That was an absolutely revolutionary idea. I had never thought of education that way, but it was an idea I will never forget.

Higher education is not about jobs or politics or sensitivity or compassion for hurting peoples or even about making the world a better place. Yes, all of those things are important, and education may help you to do that, but that's not what a university is for. A proper university education is about forming the habits of mind that allow young men and women to see beyond the trashy and transitory, and a chance to stand on the shoulders of the giants who have gone before us. It's not just about discovery or inventing new ideas, but building on the accumulated knowledge of our forebears. Education is about the pursuit of truth. That's why history and literature and philosophy are so important. And it's also why restoring a comprehensive core curriculum on every campus is essential.

If tomorrow's teachers, leaders, and business executives gain nothing from their expensive college educations but the skill to perform a certain set of tasks, or the conviction that they're the masters of their own destiny in pursuit of some utopian dream, our culture will not survive. A college education should give us the tools to discover where our own society stands in the cavalcade of history. It's not about creating anything from nothing, but about building upon the foundations of our rich cultural heritage. The greatest threat to the future of the American university is not lack of funds or even the smug behaviors of the anointed, but the notion that we are the first of our kind. By rejecting our history, with all of its victories and defeats, we betray a type of intellectual arrogance that is beneath contempt. But such arrogance is all too common in the academy today.

In one of the most memorable speeches of his illustrious career, Russell Kirk once said, "America has overcome the ideological culture of the Union of Soviet Socialist Republics. In the decade of this victory, are Americans to forswear the beneficent culture that they have inherited? For a civilization to arise and flower, centuries are required; but the indifference or the hostility of a single generation may suffice to work that civilization's ruin."[13] I can hardly imagine what Dr. Kirk would say if he were here today to see how far down that road we have already come. For even now we are standing in the ruins.

Which way do we go from here? We've passed the crossroads already.

There is another way, but we're not taking it now. To get there, we'll have to turn back and take the neglected route. If we continue down the path we're on, we will soon be submerged in a sea of ideological passions, intellectual compromise, political correctness, more and more thought control, the gulags of diversity and tolerance, and even greater disasters of moral decay. Or we can stop now, while there's still time, and seek the promise of an altogether different destiny.

A young woman at Pennsylvania State University penned a brief commentary on her personal Web site in which she said that this generation of university students is fed up with the acrimony and irrelevance they're being exposed to on campus. While she couldn't say what sort of reaction this resentment might provoke, she did say that she feels strongly that something's about to happen. She wrote:

> Frankly, I believe there will in fact be a revolution on universities, even if it has to come from the students themselves. Young students everywhere are giving out sighs of exasperation at what they are being taught—all of which has no application to their real lives. My generation is a generation that grew up under the tyranny of the Baby Boomer generation, with all of their divorce and selfishness. There is little doubt in my mind that the pain passed on to us will incite a rebellion. The only real question I can see is: which direction will that rebellion take? Those who are willing to provide leadership to college students will answer that question.[14]

Are we willing to take that challenge? Are we bold enough to demand the kinds of changes that are needed to get the academy back on track? In the end, it's not the institution, the erudition, the accumulated knowledge, the research, or even the initiation of young men and women into the life of the mind that matters most: what matters is the social, cultural, and moral heritage that we pass on to the next generation, and their capacity to accept the responsibilities of their citizenship. Most of those in control of the universities today have a very different vision, and changing course will not be easy. It will take courage and persistence. It may even take a revolution.

APPENDIX I

THE ACADEMIC BILL OF RIGHTS

I. THE MISSION OF THE UNIVERSITY

The central purposes of a University are the pursuit of truth, the discovery of new knowledge through scholarship and research, the study and reasoned criticism of intellectual and cultural traditions, the teaching and general development of students to help them become creative individuals and productive citizens of a pluralistic democracy, and the transmission of knowledge and learning to a society at large. Free inquiry and free speech within the academic community are indispensable to the achievement of these goals. The freedom to teach and learn depend upon the creation of appropriate conditions and opportunities on the campus as a whole as well as in the classrooms and lecture halls. These purposes reflect the value—pluralism, diversity, opportunity, critical intelligence, openness, and fairness—that are the cornerstones of American society.

II. ACADEMIC FREEDOM

1. *The Concept.* Academic freedom and intellectual diversity are values indispensable to the American university. From its first formulation in the *General Report of the Committee on Academic Freedom and Tenure* of the American Association of University Professors, the concept of academic freedom has been premised on the idea that human knowledge is a never-ending pursuit of the truth, that there is no humanly accessible truth that is not in principle open to challenge, and that no party or intellectual faction has a monopoly on wisdom. Therefore, academic freedom is most likely to

320

thrive in an environment of intellectual diversity that protects and fosters independence of thought and speech. In the words of the *General Report*, it is vital to protect "as the first condition of progress, [a] complete and unlimited freedom to *pursue* inquiry and publish its results."

Because free inquiry and its fruits are crucial to the democratic enterprise itself, academic freedom is a national value as well. In a historic 1967 decision (*Keyishian* v. *Board of Regents of the University of the State of New York*) the Supreme Court of the United States overturned a New York State loyalty provision for teachers with these words: "Our Nation is deeply committed to safeguarding academic freedom, [a] transcendent value to all of us and not merely to the teachers concerned." In *Sweezy* v. *New Hampshire*, (1957) the Court observed that the "essentiality of freedom in the community of American universities [was] almost self-evident."

2. *The Practice.* Academic freedom consists in protecting the intellectual independence of professors, researchers, and students in the pursuit of knowledge and the expression of ideas from interference by legislators or authorities within the institution itself. This means that no political, ideological, or religious orthodoxy will be imposed on professors and researchers through the hiring or tenure or termination process, or through any other administrative means by the academic institution. Nor shall legislatures impose any such orthodoxy through its control of the university budget.

This protection includes students. From the first statement on academic freedom, it has been recognized that intellectual independence means the protection of students—as well as faculty—from the imposition of any orthodoxy of a political, religious, or ideological nature. The 1915 *General Report* admonished faculty to avoid "taking unfair advantage of the student's immaturity by indoctrinating him with the teacher's own opinions before the student has had an opportunity fairly to examine other opinions upon the matters in question, and before he has sufficient knowledge and ripeness of judgment to be entitled to form any definite opinion of his own." In 1967, the AAUP's *Joint Statement on Rights and Freedoms of Students* reinforced and amplified this injunction by affirming the inseparability of "the freedom to teach and freedom to learn." In the words of the report, "Students should be free to take reasoned exception to the data or views offered in any course of study and to reserve judgment about matters of opinion."

Therefore, to secure the intellectual independence of faculty and students and to protect the principle of intellectual diversity, the following principles and procedures shall be observed:

1. All faculty shall be hired, fired, promoted, and granted tenure on the basis of their competence and appropriate knowledge in the field of their expertise and, in the humanities, the social sciences, and the arts, with a view toward fostering a plurality of methodologies and perspectives. No faculty shall be hired or fired or denied promotion or tenure solely on the basis of his or her political or religious beliefs.

2. No faculty member will be excluded from tenure, search and hiring committees on the basis of their political or religious beliefs.

3. Students will be graded solely on the basis of their reasoned answers and appropriate knowledge of the subjects and disciplines they study, not on the basis of their political or religious beliefs.

4. Curricula and reading lists in the humanities and social sciences should reflect the uncertainty and unsettled character of all human knowledge in these areas by providing students with dissenting sources and viewpoints where appropriate. While teachers are and should be free to pursue their own findings and perspectives in presenting their views, they should consider and make their students aware of other viewpoints. Academic disciplines should welcome a diversity of approaches to unsettled questions.

5. Exposing students to the spectrum of significant scholarly viewpoints on the subjects examined in their courses is a major responsibility of faculty. Faculty will not use their courses for the purpose of political, ideological, religious, or anti-religious indoctrination.

6. Selection of speakers, allocation of funds for speakers programs, and other student activities will observe the principles of academic freedom and promote intellectual pluralism.

7. An environment conducive to the civil exchange of ideas being an essential component of a free university, the obstruction of invited campus speakers, the destruction of campus literature, or other efforts to obstruct this exchange will not be tolerated.

8. Knowledge advances when individual scholars are left free to reach their own conclusions about which methods, facts, and theories have been validated by research. Academic institutions and professional societies formed to advance knowledge within an area of research, maintain the integrity of the research process, and organize the professional lives of related researchers serve as indispensable venues within which scholars circulate research findings and debate their interpretation. To perform these functions adequately, academic institutions and professional societies should maintain a posture of organizational neutrality with respect to the substantive disagreements that divide researchers on questions within, or outside, their fields of inquiry.

These principles only fully apply to public universities and to private universities that present themselves as bound by the canons of academic freedom. Private institutions choosing to restrict academic freedom on the basis of creed have an obligation to be as explicit as is possible about the scope and nature of these restrictions.

SEE ALSO:

The Students Bill of Rights: (http://www.studentsforacademicfreedom.org/essays/sbor.html)

[NOTE: This statement, drafted by Students for Academic Freedom, is not to be confused with legislation of the same name sponsored by

Democrats in the House of Representatives, identified in the 108th Congress as HR 236, which proposes additional funding to primary and secondary schools.]

APPENDIX II

ORGANIZATIONS & WEB SITES

Following is a list of recommended organizations and Web sites for and about issues of conscience, politics, activism, current events, faith, public policy, and academics from a generally conservative point of view. Some of these Internet addresses may be subject to change. If links should change, the organizations, individuals, and publications listed here can be located easily on the World Wide Web by most search engines.

CONCERNED ORGANIZATIONS:

Accuracy In Academia (www.academia.org)
Alliance Defense Fund (www.alliancedefensefund.org)
American Center for Law & Justice (www.aclj.org)
American Conservative Union (www.conservative.org)
American Council of Trustees and Alumni (www.goacta.org)
American Enterprise Institute (www.aei.org)
Americans for the Military (www.americansforthemilitary.com)
CATO Institute (www.cato.org)
Center for Individual Rights (www.cir-usa.org)
Center for Reclaiming America (www.reclaimamerica.org)
Center for the Study of Popular Culture (www.cspc.org)
Citizens United (www.citizensunited.org)
Clare Boothe Luce Policy Institute (www.cblpolicyinstitute.org)
Collegiate Network (www.collegiatenetwork.org)

Conservative HQ.com (www.conservativehq.com)

Conservative Political Action Committee (www.cpac.org)

Ann Coulter (www.anncoulter.org)

Cybercast News Service (www.cnsnews.com)

The Drudge Report (www.drudgereport.com)

Dinesh D'Souza (www.dineshdsouza.com)

Eagle Forum Collegians (www.eagleforum.org)

Family Research Council (www.frc.org)

The Federalist (www.federalist.com)

Foundation for Economic Education (www.fee.org)

Foundation for Individual Rights in Education (www.thefire.org)

Free Congress Foundation (www.freecongress.org)

Freedom Alliance (www.freedomalliance.org)

Frontpage Magazine (www.frontpagemag.com)

Fund for American Studies (www.tfas.org)

The Heritage Foundation (www.heritage.org)

The Hoover Institution (www.hoover.stanford.edu)

David Horowitz (www.salon.com/archives/1999/col_horo.html)

The Hudson Institute (www.hudson.org)

Human Events (www.human-events.com/home.html)

The Independent Institute (www.independent.org)

The Independent Women's Forum (www.iwf.org)

Insight Magazine Online (www.insightmag.com)

Institute for Humane Studies (www.theihs.org)

Intercollegiate Studies Institute (www.isi.org)

Ivy Leaguers for Freedom (www.ivyleaguers.org)

Judicial Watch (www.judicialwatch.org)

The Kirk Center (www.kirkcenter.org)

Rabbi Daniel Lapin (www.towardtradition.org)

Leadership Institute (www.leadershipinstitute.org)

Leadership University (www.leaderu.org)

Ludwig von Mises Institute (www.mises.org)

Media Research Center (www.mediaresearch.org)

Michael Medved (www.michaelmedved.com)
National Center for Public Policy Research (www.nationalcenter.org)
National Journalism Center (www.nationaljournalismcenter.org)
National Review Online (www.nationalreview.com)
National Rifle Association of America (www.nra.org)
National Taxpayers Union (www.ntu.org)
NoIndoctrination.org (www.noindoctrination.org)
Pacific Legal Foundation (www.pacificlegal.org)
Star Parker (www.urbancure.org/cureonline/default.html)
The Phillips Foundation (www.thephillipsfoundation.org)
The Pope Center for Higher Education Research (www.popecenter.org)
The Rutherford Institute (www.rutherford.org)
Phyllis Schlafly (www.eagleforum.org/educate/)
Tony Snow (www.creators.com/opinion/pundits/snow.asp)
Students for Academic Freedom (www.studentsforacademicfreedom.org)
Toward Tradition (www.towardtradition.org)
Town Hall (www.townhall.com)
The Vanguard (www.thevanguard.org)
The Washington Times (www.washtimes.com)
The Washington Times National Weekly Edition
    (www.washtimes-weekly.com)
The Weekly Standard (www.weeklystandard.com)
The Wilberforce Forum (www.wilberforce.org)
Walter Williams (www.jewishworldreview.com/cols/williams1.asp)
World Magazine (www.worldmag.com)
World Net Daily (www.worldnetdaily.com)
Young America's Foundation (www.yaf.org)

CAMPUS PUBLICATIONS:
American Foreign Policy (www.princeton.edu/~afp)
The American Journal (www.benladner.com)
The Amherst Spectator (www.amherst.edu/~spectate)
The Austin Review (www.austinreview.com)

The Binghamton Review (www.binghamtonreview.com)

The Boston College Observer (www.thebcobserver.com)

The Bowdoin Patriot (www.bowdoin.edu/~gop/dcf.html)

The Broadside Magazine (www.thebroadside.org)

The Brown Spectator (www.brownspectator.com)

The California Patriot (www.calpatriot.org)

The California Review (www.californiareview.org)

The Carolina Review (www.unc.edu/cr)

The Carrollton Record (www.tcrecord.com)

The Chicago Criterion (criterion.uchicago.edu)

The Claremont Independent (www.claremontindependent.com)

The College Redeemer (www.redeemernews.org)

The College Standard Magazine (www.collegestandard.net)

Common Sense (www.msucommonsense.com)

The Concord Bridge (www.concordbridge.org)

Contumacy (www.contumacy.org)

The Cornell Review (www.cornellreview.org)

The Counterweight (www.bucknellconservatives.org)

Crossroads of Boston College (bccrossroads.com/main.cfm)

CUA World (www.cuaworld.com)

The Dartmouth Review (www.dartreview.com)

Equitas (www.students.missouri.edu/~equitas)

The Examiner (www.texaminer.com)

The Fountainhead (www.thehead.org)

Gaucho Free Press (www.gauchofreepress.org)

The Georgetown Academy (www.georgetownacademy.com)

The Georgia GuardDawg (www.guarddawg.com)

The Gonzaga Witness (www.gonzagawitness.com)

The GW Patriot (www.gwpatriot.com)

The Harvard Salient (hcs.harvard.edu/~salient)

The Houston Review (www.houstonreview.com)

The Iowa Observer (www.iowaobserver.com)

The Irish Rover (www.irishrover.net)

The Irvine Review (www.irvinereview.org)

The John Galt Press (www.johngaltpress.org)

The Kenyon Observer (tko.kenyon.edu)

The Liberty (www.theliberty.org)

Light & Truth (www.yale.edu/lt)

The Madison Review (www.madisonreview.com)

The Michigan Review (www.michiganreview.com)

The Minuteman Newspaper (www.minuteman-newspaper.com)

The New Sense (www.newsensemagazine.org)

The Northwestern Chronicle (www.chron.org)

The Orange & Blue Observer (faf.union.uiuc.edu)

The Oregon Commentator (www.oregoncommentator.com)

The OSU Sentinel (www.osusentinel.com)

The Pennsylvania Independent (www.pennindy.org)

The Portland Spectator (www.portlandspectator.com)

The Primary Source (www.tuftsprimarysource.org)

The Princeton Tory (www.princetontory.com)

Punch (www.punchonline.org)

The Remnant (www.cs.wm.edu/remnant.html)

The Right Turn (students.washington.edu/right)

Sam Adams Review (www.samadamsreview.com)

The Stanford Review (www.stanfordreview.org)

The SU Review (www.sureview.org)

The Terrapin Times (www.theterrapintimes.com)

The Texas Education Review (www.texaseducationreview.com)

Texas Review of Law and Politics (www.trolp.org)

The Tiger Town Observer (www.observer.clemson.edu)

The Vanderbilt Torch (www.vutorch.org)

The Villanova Times (www.villanovatimes.com)

The Virginia Advocate (www.student.virginia.edu/~vaad)

The Wabash Commentary (www.wabashcommentary.com)

The Washington Witness (www.washingtonwitness.com)

The Yale Free Press (www.yale.edu/yfp)

OTHERS:

    The ASU Review

    The California Statesman

    The Fenwick Review

    The Flatirons Review

    The Gator Standard

    Liberty's Flame

    MSU Patriot

    The Redwood Review

    The Richmond Standard

    The Vast Right-Wing Conspiracy

    The Washington & Lee Spectator

Visit the Collegiate Network at www.collegiatenetwork.org

Acknowledgments

I'm especially grateful to the dozens of individuals—students, faculty, and concerned scholars—with whom I've spoken either face-to-face, by telephone or e-mail, or by some other form of correspondence over the past year. These are the men and women in the eye of the storm. They are the ones who know from their daily encounters and brave resistance what the struggle is really all about. Ultimately, I'm responsible for the format of their comments as they appear in this volume, but I have tried to be faithful to their observations, and I trust that the unique perspective each of them brings to the book may have a bracing and eye-opening effect on every reader.

I'm also grateful to Joseph Farah, Michael Hyatt, David Dunham, Joel Miller, and the editors and staff at WND Books, who grasped the urgency of this project from the first and have been faithful and generous supporters of my research and writing. I'm honored to be associated with the WND family and to be able to promulgate this message through the publishing and communications network of WorldNetDaily and its affiliates worldwide. We share a common interest in renewing the promise of our great nation.

Thanks to Dr. Arnold Beichman of the Hoover Institution for his words of wisdom, for his always rewarding commentary, and for perspective on the cultural transformations I have attempted to address in these pages. I also hasten to offer a word of thanks to each of the faculty members named in this work and to many others hither and yon who have been willing to speak with me candidly, but off the record, about the peculiar world of higher education in which they toil. And not least, thanks to Stephen H. Balch and my colleagues of the National Association of Scholars; David Horowitz of the Center for the Study of Popular Culture; Roger Ream of the Fund for American Studies; Alan Charles Kors, Harvey Silverglate, and Thor Halvorssen of the Foundation for Individual Rights in Education; and Gary L. Gregg and Jeffrey O. Nelson of the Intercollegiate Studies Institute for their fearless trailblazing in this wilderness.

It will be noted that some of the individuals cited in this work have asked not to be identified by name, for obvious reasons, and in those cases I've chosen other names for them. Even though most of the young people I interviewed were more than willing to have their names appear in print, I've decided not to identify those who could be put at risk. Sadly, there is still a price to pay for honesty on these campuses, and except for those protected by tenure, reputation, or sheer pugnacity, I've modified names and some few details of our conversations in order to protect the innocent. In all other ways, however, I've followed journalistic practice in relating the content of the interviews.

And, finally, a special word of gratitude to my wife, Connee Robertson Black, for her research and input in this volume, and for our many years of friendship, love, and marriage. Thanks also to our daughter Alison and son Gavin who graduated from major universities and somehow managed to emerge as responsible adults and good citizens. I'm grateful to them, as I am to all my family who have offered their encouragement over these many months.

I have now spent fully two-thirds of my life in, around, and involved one way or another with the American university. I had no idea when I took my first hapless steps across the threshold of Ransom Hall that I would spend so very many years and so many sleepless nights focused on the quest for knowledge and a better understanding of the demands of the academic enterprise. As a wide-eyed freshman, I was terrified; today I am no less so; only the source of the terror has changed dramatically, and not for the better.

It is my fervent hope that, forty years from today, the problems enu-merated in this book will no longer exist and that, except perhaps as a relic of ancient history, these words will no longer mean very much to anyone. I am not pessimistic about America's future, or even about the prospects for restoring the integrity of the academy. Our forefathers, after all, accomplished so much more in so few years. I am certain that with persistence and firm reliance upon the hand of providence that was their true shield and defender, even the seemingly impossible tasks of reform may yet be accomplished.

We're not without resources, but there's no time to waste. It's in that spirit that this work is now sent forth.

Bibliography

Martin Anderson, *Impostors in the Temple: American Intellectuals Are Destroying Our Universities and Cheating Our Students of Their Future*. New York: Simon & Schuster, 1992.

Arnold Beichman, *CNN's Cold War Documentary*. Stanford: Hoover Institution, 2000.

William J. Bennett, *Index of Leading Cultural Indicators*. New York: Touchstone, 1994.

_____, ed., *What Works: Research about Teaching and Learning*. Introduction by Dana B. Ciccone. Wooster: Wooster Book Co., 1996.

Jim Nelson Black, *When Nations Die: Ten Warning Signs of a Culture in Crisis*. Wheaton: Tyndale, 1994.

_____, *America Adrift*. Fort Lauderdale: Coral Ridge, 2002.

_____, D. James Kennedy, *Character & Destiny: A Nation in Search of Its Soul*. Grand Rapids: Harper Zondervan, 1994.

Allan Bloom, *Closing of the American Mind: How Higher Education Has Failed Democracy and Impoverished the Souls of Today's Students*. Foreword by Saul Bellow. New York: Simon & Schuster, 1987.

Harold O. J. Brown, *The Sensate Culture: Western Culture between Chaos and Transformation*. Dallas: Word, 1996.

Tammy Bruce, *The Death of Right and Wrong: Exposing the Left's Assault on Our Culture and Values*. Roseville: Prima Forum, 2003.

William F. Buckley Jr., *God and Man at Yale: The Superstitions of "Academic Freedom."* Introduction by John Chamberlain. South Bend: Gateway Editions, 1977.

_____, *Gratitude: Reflections on What We Owe to Our Country*. New York: Random House, 1990.

J. Budziszewski, *The Revenge of Conscience: Politics and the Fall of Man*. Dallas: Spence Publishing, 1999.

_____, *Written on the Heart: The Case for Natural Law*. Downers Grove: InterVarsity, 1997.

Stephen L. Carter, *The Culture of Disbelief: How American Law and Politics Trivialize Religious Devotion*. New York: Basic Books, 1993.

Peter Collier and David Horowitz, *Destructive Generation: Second Thoughts about the Sixties*. New York: Summit Books, 1989.

_____, *Surviving the PC University*. Studio City: Second Thoughts Books, 1993.

Ward Connerly, *Creating Equal: My Fight against Race Preferences*. San Francisco: Encounter Books, 2000.

Robert Conquest, *History, Humanity and Truth*. Stanford: Hoover Institution, 1993.

Maurice Cranston, *The New Left: Six Critical Essays*. Chicago: Open Court, 1971.

Dinesh D'Souza, *Illiberal Education: The Politics of Race and Sex on Campus*. New York: Vintage Books, 1992.

Shaunti Feldhaun, *The Veritas Conflict: A Novel*. Sisters: Multnomah, 2001.

Daniel J. Flynn, *Why the Left Hates America: Exposing the Lies that Have Obscured Our Nation's Greatness*. Roseville: Prima Forum, 2002.

John Taylor Gatto, *Dumbing Us Down: The Hidden Curriculum of Compulsory Schooling*. Philadelphia: New Society Publishers, 1992.

Robert P. George, *The Clash of Orthodoxies: Law, Religion, and Morality in Crisis*. Wilmington: ISI Books, 2001.

Martin L. Gross, *The End of Sanity: Social and Cultural Madness in America*. New York: Avon, 1997.

E.D. Hirsch Jr., *Cultural Literacy: What Every American Needs to Know*. New York: Vintage Books, 1988.

Victor Davis Hanson, John Heath, and Bruce S. Thornton, *Bonfire of the Humanities: Rescuing the Classics in an Impoverished Age*. Wilmington: ISI Books, 2001.

John Earl Haynes and Harvey Klehr, *In Denial: Historians, Communism & Espionage*. San Francisco: Encounter, 2003.

Paul Hollander, *Understanding Anti-Americanism: Its Origins and Impact at Home and Abroad*; Edited with an introduction by Paul Hollander. Chicago: Ivan R. Dee, 2004.

_____, *Political Pilgrims: Travels of Western Intellectuals to the Soviet*

Union, China, and Cuba, 1928-1978. Lanham: University Press of America, 1990.

Intercollegiate Studies Institute, *Choosing the Right College: The Whole Truth about America's 100 Top Schools*. Wilmington: ISI Books, 2003.

Charlotte Thomson Iserbyt, *The Deliberate Dumbing Down of America: A Chronological Paper Trail*. Ravenna: Conscience Press, 1999.

Paul Johnson, *Intellectuals*. New York: Harper & Row, 1998.

Donald Kagan, *Decline & Fall of the Roman Empire: Why Did It Collapse?* Englewood: D.C. Heath, 1962.

Zachary Karabell, *What's College For? The Struggle to Define American Higher Education*. New York: Basic Books, 1998.

Morton Keller and Phyllis Keller, *Making Harvard Modern: The Rise of America's University*. New York: Oxford University Press, 2001.

Kirk Kilpatrick, *Why Johnny Can't Tell Right from Wrong: Moral Illiteracy and the Case for Character Education*. New York: Simon & Schuster, 1992.

Roger Kimball, *Tenured Radicals: How Politics Has Corrupted Our Higher Education*. New York: Harper & Row, 1990.

_____, *The Long March: How the Cultural Revolution of the 1960s Changed America*. San Francisco: Encounter Books, 2000.

Russell Kirk, *The Conservative Mind: From Burke to Eliot*. 7th Revised Edition. Washington, DC: Regnery Gateway, 1993.

_____, *Enemies of the Permanent Things*. New Rochelle: Arlington House, 1969.

_____, *Reclaiming a Patrimony: The Heritage Lectures*. Vol. 13. Washington, DC: Heritage Foundation, 1982.

_____, *The Roots of American Order*. Washington, DC: Regnery Gateway, 1991.

Alan Charles Kors and Harvey A. Silverglate, *The Shadow University: The Betrayal of Liberty on America's Campuses*. New York: Free Press, 1998.

Hilton Kramer and Roger Kimball, ed., *The Betrayal of Liberalism: How the Disciples of Freedom and Equality Helped Foster the Illiberal Politics of Coercion and Control*. Chicago: Ivan R. Dee, 1999.

Christopher Lasch, *The Revolt of the Elites*. New York: W.W. Norton, 1996.

_____, *The Culture of Narcissism: American Life in an Age of Diminishing Expectations*. New York: Warner Books, 1980.

John Leo, *Incorrect Thoughts: Notes on Our Wayward Culture*. New Brunswick: Transaction Publishers, 2000.

_____, *Two Steps Ahead of the Thought Police*. New Brunswick: Transaction Publishers, 1998.

Harvey C. Mansfield Jr., *America's Constitutional Soul*. Baltimore: Johns Hopkins University Press, 1991.

_____, *Responsible Citizenship: Ancient and Modern*. Eugene: University of Oregon Humanities Center, 1994.

Cary Nelson, *Manifesto of a Tenured Radical*. New York: NYU Press, 1997.

Norman R. Phillips, *The Quest for Excellence: The Neo-Conservative Critique of Educational Mediocrity*. New York: Philosophical Library, 1978.

Julie A. Reuben, *The Making of the Modern University*. Chicago: University of Chicago Press, 1996.

Jean-François Revel, *Democracy Against Itself: The Future of the Democratic Impulse*. Translated by Roger Kaplan. New York: Free Press, 1993.

Alvin J. Schmidt, *The Menace of Multiculturalism: Trojan Horse in America*. Westport: Praeger, 1997.

Wendy Shalit, *A Return to Modesty: Rediscovering the Lost Virtue*. New York: Free Press, 1999.

John Silber, *Straight Shooting: What's Wrong with America and How to Fix It*. New York: Harper & Row, 1989.

Thomas Sowell, *A Conflict of Visions: Ideological Origins of Political Struggles*. New York: Basic Books, 2002.

_____, *Choosing a College: A Guide for Parents and Students*. New York: Perennial Library, 1989.

_____, *The Quest for Cosmic Justice*. New York: Free Press, 1999.

_____, *Barbarians Inside the Gates—and Other Controversial Essays*. Stanford: Hoover Institution, 1999.

Jacques Steinberg, *The Gatekeepers: Inside the Admissions Process of a Premier College*. New York: Penguin, 2002.

Charles Sykes, *Dumbing Down Our Kids: Why America's Children Feel Good about Themselves but Can't Read, Write, or Add*. New York: St. Martin's Press, 1996.

_____, *A Nation of Victims: The Decay of the American Character*. New York: St. Martin's Press, 1992.

_____, *Profscam: Professors and the Demise of Higher Education*. Washington, DC: Regnery Gateway, 1988.

Alexis de Tocqueville, *Democracy in America*. J.P. Mayer, ed.; Translated by George Lawrence. New York: Harper & Row, 1969.

Paul C. Vitz, *Faith of the Fatherless: The Psychology of Atheism*. Dallas: Spence Publishing, 1999.

Peter Wood, *Diversity: The Invention of a Concept*. San Francisco: Encounter Books, 2003.

Notes

FOREWORD
1. Christopher Lasch. *The Revolt of the Elites*. New York: W. W. Norton, 1996. 179.
2. Lasch. *The Revolt of the Elites*. 180.

CHAPTER 1: A Crisis on Campus
1. Alan Charles Kors and Harvey A. Silverglate. *The Shadow University: The Betrayal of Liberty on America's Campuses*. New York: Free Press, 1998, pp. 3-6.
2. Paul Hollander. *Survival of the Adversary Culture: Social Criticism & Political Escapism in American Society*. New Brunswick, New Jersey: Transaction Publishers, June 1991.
3. From a list compiled by *Education Reporter*, a publication of Eagle Forum (www.eagleforum.org).
4. John Leo. "The New Trivial Pursuit." Universal Press Syndicate. 30 August 1999.
5. Paul Vitz, et al. "A Nation at Risk." A Report of the National Commission on Excellence in Education. Washington, DC: U.S. Department of Education, 1983.
6. U.S. Department of Education, National Assessment of Educational Progress (NAEP): "The Nation's Report Card." NCES Number: 90423, 26 September 1990.
7. Carol Innerst. "Schools 'Really Bad' Says AFT Leader." *Washington Times*. 5 July 1990. Cited in Bennett, *Index of Leading Cultural Indicators*, p. 89.
8. David Horowitz. "Missing Diversity." *FrontPage*. 18 June 2002.
9. René Grousset. *Bilan de l'histoire, 1946*. Translated by A. & H. Temple as *The Sum of History*. Westport, Connecticut: Hyperion, 1979, p. 18.
10. Victor Davis Hanson. "Bomb Texas." *Commentary*. 16 January 2003.
11. Jim Nelson Black. *When Nations Die: Ten Warning Signs of a Culture in Crisis*. Wheaton, Illinois: Tyndale, 1994, p. 122.
12. Jean-François Revel. *Democracy against Itself: The Future of the Democratic Impulse*. Translated by Roger Kaplan. New York: Free Press, 1993, p. 258.
13. Alexis de Tocqueville. *Democracy in America*. J.P. Mayer, ed.; Translated by George Lawrence. New York: Harper & Row, 1969, pp. 464-5.

14. Sen. Joseph Lieberman. "Opening Statement on the Rising Cost of College Tuition." Committee on Governmental Affairs: United States Senate, 9 February 2000. (www.senate.gov/~gov_affairs/ 020900_lieberman.htm)
15. Robert H. Bork. *Slouching towards Gomorrah: Modern Liberalism and American Decline*. New York: HarperCollins, 1996, p. 193.
16. John Berthoud. "The NEA's Fiscal Agenda: Bad News for Kids." Alexis de Tocqueville Institute, 1 July 1996.
17. See a discussion of the "Academic Bill of Rights" drafted by Students for Academic Freedom in Chapter Six and the actual text of the document in Appendix I.

CHAPTER 2: A Trajectory of Decline

1. Ellen Sorokin. "Cultural Knowledge Down over Five Decades." *Washington Times*. 20 December 2002.
2. Russell Kirk. *The Conservative Mind: From Burke to Eliot*. 7th Revised Edition. Washington, DC: Regnery, 1993, p. 480.
3. "Losing the Big Picture: The Fragmentation of the English Major since 1964." A Report of the National Association of Scholars, 575 Ewing Street, Princeton, New Jersey 08540-9371. 2002.
4. Mona Charen. "Don't Know Much about History." Creators Syndicate. 15 July 2003.
5. Denise K. Magner. "George Washington Is Last in Minds of College Students, Survey Suggests." ACTA: 22 February 2000. (http://www.goacta.org/press/articles/CHE/CHE2-22-00.htm)
6. Diane Ravitch. "Statement on 2001 NAEP U.S. History Report Card." National Assessment Governing Board, 9 May 2002. (http://www.nagb.org/naep/history_ravitch.html)
7. Don Feder. "For Public Education, America Is History." Creators Syndicate. 27 May 2002.
8. As reported in the *Weekly Standard*, 6 May 2002; cited by Feder, *op.cit.*
9. "Losing the Big Picture," *op. cit.*
10. Edward Feulner. "Lower Education." Heritage Foundation. 25 March 1996.
11. Russell Kirk. "Prospects for Conservatives: Cultivating Educational Wastelands." Heritage Foundation: Lecture 285, 14 June 1990.
12. Greg Winter. "College Loans Rise, Swamping Graduates' Dreams." *New York Times*. 28 January 2003, A16.
13. Dennis Prager. "Don't Waste Your Money on an Expensive College." 11 Febraury 2003.
14. Prager. "Don't Waste Your Money on an Expensive College."
15. Eugene Ham, James Bowman, et al. "The Lost Art of Educating Children." *Women's Quarterly* magazine of the Independent Women's Forum: Vol. 25, Autumn 2000.

CHAPTER 3: The Agenda Is Reeducation

1. "Survival Message For College Students." *Education Reporter*: A publication of Eagle Forum. 29 August 2001.

2. Phyllis Schlafly. "The Dangers and Frauds of Diversity." Copley News Service. 3 April 2002.
3. Schlafly. "The Dangers and Frauds of Diversity."
4. Two important surveys reflect bias in campus attitudes: Luntz Research and the Center for Popular Culture, "Professor Survey" of Ivy League campuses (http://www.studentsforacademicfreedom.org/); and David Horowitz and Eli Lehrer, "Political Bias in the Administrations and Faculties of 32 Elite Colleges and Universities" (http://www.frontpagemag.com/Content/read.asp? ID=55).
5. Daniel Pipes. "Profs Who Hate America." *New York Post*. 12 November 2002.
6. Dan Flynn. "Masters of Deceit." *FrontPage* magazine. 3 June 2003. (http://www.frontpagemag.com/Articles/ReadArticle.asp?ID=8145)

CHAPTER 4: Dumbing Down

1. Charlotte Thomson Iserbyt. *The Deliberate Dumbing Down of America: A Chronological Paper Trail*. Ravenna, Ohio: Conscience Press, 1999.
2. John Dewey. "My Pedagogic Creed." *The School Journal*. Vol. LIV, No. 3: 16 January 1997, pp. 77-80.
3. Iserbyt. *The Deliberate Dumbing Down of America*.
4. Chester M. Pierce, M.D. Keynote address, The Association for Childhood Education International. Denver, 1972.
5. For a detailed discussion of this book and the issues, see Alan Caruba's excellent four-part review, "The Subversion of Education in America," from which these comments are drawn. (http://www.anxietycenter.com/)
6. William J. Bennett. *Index of Leading Cultural Indicators*. New York: Touchstone, 1994, p. 86. Source of statistics: U.S. Department of Education, National Center for Education Statistics, National Assessment of Educational Progress, 1992 Trial State Assessment, 1993.
7. Gary Crosby Brasor, Review (*Cloning of the American Mind: Eradicating Morality Through Education*, by B.K. Eakman. Lafayette, Louisiana: Huntington House Publishers, 1998) in *Academic Question*, journal of the NA. Vol. 12, No. 1, 1998-99.
8. John Taylor Gatto. *Dumbing Us Down: The Hidden Curriculum of Compulsory Schooling*. Philadelphia: New Society Publishers, 1992.
9. Brooks Alexander. "The Rise of Cosmic Humanism: What Is Religion?" *SCP Journal*. Vol. 5, Winter 1981-82, p. 4.
10. Walter Williams. "Improve Education: Fire the Experts." Creators Syndicate. 26 August 2002.
11. Karl Zinsmeister. "The 60s Rules in Public Schools." *American Enterprise*. May/June 1997.
12. Williams. "Improve Education: Fire the Experts."
13. Williams. "Improve Education: Fire the Experts."
14. Harvey C. Mansfield Jr. "To B or Not to B?" *Wall Street Journal*. 20 December 2001.
15. Christopher Lasch. *The Culture of Narcissism: American Life in an Age of Diminishing Expectations*. New York: Warner Books, 1980.
16. Charles Sykes. *Dumbing Down Our Kids: Why America's Children Feel Good about Themselves but Can't Read, Write, or Add*. New York: St. Martin's Press, 1996.
17. Martin L. Gross. *The End of Sanity: Social and Cultural Madness in America*. New York: Avon, 1997, p. 116.

18. Thomas Sowell. "Artificial Stupidity." Creators Syndicate. 26 March 2003.

19. Charles Francis Potter. *Humanism: A New Religion*. New York: Simon and Schuster, 1930, p. 128.

CHAPTER 5: The New Orthodoxy

1. "Race-Conscious Admissions Programs: A National Survey." Marist College Institute for Public Opinion, January 2003. (http://www.maristpoll.marist.edu/usapolls/030609MT.pdf)

2. John Leo. "Admission Policies That Subvert Their Purposes." Creators Syndicate. 3 February 2003.

3. For an insider's view of the admissions process, see: Jacques Steinberg. *The Gatekeepers: Inside the Admissions Process of a Premier College*. New York: Penguin, 2002.

4. Thomas Sowell. "For What Purpose?" Creators Syndicate. 6 February 2003.

5. For a comprehensive and startling chronicle of what this widely used indoctrination program entails, see the cover story feature: Lynn Vincent. "BMOC: Big Mandate on Campus: College 'Diversity' Activists Grab Freshmen at Orientation—and Won't Let Go until Everyone Holds the Same View." *World Magazine*. Vol. 17, No. 35, 14 September 2002. (Available online at http://www.worldmag.com/. Registration required.)

6. Alan Charles Kors and Harvey A. Silverglate. *The Shadow University: The Betrayal of Liberty on America's Campuses*. p. 217.

7. Denise M. DeLancey. "Professor Tells What He Learned in the Ivy League." *Education Reporter*. No. 140, September 1997.

8. Alan Charles Kors. "Thought Reform 101: The Orwellian Implications of Today's College Orientation." *Reason*. March 2002. (http://reason.com/0003/fe.ak.thought.shtml)

9. See also: Wendy McElroy. "America's Re-education Camps." Associated Press. 9 May 2001. (http://www.foxnews.com/story /0,2933,24276,00.html)

10. Princeton alumnus Charles Robertson donated $35 million to the Woodrow Wilson School of Government to prepare grads for government careers. That endowment grew to $550 million, yet only a fraction of graduates were so directed. In 2002, Robertson put a hold on funds and sued the university. For more on this incident, see: Argelio Dumenigo. "Robertson Family Sues Princeton over Management of $550-Million Foundation." *Princeton Alumni Weekly*. 11 September 2002. (http://www.foxnews.com/story/0,2933,24276,00.html)

11. Visit the Madison Program Web site at http://www.princeton.edu/academics/departments.

12. Walter Williams. "America's Academic Tyrants." Creators Syndicate. 3 September 2003.

CHAPTER 6: Changing the Curriculum

1. Stephen H. Balch and Rita C. Zurcher. "The Dissolution of General Education: 1914-1993." National Association of Scholars, updated 1999. (http://www.nas.org/reports/disogened/excont.htm)

2. Cheryl K. Chumley. "Education Foundation Highlights 'Ridiculous' Classes." CNSNews.com. 3 September 2000.

3. Stanley K. Ridgeley. "Education 451." *Education Reporter*. No. 179, December 2000. (http://www.eagleforum.org/educate/ 2000/dec00/ed-451.shtml)

4. Rob Asbell. "Students Speak Out for Academic Bill of Rights." Remarks by Representative Jack Kingston, 24 October 2003. (http://www.gop.gov/item-news.asp?docId=59142)

5. Thomas C. Reeves. "The Academic Bill of Rights: Not Exactly McCarthyism." History News Network. 23 September 2003. (http://hnn.us/articles/1731.html)

6. "Academic Bill of Rights: A Statement of Committee A on Academic Freedom and Tenure." American Association of University Professors. December 2003. (http://www.aaup.org/statements/SpchState/billofrights.htm)

Chapter 7: Rewriting History

1. See: Linda Starr. "Students Flunk U.S. History Test: Congress Calls on Teachers To 'Redouble Efforts,'" *Education World*. 7 July 2000. (http://www.education-world.com/a_issues/issues100.shtml)

2. Tamara Henry. "Kids Get 'Abysmal' Grade in History." *USA Today*. 10 May 2002.

3. C. Bradley Thompson. "The Historians vs. American History." CNSNews Commentary. 26 February 2003.

4. Melanie Smith and John Cise. "Indoctrination 100 AC: Graduation Requirement Misrepresents History, Culture." *California Patriot*. December 2003. (http://www.calpatriot.org/december03/ac.htm)

Chapter 8: A Moral Freefall

1. Wendy Shalit. *A Return to Modesty: Rediscovering the Lost Virtue*. New York: Free Press, 1999, p. 28.

2. Candace de Russy. "Sex and Bondage 101." *Women's Quarterly*, Journal of the Independent Women's Forum. Summer 1998. (http://www.iwf.org/)

3. Dan Flynn. "Indecent Northern Exposure." *Campus Report*. February 1998. (http://www.academia.org/campus_reports/1998/ february_1998_1.html)

4. Ben Shapiro. *Brainwashed: How Universities Indoctrinate America's Youth*. Nashville: WND Books, 2004.

5. Ben Shapiro. "Militant Gay English on the Rise." Creators Syndicate. 20 August 2003.

6. Staff report. "Amherst High School Begins Course on Gay Literature." MassNews.com. May 2002. (http://www.massnews.com/ 2002_editions/Print_editions/05_May/05_May_gay_lit.shtml)

7. Staff report. "High School Hosting 'Porn' Play: Local Residents Protest Eve Ensler's 'V-Monologues'." WorldNetDaily.com. 11 February 2004. (http://www.worldnetdaily.com/news/ article.asp?ARTICLE_ID=37058)

8. Staff report. "High School Hosting 'Porn' Play."

9. Candace de Russy. "Sex and Bondage 101."

10. Joshua P. Rogers. "Mansfield Decries Harvard's Sex Scene." *The Harvard Crimson*. 4 December 2003.

11. Gary Gately. "College Students Ignoring Risks of Unprotected Sex." DiscoveryHealth.com. 22 August 2003. (http://health.discovery.com/news/healthscout/article.jsp?aid=514693&tid=24)

12. Gary Gately. "College Students Ignoring Risks of Unprotected Sex." *HealthDay Reporter*. 22 August 2003. (Sources cited in the article include: Helen E. Johnson, author and parent relations consultant to colleges and universities, Chapel Hill, North Carolina, and Charlotte A. Gaydos, M.S., M.Ph., Dr.Ph., associate professor of medicine at Johns Hopkins University School of Medicine, Baltimore.)

13. "Rethinking Rites of Passage: Substance Abuse on America's Campuses: A Report by the Commission on Substance Abuse at Colleges and Universities." National Center on Addiction and Substance Abuse. June 1994.

14. "Analysis: College Days Filled with Peril." MedServ Medical News. 8 September 2003. (http://medserv.no/modules.php?name= News&file=article&sid=2543)

15. Meg Meeker. *Epidemic: How Teen Sex Is Killing Our Kids*. Washington, DC: Lifeline, 2002. Information cited here is from a review by Johannes L. Jacobse for the Web site OrthodoxyToday.org.

16. The American Foundation for Suicide Prevention. (http://healthyliving.allinfo-about.com/suicide.html)

17. Alan Lipschitz, M.D. "College Student Suicide." 1 August 2003. (http://www.afsp.org/research/articles/lipsch2.html) Dr. Lipschitz is author of "A College Suicide: A Review Monograph." New York: AFSP, 1990.

18. "Campuses Expand Suicide Prevention: More Students Report Thoughts of Taking Their Own Lives." Associated Press. 18 November 2003.

19. Harold O. J. Brown. *The Sensate Culture: Western Culture between Chaos and Transformation*. Dallas: Word, 1996, p. 184.

20. Brown. *The Sensate Culture*. p. 185.

21. Brown. *The Sensate Culture*. p. 185.

22. President John Adams. "Address to the Military." 11 October 1798. In *The Works of John Adams, Second President of the United States*, Charles Francis Adams, ed., Vol. IX. Boston: Little Brown, 1851, p. 229.

23. Lasch. *The Revolt of the Elites*. pp. 213-14.

24. Lasch. *The Revolt of the Elites*. pp. 222-23.

25. Andrea Billups. "College Students Want More Talk of Morality, Patriotism." *Washington Times*. 1 July 2000. (See the full report at http://www.gofast.org/.)

CHAPTER 9: Politics and Religion

1. Jerry L. Martin and Anne D. Neal. "Defending Civilization: How Our Universities Are Failing America and What Can Be Done About It." Report of the American Council of Trustees and Alumni. Washington, DC: 11 November 2001; revised February 2002. (http://www.goacta.org/)

2. Martin and Neal. "Defending Civilization."

3. Herbert London. "Anti-Americanism." Hudson Institute. 11 August 2003.

4. Herbert Marcuse. *Counter-Revolution and Revolt*. New York: Beacon Press, 1972, p. 17.

5. Michael Lerner, a Clinton adviser on social policy and inventor of the term "politics of meaning," explained in his 1998 review of a new collection of Marcusian writings why the Marxist professor was such an inspiration to the Left. Lerner writes, "Marcuse remained an inspiration to many of us because he unashamedly embraced the need for utopian vision and a revolutionary

metaphysics that could recognize human needs that transcend economic security, individual rights, or the struggle for inclusion and non-discrimination within an oppressive social reality." See: Michael Lerner. "Marcuse at 100." *Tikkun*. September–October 1998.

6. Christopher Chow. "American Flag Banned on Colleges across the Nation." *Campus Report*. November 2001.
(http://www.academia.org/campus_reports/2001/nov_2001_1.html)

7. Paul Craig Roberts. "Abolishing America: Academe vs. Patriotism." Creators Syndicate. 28 October 2001.

8. "Berkeley Study Links Reagan, Hitler." WorldNetDaily.com. 23 July 2003.
(http://www.worldnetdaily.com/news/printer-friendly.asp?Article_ID=33714)

9. John O. McGinnis and Matthew Schwartz. "Conservatives Need Not Apply." *Wall Street Journal*. 1 April 2003.

10. Karl Zinsmeister. "The Shame of America's One-Party Campuses: A Report by the American Enterprise Institute and the Center for the Study of Popular Culture." *American Enterprise*. September 2002.

11. Christopher Chow. "New Study Reveals Extreme Partisan Bias Among Faculty." *Campus Report*. 10 November 2003. (http://www.academia.org/campus_report/october_2002_5.htm)

12. Jordan L. Hylden and John H. Jernigan. "Leaning Ivory Tower: The Most Troubling Bias among Academics Is Not Political but Religious." *Harvard Political Review*. Vol. 30, No. 2, Summer 2003, p. 13.

13. Richard T. Halvorson. "Confessions of a Skeptic." *Harvard Crimson*. 7 April 2003. (http://www.thecrimson.com/ article.aspx?ref=347399)

14. John Leo. "Splitting Society, Not Hairs." Universal Press Syndicate. 8 December 2003.

15. Bradford P. Wilson. "The Culture Wars in Higher Education." *Phi Kappa Phi Journal*. Winter 1999, p. 17-18.

16. Thomas Sowell. "Drawing a Firm Line: Acceptance Address for the 1998 Sidney Hook Memorial Award of the National Association of Scholars." *Academic Questions*. Vol. 11, No. 3, Summer 1998, pp. 53-54.

17. Julie Ruben. *The Making of the Modern University: Intellectual Transformation and the Marginalization of Morality*. Chicago: University of Chicago Press, 1996, p. 265.

18. Russell Kirk. "Renewing a Shaken Culture." Heritage Foundation, Lecture #434. 11 December 1992. (http://www.heritage.org/)

CHAPTER 10: The Grand Delusion

1. Karl Marx and Friedrich Engels. *The Communist Manifesto*. Introduction by A. J. P. Taylor. Baltimore: Penguin, 1967.

2. Marx and Engels. *The Communist Manifesto*. p. 91.

3. Harvey C. Mansfield Jr. "To B or Not to B?"

4. Jennifer A. Lindholm, Alexander W. Astin, Linda J. Sax, and William S. Korn. "The American College Teacher: National Norms for 2001-2002." Higher Education Research Institute, UCLA Graduate School of Education & Information Studies, 3005 Moore Hall, Box 951521, Los Angeles, California 90095-1521.

5. Bradford Wilson. "Free Speech, Civility, and the Campus Community." National Association of Scholars. 9 September 2003.

6. Robert Conquest. "Liberals and Totalitarianism." In: Hilton Kramer and Roger Kimball. *The Betrayal of Liberalism: How the Disciples of Freedom and Equality Helped Foster the Illiberal Politics of Coercion and Control.* Chicago: Ivan R. Dee, 1999.
7. Thomas Sowell. "Dissenting from Liberal Orthodoxy: A Black Scholar Speaks for the 'Angry Moderates.'" Reprint 59, American Enterprise Institute, 1150 Seventeenth Street, N.W., Washington, DC 20036.
8. Anne D. Neal. "Intellectual Diversity Endangered." Center for Individual Freedom. 7 November 2003. (http://www.cfif.org/ htdocs/freedomline/current/guest_commentary/student_right_to_learn.htm)

Chapter 11: A Mandate for Change

1. Tammy Bruce. *The Death of Right and Wrong: Exposing the Left's Assault on Our Culture and Values.* San Francisco: Prima, 2003.
2. "NAS/Zogby Poll Reveals American Colleges Are Teaching Dubious Ethical Lessons." National Association of Scholars. 22 July 2002. (http://www.nas.org/print/pressreleases/hqnas/releas_02jul02.htm)
3. "Top Ten Things Professors Do To Skew You." Internet Survey by the Independent Women's Forum. 5 April 2004. (http://www.iwf.org/issues/issues_detail.asp?ArticleID=559)
4. Winston Churchill. "The Iron Curtain Speech: 1946." National Center for Public Policy Research. (http://www.nationalcenter.org/ChurchillIronCurtain.html)
5. Michael J. Thompson. "Who Won the Cold War?" *Auburn Plainsman.* 5 September 2003. (http://www.theplainsman.com/vnews/display.v/ART/2003/09/05/3f57963178169)

Chapter 12: The Coming Revolution

1. Malcolm Gladwell. *The Tipping Point: How Little Things Can Make a Big Difference.* Boston: Little Brown, 2000.
2. Tanya Schevitz. "Cramped Speech at UC Berkeley." *San Francisco Chronicle.* 10 May 2002. (http://www.campus-watch.org/article/id/7)
3. Hugh Hewitt. "Larry Summers Is Bucking the Faculty and Trying To Remake Undergraduate Education at Harvard." *National Review Online.* 12 June 2003.
4. Kors and Silverglate. *The Shadow University.* p. 354.
5. David Horowitz. "The Problem with America's Colleges and the Solution." FrontPageMagazine.com. 3 September 2002. (http://www.frontpagemag.com/Articles/ReadArticle.asp?ID=2637)
6. Stanley Kurtz. "Taking Back the Academy: How Bush Can Kill PC." *National Review Online.* 9 February 2001.
7. "Speech Codes and Censors." *Wall Street Journal.* 10 June 1992, A14.
8. Sheena Engle. "Political Interest on the Rebound among the Nation's Freshmen." Higher Education Research Institute, UCLA. 26 January 2004. (http://www.bruinnews.ucla.edu/ page.asp?RelNum=4860)
9. David J. Bobb. "The Good, the Bad, and the Politically Correct." *Campus.* Vol. 10, No. 1, Fall 1998, p. 21.
10. Steve Brown. "Conservative Students in Texas Place Liberal Profs on Watch List." CNSNews.com. 6 November 2003.

11. Check out the complete list of Collegiate Network publications in Appendix II, and visit them online for a better look at what's really happening on these campuses. For students who may be considering enrollment at one of these schools, off-campus

subscriptions are usually available at a nominal cost.

12. Valerie Richardson. "Coming Out Day for Conservatives." *Washington Times*. 3 February 2004. (http://www.washtimes.com/ national/20040203-103504-2926r.htm)

13. Russell Kirk. "Renewing a Shaken Culture." Heritage Foundation, Lecture #434. 11 December 1992.

14. Amber Pawlik. Pennsylvania State University, Class of '04. Used by permission.

Index